FRENCH ENTRÉE 9

NORMANDY *Encore*

A **P & O European Ferries** guide

FRENCH ENTRÉE 9
NORMANDY
Encore

A **P & O European Ferries** guide

Patricia Fenn

Quiller Press

St Paterne.

First published 1991 by Quiller Press Ltd
46 Lillie Road, London SW6 1TN

Line drawings: Ken Howard and Tony Cooke
Area and port maps: Paul Emra
Design and production in association with
Book Production Consultants, Cambridge

ISBN 1-870948-22-X

Printed in Great Britain by Clays Ltd., St. Ives plc

Contents

Notes on using the book **6**
Raisons d'être **7**
Entrée to the Entrées **8**
Tips for beginners **10**
Normandy: introduction **14**
   Food **15**
   Cheeses **18**
   Drink **21**
Arrows **23**
Maps **26–29**

NORMANDY   **30–255**

Wines and Spirits by John Doxat **256**

Glossary of cooking terms and dishes **264**

Notes on using the book – and an appeal

1 The area maps are to help the reader to find the place he wishes to visit on his own map. Each place is given a reference on the relevant area map, but they are not designed to replace a good touring map.

2 A number in brackets at the beginning of a telephone number is the area dialling code, used when making calls from outside the area.

3 o.o.s. stands for 'out of season'; cl. for 'closed'. Other abbreviations, such as f for francs, are standard.

4 L, M or S in the margin stand for 'L' = Luxury, 'S' = Simple and 'M' for those in between.

5 H stands for Hotel; R for Restaurant and C for Chambre d'hôte in combination with 4 above, ie (H)S, (R)L etc.

6 stc means service and taxes are included (*service et taxes compris*).

7 The ➤ symbol means the establishment fulfils exceptionally well at least one of the author's criteria of comfort, welcome and cuisine.

8 P stands for parking, Ⓣ for Tourist Office and Ⓜ for market day.

9 Credit cards: *A* = Access, *AE* = American Express, *V* = Visa, *DC* = Diners Club, *EC* = Eurocard and *CB* = Carte Bleue.

10 The figures given in the address, eg. 62000, are the postal codes, which should be used in all correspondence.

Author's appeal

In order to keep *French Entrée* up to date I need all the latest information I can get on establishments listed in the guide. If you have any comments on these or any other details that might supplement my own researching I should be most grateful if you would pass them on.

Please include the name and address of establishment, date and duration of visit. Also please state if you will allow your name to be used.

Patricia Fenn,
Quiller Press
46 Lillie Road
London SW6 1TN

RAISONS D'ÊTRE

F.E. 9 is different from the other French Entrées in that it covers the same area as a previous guide – Normandy. This brings the advantage of six years' close association with the region and six years' reports from readers. Their approvals, disapprovals and new ideas have been weighed and, where appropriate, incorporated, but ultimately French Entrée remains wilfully subjective, with its author's preferences and prejudices admitted.

Its aim remains the same – to paint a comprehensive picture of Normandy's hotels, restaurants, scenery and diversions, and to leave the reader to decide which is right for him. The assumption is that we all have different requirements on different occasions. Take the kids and you're thinking budget; take the bride and the sky's the limit. Less-than-perfects are included. If your ideal hotel/restaurant is closed, too far or too dear, you need help with an alternative.

Look elsewhere on the shelves for a quick symbolised reference book, or one for a particular income group. Snatch this one up if you want to know exactly what's on offer before *you* make the choice.

ENTRÉE TO THE ENTRÉES

Categories: Hotels, restaurants and b. and b.s are graded into three categories: **L** for Luxury, **M** for Medium and **S** for Simple, but always the prime criterion for recommendation is value for money. Service with a smile scores top marks.

Normandy is increasingly well-endowed with chambres d'hôte – literally guest-rooms, or b. and b.s – and these have proved particularly popular with F.E. readers, who have enjoyed meeting their French hosts, sampling their life-styles and paying a remarkably modest bill. A relatively new phenomenon is the rise and rise of the luxury b. and b.s – châteaux and manor-houses, whose owners have converted old bedrooms into extremely comfortable accommodation, often better value then luxury hotels and invariably more interesting, but *special*. If you like your Bloody Mary to arrive at a snap of the fingers, forget this category.

Few chain hotels are included because (a) they are not difficult to locate without any help from me and (b) I happen to prefer a degree of individuality and owner-management to even the most efficient plastic uniformity.

Readers of previous F.E.s may be disappointed to find that here there is no 'Hotel of the Year'. The idea was very popular. Too popular sometimes, when the hotel became swamped with Brits, partly defeating the object, or, in one case, flushed with success, the hotel promptly upgraded itself, causing grave offence to readers expecting a bargain. Even worse was F.E.8's choice in the Loire, whose owner sold out one month after publication! I am still dealing with the indignant letters on this one.

The advent of châteaux b. and b.s has further compounded the problem, since they are all so good that each deserves special mention.

There are fewer recommendations in the **L** grade, particularly in hotels, than before. This is because their soaring prices put them out of bounds except for special occasions. Nevertheless for a celebration (or on expense account) £100 is still better spent in a grand hotel in Normandy than back home. The L b. and b.s, now costing between 350 and 750f, are still bargains. Catch them before the rest of the world does.

The **L** restaurants are another matter. To sample Michel Bruneau's cooking at La Bourride in Caen will be an unforgettable experience and worth every penny of the £30-odd bill. If this amount is totally out of court, seek out the cheaper menus, which, especially at lunchtime, give a good idea of the top chefs' exceptional talents. Where else can you find a four-course meal for £13, cooked by a chef like Alain Cornet at Château d'Audrieu? Can his second Michelin star be far away? Can you afford not to go now?

The **M** category covers the majority of Hotels, safe and not too expensive. One Hotel of the Year that has never let me down is the Auberge de l'Abbaye at Hambye, which would still be a prime choice for the title. I cannot praise this early discovery too highly. It epitomises all that I personally look for in a little French hotel, with rooms costing under 200f. A new find that I predict will be a hit is Le Mesnil Grand at Négreville. Remember you read it here first!

M restaurants are the kind that most French bourgeois would choose (they tend to be more snobbish about restaurants: Brits boast about the modesty of their bill; the French would never.) There are some bargains and some new discoveries here. One of my favourites is the Relais du Lion d'Or at Le Lion d'Or. Not only is their 85f menu a winner, but the ambiance and welcome well merit a detour. In the big cities, where workers as well as tourists eat, this category is well represented. For under £10, Les Maraîchers in Rouen or Le Boeuf Ferré in Caen will demonstrate that real French food, as served to real French people, is alive and well.

It is the **S** categories that cause me most pleasure and most pain. Pleasure because there is great satisfaction in finding somewhere like the Belvédère in Honfleur, with double rooms from £16 or the re-vamped Bouquet de Cosqueville at Cosqueville for even less, and to eat and sleep cheaply and soundly at that old faithful Le Vieux Donjon at Brionne. New discovery Le Grain de Sel at Dragey and the Manoir de l'Acherie at Acherie have menus for about £5, and that old favourite La Sélune at Ducey for only slightly more. These are stalwarts and arrowed accordingly, but obviously in this category there are often more short cuts and subsequent disappointments, particularly with hotels. One bad meal, you can forget; one night with bedbugs you can't. Extra care must be taken in checking; this applies especially to the hundreds of **S** chambres d'hôte. There is a limit to just how simple you can get.

Tips for beginners

Maps and guides

Good maps are essential and I must stress that those in the front of this book are intended only as an indication of where to find the entries. They should be used in conjunction with the appropriate Michelin maps: 231 covers all Normandy; 52, 54, 55 will deal with smaller areas.

The red Michelin, apart from all its other virtues, has useful town maps. It's a bit slow to spot a newcomer though, unlike its rival Gault-Millau. This gives more specific detail but has less comprehensive coverage and is strongly biassed in favour of *la nouvelle cuisine* (its authors did invent the label in the first place); it is useless for the really basic hotels and restaurants.

Logis de France do a good guide to their hotels, obtainable at the French Government Tourist Bureau at 178 Picadilly. This is the place to go for general advice, free maps and brochures and details of the admirable gîtes system, which provides simple self-catering accommodation in farmhouses and cottages. We have stayed in gîtes all over France and found them invariably reliable and cheap, and often more comfortable and interesting than hotels, but you have to be quick off the mark to book the best in peak season.

Chambres d'hôte are listed in *French Country Welcome*, price £8.95.

Booking

Sunday lunch is the Meal of the Week, when several generations settle down together to enjoy an orgy of eating, drinking, conversation and baby-worship that can well last till teatime. You should certainly book then and on fête days. Make tactical plans and lie low, or it could be a crêpe and a bed in the car. French public holidays are as follows:

New Year's Day	France's National Day, 14 July
Easter Sunday and Monday	
Labour Day, 1 May	The Assumption, 15 August
VE Day, 8 May	All Saints' Day, 1 November
Ascension Day	Armistice Day, 11 Novembe
Whit Sunday and Monday	Christmas Day

If you wish to book ahead and do not speak French, try and

find someone who does to make a preliminary telephone call. If necessary, write in English and let them sort it out, but make sure when you get the confirmatory letter that you understand what you've booked. Many hotels nowadays wil ask for a deposit. My method is to send them an English cheque; they then either subtract the equivalent from the bill or return the cheque.

Make good use of the local tourist bureaux, clearly indicated in the centre of every town, where you will find English spoken. Let them do the booking for you if you have problems. This is the place to pick up maps and brochures.

Closing Times The markets, like the rest of the town, snap shut abruptly for lunch. I regularly get caught out by not shopping early enough; if it's going to be a picnic lunch, the decision has to be made in good time. From 12 p.m. to 2.30, and sometimes 3, not a cat stirs. At the other end of the day it's a joy to find shops open until 7 p.m. Mondays tend to be almost as dead as Sundays and it's likely to prove a grave disappointment to allocate that as a shopping day.

It does not pay to be casual about the weekly closure (*fermeture hebdomadaire*) of the restaurants. It is an excellent idea to ensure that not every restaurant in the same town is closed at the same time, but do check before you venture. Thwarted tastebuds are guaranteed if you make a special journey only to find the smug little notice on the door. 'Sun. p.m. and Mon.' are the most common and often it will take a good deal of perseverance to find a possibility open then.

Changing Money Everyone has their pet method, from going round all the banks to get a few centimes advantage, to playing it the easy and very expensive way of getting the hotel to do it. It depends on how much is involved and how keen a dealer you are as to how much trouble is worth it. I change mine on the boat, where I have always found the rate to be very fair. If you get caught outside banking hours, the *bureaux de change* stay open late.

Telephoning Most of the public telephones in France actually work. You put your 1f piece in the slot and watch it roll down for starters, then as many more pieces as you estimate you will need. If it's too much, out it all comes at the conclusion of the conversation.

To dial UK from France: 19, wait for tone, 44, then STD code minus 0, then number.

Inter-departmental:
Province to Province: Dial just 8 figures (e.g. 21.33.92.92.)
Province to Paris: Dial 16, then 1, then 4 followed by 7 figures (e.g. 16.1.4XX.XX.XX)
Paris to Province: Dial 16, then the 8 figures
Please note that all numbers you refer to should be 8 figures only (e.g. 21.86.80.48 not (21) 86.80.48).
To dial France from UK: 010, pause, 33, 8-figure code.
Emergencies: Fire 18; Police 17; Operator 13; Directory Enquiries 12.

Markets We Brits go to France to sleep cheaply, eat well and to shop. The markets are more than just a utility – they are part and parcel of the French scene, and everyone loves them. Take your time strolling round the colour and hubbub, and experience the pleasure of buying from someone who knows and cares about his wares. The man selling you a kitchen knife will be an expert on knives and will want to know what you need it for; the cheesemonger will choose for you a cheese ready for eating today or in a couple of days' time, back home. Trust them. Choose for yourself the ripest peach, the perfect tomato, and buy as little as you need and no more, so that you can buy fresh again tomorrow. Stock up on herbs and spices, pulses and dried fruits, soap scented with natural oils, honey from local bees, slices of farmers' wives' terrines – every village a veritable Fortnums on market day. The day of the market in the nearest town is listed in most entries – (M)

Take with You Soap (only the grander hotels supply if) and a decent towel if you're heading for the S group and can't stand the handkerchief-sized baldies. If self-catering, take tea, orange juice, breakfast cereals, biscuits, Marmite, marmalade – all either expensive, or difficult to locate, or horrible.

Bring home The list of Best Buys doesn't change much. Obviously wine, but not the more expensive varieties which are, surprisingly, cheaper in England. Be a lager lout and take as much as you can carry. Coffee is much cheaper; jams, plain chocolate, stock cubes are worth considering, as are electrical goods, ironmongery, kitchen gadgets, glass ware. Best of all are impulse buys in the markets.

Breakfast A sore point. The best will serve buttery croissants, hot fresh bread, home-made preserves, a slab of slightly salted butter, lots of strong coffee and fresh hot milk, with fresh orange juice if you're lucky. The worst – and at a price of between 15 and 40f this is an outrage – will be stale bread, a foil-wrapped butter pat, plastic jam, a cup of weak coffee and cold sterilised milk. Synthetic orange juice can add another 10f to the bill. If you land in an hotel like this, get out of bed and go to the café next door.

Tipping

Lots of readers, used to the outstretched British hand, worry about this. Needlessly – 's.t.c.' should mean what is says – all service and taxes included. The only exception perhaps is to leave the small change in the saucer at a bar.

Garages and Parking

Considerably older and wiser since I started travelling so often, I now have sympathy with readers who insist on a garage. I have to tell you that my locked car has been twice broken into and once stolen altogether (recovered three weeks later with £2000 worth of damage). The latter disaster was from a well-lit street outside a very grand hotel, so my experience is altogether different from that of a reader who advises street parking after having all his belongings pinched from a car in an underground car-park. I can only advise removing any valued belongings, however tiresome that may be, and taking out adequate insurance.

Thanks

To all my friends, old and new, in the regional tourist boards in France, and especially to Heidi Thorley, the Normandy representative in England, and to Pauline Hallam of the French Government Tourist Office at 178 Picadilly.

What Next?

I am pleased to be able to report that the French Entrée series is blossoming. F.E.10, due out later this year, will cover the South of France; F.E.11, for early 1992, will be Paris. A separate book on Chambres d'Hôte will follow, and so will a variation on the theme: Entrées to the Algarve, Majorca and Malta (with others to come). Any suggestions for these areas will be welcome.

Other Entrées

5 – Brittany
6 – Coast to Capital, Boulogne, Picardy, Somme
7 – Calais, Ardennes, Champagne, Bruges
8 – The Loire
     None of these, and especially F.E.9 would have been possible without readers' help. Please write to Quiller Press Ltd., 46 Lillie Road, London SW6 1TN, if you have any comments, favourable or otherwise, and stating if you object to being quoted. I do try and answer each letter personally but please be patient!

NORMANDY

So vast a province is Normany, so rich in culture, scenery, hotels and restaurants, and so extensive was the raw material for this new guide, that we did consider publishing two books, one each for Upper and Lower Normandy. The pros were that these would be slimmer and more manageable volumes (and we might sell two books instead of one!), but the cons – the confusion that would ensue – prevailed, and the result is 50% more copy than in the old F.E.3.

Normand

As I have had the opportunity to spend a further two years researching F.E.9, I have come to appreciate even more the infinite variety on offer. It is still difficult to realise that the wild granite rocks and cliffs of the NW Manche can be in the same country, let alone the same province, as the flat chalk plains of the Caux area in the Seine-Maritime, or the lush green hills of Calvados with its archetypal timbered cottages and contented cows. Deauville's sophistication contrasts with the bucket-and-spade holiday atmosphere of west-coast resorts like Carteret and Coutainville.

France's No. 1 tourist attraction is in Normandy – the incomparable Mont St. Michel. So are the historic landing beaches, now further illuminated by the magnificent Mémoriale in Caen. William the Conqueror's tomb in his glorious cathedral is in Caen too; rival Rouen has the site of Joan of Arc's last moments and its cathedral will be more than ever an essential place of pilgrimage after the Royal Academy's unique Monet exhibition, which illustrated it in so many guises.

It is not surprising that the Seine estuary attracted artists like the Impressionists, inspired by the light and picture-book fishing villages like Honfleur. Monet's home at Giverny, Proust's inspiration at Cabourg, Flaubert's many associations in the Seine-Maritime, are all good reasons to visit.

Further south, in the départements of Orne and Eure, lies a Normandy still to be discovered by the tourists. Time-warped villages, feudal châteaux, vast stud farms, many rivers, empty green lanes, modest country auberges are all here, waiting to be explored.

Prices have risen, of course, but a holiday in Normandy should still cost considerably less than its equivalent back home. And just think what you get for your money!

FOOD

Sailors and farmers by tradition and inclination are our Norman cousins, and fishing and farming are still two of the province's main occupations. No surprise to find that Norman cuisine centres around these two richnesses. A first plâteau de fruits de mer is an unforgettable experience; nowhere are they better than in Normandy and Brittany. Simple, fresh, local is the key.

Perhaps it is the very abundance of prime ingredients that hinders Normandy from ranking as a top gastronomic province. If there were but one goat grazing on the hill and thin vegetables fighting through barren soil, anything that moved or grew would be pressed into imaginative culinary service. But the Norman larder overflows with tender lamb from the salt marshes, thick yellow cream from the indulged Norman cow, with lobsters from the Cotentin rocks fit for the best tables in Paris, and sole brought flapping from the Dieppe catch. When cauliflowers and artichokes and baby beans proliferate in this natural market garden (when they say a stick poked in the ground will burst into leaf overnight) and a surplus of apples and pears plop to the ground for want of picking, there can be lilttle temptation to conjure and scrape marvels of gastronomic improvisation. Escoffier had no need to preach 'Faites simple' to the Normans.

The products of cow and apple – butter, cream, cider and Calvados – appear repeatedly (some might say monotonously) in the cooking. Sauce normande literally covers a multitide of sins. At worst it can be merely cream sloshed indiscriminately with no attempt to blend and enhance, at best an unctuous glossiness made by whisking the cream and butter into a cider sauce and used to coat, not drench, the vegetables or, with fish stock added, the fish.

The fecund Pays d'Auge gives its name to a sauce combining cream and apple. The two most common bases are chicken and veal escalope, but turbot vallée d'Auge is a traditional dish for first communion celebrations around Étretat. The Caux area of upper Normandy is potato country and you can expect to see them included in any dish labelled Cauchoise, along with the cream. A simple but perfect Salade Cauchoise is made by dressing the freshly boiled potatoes with vinegar and seasoning while they are still hot and tossing them in crème fraîche, with additions like ham and celery to make a substantial meal.

Crème fraîche, an unknown quality still to most British shops, is a key ingredient to Norman cooking and always top of my French shopping list. It has a slightly fermented tang, too sour for some tastes, but I much prefer its slight tartness to sweet cream. It also has the added virtue (or vice) of a high butterfat content that naturally thickens any sauce made from it and can be boiled to a wonderfully concentrated reduction if required. It keeps well too – up to three weeks for savoury dishes, though best used fresh and light for desserts.

A familiar sight in the apple orchards is a fat pig happily

rootling amongst the windfalls. When his time comes to be despatched by the local charcutier, some of his more obscure parts will go into a variety of sausages, like the smoked andouilles from Vire, or the boudin noir, coloured with blood and enriched with cream. Butchers from the North of England compete in – and sometimes win – the boudin competition held in Mortagne every year. Imagine the scene! I shall go one day. The strong-flavoured liver of the pig goes into terrines, along with the pork fat, their richness spiked with a lacing of Calvados.

From Rouen comes canard rouennais. I don't know anyone in Normandy nowadays who sticks by the rules and smothers the duck so that its blood is retained, but duck presses survive which squeeze the bones to supply the juice to enrich the red wine and cognac (for Calvados) sauce. The bird should be a special variety, half domestic, half wild, but again the original concept is loosely interpreted. The Hôtel de la Poste at Duclair used to be famous for serving the bird in fourteen different ways, but generally the most you can expect now will be any kind of duck roasted and served with a wine sauce, with luck, thickened with a purée of the duck's liver.

Mussels breed abundantly along the coast and the tiny juicy variety from these cold northern waters are far better than the inflated southern kind. The Norman way of preparing them, of course, is to add cream and kneaded butter to the broth and to serve them 'à la crème'. Very, very good too. If you see 'dieppoise' attached to a dish, it will probably involve the baby grey shrimps hauled in at Dieppe. I prefer marmite dieppoise, a fish stew usinig white fish, shelled mussels and peeled shrimp, and made piquant with spices (echoes of Dieppe's early eastern seafaring forays) to the over-rated bouillabaisse from the Mediterranean.

Tarte aux pommes is the ubiquitous dessert and comes in legions of shapes and guises. Many is the slice of blackened cardboard pastry topped with thin leathery apple slices I've choked on in the interests of this book. My favourite recipe uses a rich buttery eggy pastry, and tops it with almond cream which browns and bubbles through the fanned apple slices. (The French use dessert apples for cooking, incidentally.)

Crème pâtissière, another base, can be solid yellow plastic or delicately nutmegged creamy 'real' custard. Check the windows of the pâtissier before you buy. Chances are if his custard is synthetic so will be the rest of his products.

Tarte aux demoiselles Tatin is often found in Normandy,

but in fact has its origin in the Loire region, where the blessed Tatin daughters accidentally burned and caramelised their sugar and turned their tart upside down to disguise their carelessness. Delicious if well done, but time-consuming to get right and short cuts can be disastrous. Another version purées the apples and covers them with a latticework of pastry. Lovers of apple dumplings will be pleased to find a Norman version, known as 'bouillons'.

CHEESES

Consider French cheeses and the first region that springs to mind must be Normandy. The northern grass is lushest and greenest and the bespectacled Norman cows that chew it are promotional poster clichés. To be true Norman, they must be brown and white with a brown patch over at least one eye.

To understand why the quality of cheeses varies at different times of the year, one must consider the date when the cows are put out to pasture and the length of time it takes to make the cheese. Many French will reject a cheese because it is not 'in season'. Just as wine buffs know the soil and microclimate of every vineyard and how long the wine will take to age correctly, so will the cheese purist know at what season the grass sprouts, not once but twice a year, and when the meadows break into flower. He will know about individual cheese-making methods within a limited area, sometimes no larger than a few fields. Vegetation, climate, rainfall, subsoil and breed all add up to subtleties never dreamt of when you ask for a slab of Irish Cheddar in your local Co-op.

There are really only four outstanding names in Normandy. Camembert, Pont l'Evêque, Livarot and the cream cheese loosely referred to by the name of the area from which most of them derive – Neufchâtel. However, within these varieties there are many distinctions and it's worthwhile remembering what to look for.

Camembert

There are around 2000 brands of Camembert produced in France and the Germans and even the Russians have the cheek to sell their versions to the hypermarchés. But of course no Camembert is as good as Normandy Camembert, and the best of all is that which comes from the Auge country, between the rivers Touques and Dives.

A comparison between commercial Camembert and

unpasteurised *fermier* is like chalk and cheese. Sadly, it is not easy to seek out the farm variety – young Normans have no wish to dedicate seven days a week to cheese-making as their parents did. The best has an appellation V.C.N. (*véritable Camembert de Normandie*) and if you do have a choice, it is well worth the extra money.

The origins of Camembert are hotly disputed. Certainly it is named after a village near Vimoutiers, where a monument stands to Marie Harel – generally credited with having 'invented' this delicacy in 1791. Local lore, however, has it that farmers' wives in the area had been perfecting its smooth creaminess for generations before.

Napoleon III was presented with a cheese specially made for him in the village of Camembert in 1855. After tasting it, he is said to have kissed the waitress who served it to him. Fifty years later, a Monsieur Ridel designed the familiar little circular wooden box, so that the cheese could be packed and enjoyed at some distance from the farms.

Smell is a good guide to buying the perfect Camembert, but it isn't easy to describe smells in cheesy terms – 'Like the feet of a god' was one attempt. 'A tangy fragrance with no trace of ammonia' is the best I can do. Correctly it should bulge but not run when cut, but British taste tends to prefer it riper than the French and I certainly like mine oozing a bit. Its surface should be very even, downy white, with touches of red. Best seasons are late spring, autumn and winter.

Pont-l'Evêque

Probably the oldest cheese in Normandy and still made almost entirely in the farms of the *pays d'Auge*, with commercial producers beginning to try and emulate.

Small, squat, soft and tender, with golden rind, it has a pronounced tang, should feel supple when pressed and smell 'savoury with some bouquet' as the king of the cheese-makers, Pierre Androuet, puts it. He also advises to avoid one with a 'cow-barn odour', which shouldn't be too difficult.

From the same stable, or should I say barn, comes a larger version, the Pavé de Moyaux, which is said to be the ancestor of Pont-l'Evêque. It has a brighter yellow rind and a smell of 'cellars and mould'. If that hasn't put you off, Androuet prefers it to its parvenu descendant.

The generic name for these square cheeses of Lower Normandy is Pavé d'Auge. They are all at their best during summer, autumn and winter.

Livarot

Another cheese with a long history, probably devised originally, like so many good things, in a monastery. It has a stronger, spicier smell than Pont-l'Evêque, due perhaps to its being aged in airtight cellars lined with hay. Production, which is still mainly in farms around the valleys of the Viette and Vie, declines each year and attempts are being made to reproduce the brown-rinded cylinders commercially. If you hear a cheese referred to as a 'Colonel' it will be Livarot, the five bands of sedge which enclose it evoking the five service stripes.

Best seasons are late spring, autumn and winter. Avoid any with a dry or sticky rind, and consistency must be neither chalky, nor runny. Petit Lisieux is similar.

Neufchâtel

The group of cream cheeses loosely termed Neufchâtel, after the town, come from north of the Seine, in the *pays de Bray*. They make a tempting sight on the market stalls, in towns like Gisors, in their varying shapes and sizes – hearts, discs, obelisks. Look out for *triple boudard*, supposed to be the shape of the bung of a cider barrel (*bonde*), with a very pronounced fruity flavour. Its best season, like all these creamy cheeses, is late autumn.

My own weakness is for Brillat-Savarin, which comes from Forges-les-Eaux. This one not only looks but smells appealing, which is more than can be said for most, with a downy white rind and delicate creamy nose; it is not for the cholesterol-conscious – a triple cream with a wicked 75% fat content. An upstart little cheese, it was invented by the grandfather of Pierre Androuet between the wars.

Farms selling their own produce (cheese, cider and calvados) can be identified by their green and yellow sign: *Vente de Produits Fermiers*. Following the indications in the *pays d'Auge* for the *Route du Fromage* makes a good excuse for an excursion, and penetrates deeply into the most gorgeous bucolic countryside.

Finding your favourites

You can obtain a brochure from either a local tourist office or from the French Government Tourist Office at 178 Piccadilly, London, W1. The brochure lists dozens of cheese-makers and épiceries from which to buy the produce.

In the village of Camembert, you can visit Robert Durand at La Herronière. He sells Camembert and local cider, and is open weekdays (tel: 33.39.08.08).

At Boissey, on the D 4 between St Pierre-sur-Dives and Livarot, try Denis Thébault at La Houssaye. He sells Livarot and Pont-l'Evêque. Open weekdays (tel: 31.20.64.00).

In Livarot itself, for the cheese of that name, call at the Ferme du Héricourt, 3 rue Marcel Gambier. Closed Mondays.

Good markets at which to enjoy selecting the perfect cheese are at St Pierre-sur-Dives on Mondays and Livarot on Thursdays.

DRINK

Cider and Calvados are to the apple and to Normandy what wine and brandy are to Bordeaux. You cannot eat a cider apple – far too mouth-puckering – but you can see the trees through Normandy, wizened and bent with their load of tiny red apples. If you explore some of the side roads in the Auge Region you will come across signs indicating *Route du cidre*. There is one from Beuvron-en-Auge, which leads through delightful little villages set on hilltops above the sloping orchards, with *dégustation cidre fermier* signs on every farm gate. Quite an experience to sit in the farm kitchen at the scrubbed table and sample the golden liquid.

In autumn the presses go from farmer to farmer, each extracting from the neat glowing piles the juice which he will then mix with a proportion – usually about a third – of sweet apple juice to make his own blend of 'cidre bouché'. Left to ferment in the bottle, this is the champagne of cider. An everyday version, a kind of cider plonk known as petit bère, is made by adding a lot more water and passing the lot back through the apple pulp again.

Lovers of German *Spätlese* wines would appreciate that the best cider comes from the latest apples, with a touch of frost to concentrate the flavour.

Like wine-making there is a lot of judgment and a little luck in producing a good vintage, but perhaps in Normandy the farmers attach more importance to considerations like the moon being in the right quarter and the wind blowing from the right direction before perfect bottling can be achieved than would their aristocratic counterparts in Épernay.

Young Calvados is for stronger stomachs than mine. Not for nothing has the glass of the firewater offered between courses been named a 'trou normand'. It may well make room for more food but you can actually feel it burning the hole! However, a mature Calva, stored in oak for ten to fifteen years, is another matter – a smooth, golden, fruity and distinctly soothing digestif. Look for an appellation contrôlée label as an indication of quality – and don't drive afterwards!

ARROWS

These are for entries which consistently meet all or most of my standards of comfort, fine cooking, welcome and value for money.

Acherie. *Manoir de l'Acherie* (HR)M.
Aignerville. *Manoir de l'Hormette* (C)L.
Alençon. *Au Petit Vatel* (R)M-L.
Les Andelys. *La Chaine d'Or* (HR)M.
Arromanches. *La Marine* (HR)S.
Audrieu. *Château d'Audrieu* (HR)L.
Bagnoles-de-l'Orne. *Hotel Lutétia* (HR)M.
La Baleine. *L'Auberge de la Baleine* (R)S.
Balleroy. *Manoir de la Drôme* (R)M. *Hotel des Biards* (HR)S.
Barfleur. *Hotel Le Conquérant* (H)M.
Bayeux. *La Rapière* (R)S-M. *Family Home* (C)S.
Bénouville. *Manoir d'Hastings* (HR)L.
Beuzeville. *Auberge du Cochon d'Or* (HR)S. *Le Petit Castel* (H)M.
Bézancourt. *Château du Landel* (HR)M.
Boucéel. *La Ferme de l'Etang* (C)S.
La Bouille. *Le St. Pierre* (H)M(R)L. *Hotel de la Poste* (HR)M. *Maison Blanche* (R)M.
Breuil-en-Auge. *Le Dauphin* (R)M.
Le Breuil-en-Bessin. *Le Château de Goville* (HR)M.
Brionne. *Auberge Vieux Donjon* (HR)S.
Caen. *La Bourride* (R)L. *Le Boeuf Ferré* (R)S-M.
Carteret. *La Marine* (H)M (R)M-L.
Champeaux. *Au Marquis de Tombelaine* (R)M.
Cherbourg. *Le Grandgousier* (R)M.
Clécy. *Le Moulin du Vey* (HR)M. *Auberge du Châlet de Cantepie* (R)M.
Conteville. *Auberge du Vieux Logis* (R)L.
Cosqueville. *Au Bouquet de Cosqueville.* (HR)S.
Crépon. *Ferme de la Rançonnière* (C)L.
Dragey. *Le Grain de Sel* (R)S-M.
Ducey. *Auberge de la Sélune* (HR)M-S.
Fécamp. *Le Grand Banc* (R)S.
Goury. *Auberge de Goury* (R)M.
Granville. *Le Phare* (R)M. *Le Michelet* (H)M.
Hambye. *Auberge de l'Abbaye* (H)S(R)M.
Honfleur. *Le Castel Albertine* (H)M-L. *Le Belvédère* (H)S(R)M. *Au P'tit Mareyeur* (R)M. *L'Assiette Gourmande* (R)M. *Le Bistrot du Port* (R)M-S. *Château de Prêtreville* (H)M.

Joburg. *Les Grottes* (R)M.
Jumièges. *Restaurant du Bac* (R)S-M.
Leaupartie. *Suzanne Guérin* (C)S.
Le Lion d'Or. *Le Relais du Lion d'Or* (R)S-M.
Lisieux. *La Ferme du Roy* (R)M.
Maisons. *Manoir du Carel* (C)L.
Marigny. *Restaurant de la Poste* (R)M.
Mesnil-Val. *La Vieille Ferme* (HR)M.
Mortagne-au-Perche. *Hostellerie Genty Home* (HR)M.
Château des Carreaux (H)M.
Négreville. *Le Mesnil Grand* (HR)M.
Notre-Dame-de-Courson. *Château de Belleau* (HR)M.
Pierrefitte-en-Auge. *Les Deux Tonneaux* (R)S.
Pont Audemer. *Auberge du Vieux Puits* (H)M (R)L.
Pont d'Ouilly. *Auberge St. Christophe* (HR)S. *Hotel du Commerce* (HR)S.
Prêtreville. *See* **Honfleur.**
Putanges-Pont Ecrépin. *Hotel Lion Verd* (HR)S.
Quinéville. *Château de Quinéville* (HR)M.
Rainefreville. *Le Clos Cacheu* (C)L.
Rouen. *Colin's Hotel* (H)M. *La Couronne* (R)L. *L'Orangerie* (R)M. *Les Maraîchers* (R)M-S. *Charles* (R)S. *Bertrand Warin* (R)L. *Beffroy* (R)L.
St. André d'Hébertot. *Auberge du Prieuré* (HR)M.
St. Aubin-du-Perron. *Château du Perron* (C)L.
St. Christophe. *See* **Pont d'Ouilly.**
St. Georges-de-la-Rivière. *Manoir de Caillemont* (C)L.
St. Germain-de-Tournebut. *Au Bon Accueil* (R)S.
St. Paterne. *Le Château de St. Paterne* (C)L.
St. Pierre-sur-Dives. *Restaurant du Marché* (R)S.
St. Vaast-la-Hougue. *Hotel France et Fuchsias* (HR)M.
Thury-Harcourt. *Suisse Normande* (R)S.
Verneuil-sur-Avre. *Le Saumon* (HR)M. *Le Clos* (HR)L.
Vernon. *Restaurant de la Poste* (R)S.
Veules-les-Roses. *Les Galets* (R)L.
Villequier. *Hotel de France* (HR)S.

Here are some readers' recommendations which arrived too late for checking, but sound interesting. All reports welcome.

Dieppe. *Le Bas Fort Blanc* (R)M. Peter Rheinberg.
Commes (1 km from Port en Bessin). *La Goulette* (HR)S. Charles-Henry de Valbray.
Rumesnil, Cabremer (Auge). *Suzanne Lesuffleur* (C).
Etreham, near Bayeux. *Manoir de Ribot* (HR)M.
Pont Audemer. *La Ricardière* (C)L.
Chemilly (between Mamers and Belleme). *La Petite Auberge* R(S).

Tourouvre *Hotel de France* (HR)S.
Bellême. *Restaurant de la Paix* (R)M.
Colleville-sur-Mer. *Ferme-Auberge du Loucel* (R)S. Mme Corpet.
Sully, near Bayeux. *Château de Sully* (HR)M.
Le Havre. *Le Traiteur* (R)S. Roger Hunstone.

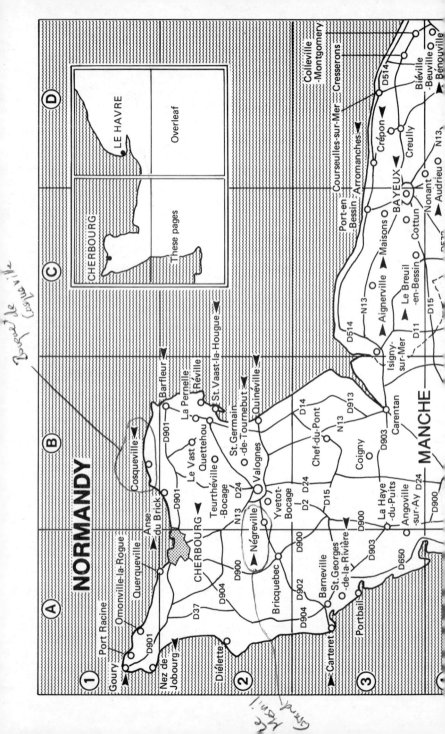

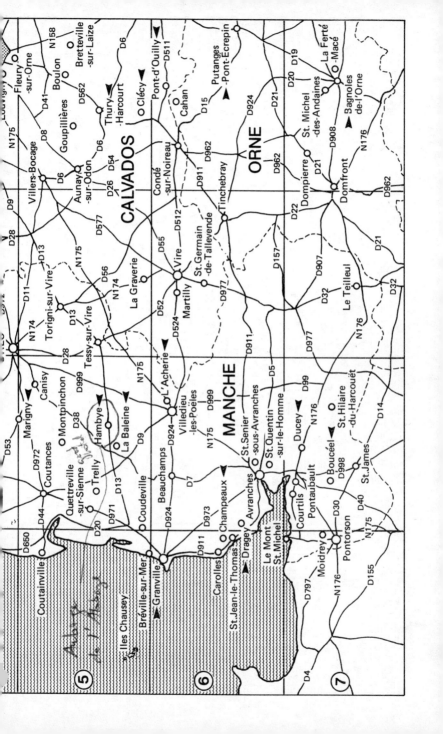

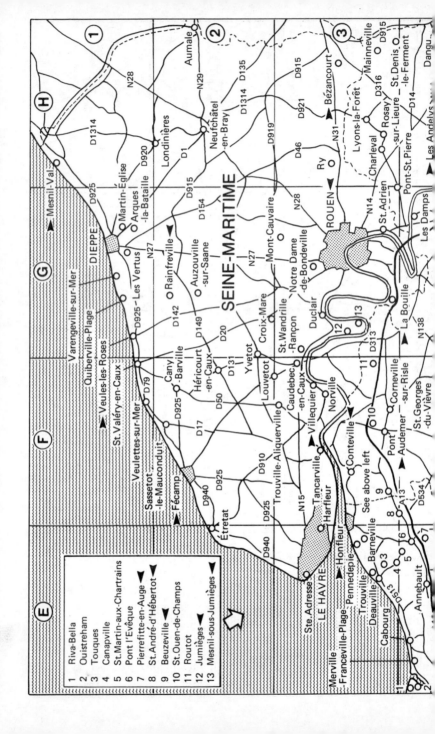

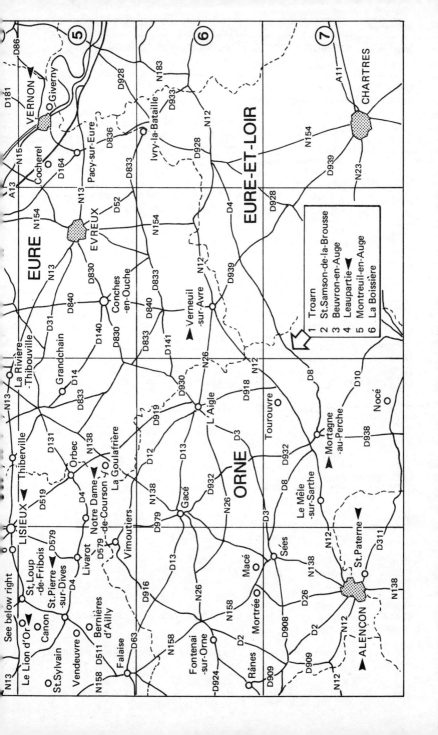

Map 6B ACHERIE 50800 Villedieu-les-Poëles, Manche. 4 km E of Villedieu by D 554

➤ Manoir de l'Acherie
(HR)M *33.51.13.87 Cl. Mon.; Feb. school hols; 26/6–10/7 CB*

This little Logis de France, strategically situated in pleasant peaceful countryside on a popular route south, is a fine 17C manor-house, well restored. It retains its appealing rusticity, with thick stone walls, monumental fireplace and old beams.

M. Cahur, the patron, used to be a charcutier, and now continues his craft in preparing for his restaurant robust country food – terrines, boudins and andouillettes. Lots of charcoal grills, and home-made cider. Excellent menus from 55f, with the 85f version particularly recommended.

The rooms are a bit dull, but very clean and well-equipped, with facilities for the handicapped. Good value at 240–300f.

'We all agreed that the best meal of our stay was at the Manoir de l'Acherie. The buildings and gardens are beautifully kept and pleasantly lit at night, whilst the main dining area is spotlessly clean and very welcoming. The main meat courses were cooked on a huge log fire. Service was excellent and the staff were helpful and friendly. Even though we had the cheapest meal, it included succulent steaks and local speciality sausages. The choice of sweets included about twenty variations.' Bryan Hugill.

An arrow for good cooking in a popular tourist area.

Map 6F L'AIGLE 61300 Orne. 54 km E of Argentan

Ⓣ *pl. F. de Beina (summer) 33.24.12.40* Ⓜ *Tues.*

Its odd name refers to the old trade of making pins and needles here. On the river Risle, it is not a very noteworthy town since the 1944 bombing.

Le Dauphin
(HR)M *pl. de la Halle 33.24.43.12 Open every day AE, DC, EC, CB*

A solid erstwhile relais de la poste, which I have always found somewhat gloomy. It has now had a facelift however and I am told that the rooms are much improved. 200–400f.

Nothing wrong with the cooking, which has earned a long-established Michelin star for M. Bernard. He now combines his traditional recipes with some more modern cooking, on menus from 110f.

Auberge St. Michel
(R)M *St. Michel-Tuboeuf, on the N 26 33.24.20.12 and 33.84.80.66 Cl. Wed. p.m.; Thurs.; and ten days in Feb. CB, EC*

In the shade of the forest a few km E of L'Aigle; a summer meal, served on the terrace of this little Norman inn, can be a delightful experience. There is a 68f weekday menu, but the 92f version is best.

Map 3C   **AIGNERVILLE** 14710 Trevières, Calvados. 15 km NW of Bayeux

---

A hamlet in deepest countryside.

Manoir de l'Hormette
(C)L *31.22.51.79   Cl. 16/11–15/3, except by special request*

Make sure, whatever you do, that you have a good map or clear instructions before you even attempt to locate l'Hormette. Mme Corpet assured me that none of her other guests ever got lost, but we circled around for some time, always assisted by local advice, before we discovered the lane leading to this nice old farmhouse.

L'Hormette dates from the 17C and its farm buildings enclose a very hygienic courtyard filled with flowers. Everywhere is immensely spick and span and never a mucky boot in sight. Mme Corpet has been a leading light in the château b. and b. business, pioneering the Normandy group and acting as secretary to their various organisations. She speaks fluent English and is an excellent source of local information of every kind. She is also an unusually good cook and has the unique distinction among b. and b. châtelaines of appearing in the Gault et Millau guide. She charges 200f for dinner, which should not be missed, but must be reserved in advance, including wine before, during and after, and coffee. Her immaculate bedrooms cost from 370 to 400f, with breakfast, including three kinds of home-made jam, another 40f.

Arrowed for all-round excellence in a popular tourist area.

Map 7E   **ALENÇON** 61000 Orne. 220 km from Le Havre

ⓣ *Maison d'Ozé 33.26.11.36*   Ⓜ *Tues., Wed., Thurs., Sat.*

A delightful old town, of manageable size. Narrow, ancient, cobbled streets, mellow stone courtyards, black Norman timbered houses, window boxes full of geraniums, splashing fountain (modern – hideous) in the main square, pedestrianised centre, all guarded over by the massive cathedral, make it a very agreeable place to pass an hour or so.

The information Bureau is now agreeably sited in the 15C Maison d'Ozé, whose colourful garden makes a serene retreat in which to study maps and ideas. Perhaps a visit to the École Dentellière might appeal, to see the delicate Point d'Alencon lace. The school in the rue Pont Neuf, is open 10–11.30, 2–5, except Sun. and Mon. The art of lace-making is dying, alas, and now a scrap of the intricate work costs, if not a king's ransom, more than a tourist's. The State keeps the school going more for prestige than as a commercial enterprise. Some of the lace is exhibited in the Musée de Beaux Arts in the 18C Hôtel de Ville, whose somewhat mixed collection of paintings includes a Ribera – 'Christ Bearing the Cross' – and a Géricault – 'Naufragé'.

Nôtre Dame is one cathedral that I prefer to view from the outside (preferably sitting at the café in the square). The flamboyant porch is the best bit. Inside interest centres on the chapel to St. Thérèse, who took her first communion there, and the 16C stained-glass windows in the nave.

Alençon makes an excellent touring centre, from which to explore lower Normandy, especially the *Perche* region, with delightful little towns like *Sées* and *Mortagne* within easy reach. It is set between the forests of *Écouve* and *Perseigne*, with the *Alpes Mancelles* (the name is grander than the Alpes) and the newly designated *National Park of Normandy-Maine* to the west. *Château d'Ô*, *Médavy* and *le Pin d'Haras*, the national stud and stunning 18C château, are pleasant drives to the north. I thoroughly recommend a stay here, particularly combined with:

Le Chapeau Rouge
(H)M   *1 bvd. Duchamp   33.26.20.23   EC, V*

An attractive little white hotel, sited right in the centre of the town (good) on the busy Le Mans exit road (possibly bad). The rooms have been recently renovated and are good value at 120–250f, but you'd have to keep your windows closed to get a good night's sleep.

Le Grand Cerf
(HR)M   *21 r. St. Blaise   33.26.00.51   Cl. Sun. o.o.s. and 23/1–14/2   CB, AE, EC*

An attractive 19C building in the centre of the town, with comfortable rooms and a restaurant of sorts. Rooms 140–340f. Meals from 80f.

Le Grand St-Michel
(HR)S   *7 r. du Temple   33.26.04.77*

I was very pleased to have firm confirmation that my hunch about this pleasantly old-fashioned, cheap hotel in a central quiet street would be a good bet:
'A bargain in every way, especially the food. We found the setting ideal, so close to the centre and yet utterly quiet. We had a room with shower for 103f. The menu at 50f. was quite the best value we encountered. This included four courses with a full cheeseboard. The hors d'oeuvre trolly was a feast in itself. Madame, who served, is extremely lively and friendly, and speaks perfect English. Highly recommended.' –Susan Leyden.

➤ Au Petit Vatel
(R)M-L   *72 pl. du Cdt. Desmeulles   33.26.23.78   Cl. Sun. p.m.; Wed.; 3 weeks in Feb.; 15/8–1/9*

One of my favourite Norman restaurants, largely due to the geniality of its chef-proprietor, Michel Lerat. He not only cooks extremely well, but actually cares if you enjoy your meal. You have only to witness the locals arriving at his little restaurant on the outskirts of the town and notice the genuine welcome they receive (a *great* deal of kissing goes on), to guess that this is a favourite Alençon institution.

The dining rooms are pretty, decorated nowadays in pink, and I guarantee a happy atmosphere. The cuisine is traditional Norman, but never dull. Fish are particularly good, as are the desserts. Menus from 118f, carafe wine. Arrowed for good food and welcome.

Map 4H **LES ANDELYS** 27700 Eure. 40 km SE of Rouen; 115 km from Le Havre

---

Ⓣ *1 r. Ph.-Auguste 32.54.41.93* Ⓜ *Mon. Visits to château: 9–12; 2–6, except Tues. and Wed. mornings, from 15/3–15/11*

The town with everything. Away from the industrial sprawl, near the autoroute to Paris, sheltered from the north and east by the jagged

Les Andelys

white escarpment sliced by the ever-fascinating Seine, and dominated by the impressive Gaillard Castle, its setting is probably the most attractive in the Seine Valley.

Richard the Lionheart, King of England, Duke of Normandy, thought so too. He built his fortress here in 1196, high on the commanding cliff-top and successfully barred the way to Rouen from the French King Philippe-Auguste. So massive was its foundation, so formidable its site, that it held Philippe at bay for seven years, by which time King John had succeeded to the English throne. Philippe assembled all his forces and eventually the castle yielded to his battering.

I would rate a visit to the ruins top priority in a visit to this area. The view from the summit is literally breathtaking, no matter whether you approach it by a long puff up the hill behind the Tourist Bureau or by car, 3 km via Le Grand Andelys. Far below the loops of the Seine lie shining, to left, to right and to centre; Le Petit Andelys nestles in the crook and the river barges passing slowly in and out of the range of vision, as though pulled by an invisible string, add animated perspective. A couple of hours could pass by very easily here, walking, clambering, photographing, picnicking. Don't miss it.

➤ **La Chaine d'Or**
(HR)M   *27 r. Grande   32.54.00.31   Cl. Sun. p.m. and Mon.; 1/1–2/2   EC, V*

If Les Andelys is the town with everything, La Chaine d'Or is the hotel with ditto. Its situation, right on the bank of the river, could not be bettered; it is a charming 18C building, with large windows in the dining room making the best of the view. Inside all is warm and mellow, and prosperity has meant that the furnishings now are delightfully in keeping – pink table cloths, pink curtains, everything rosy.

All the bedrooms are being revamped, which could spell disaster, since I particularly liked the slightly faded, spacious feel of the old ones. However Madame Foucault assures me that the character will not be changed – only the mod cons – so we shall have to reserve judgement.

Certainly the food is vastly improved, but at a cost. The menu is now 200f, or a very limited mid-week 120f version, with a choice of only two entrées. Afternoon tea costs £2 a cup. Only a few years ago I was able to recommend a 55f menu, so the changes are obvious. When I first found La Chaine d'Or for F.E.3, it was a simple little inn, in a fantastic position, with modest prices, and I arrowed it unhesitatingly. Then grumbles began because of the rocketing prices, and the arrow had to be removed in subsequent editions. It is now quite obvious that the Foucaults are highly ambitious patrons, and they have succeeded in upgrading their hotel considerably, with consequent price increases. Their hotel should now be viewed from an altogether new standpoint and considered as a far-from-cheap but unique option. It has attracted more correspondence (most of it favourable, particularly about the food) than any other hotel in F.E.3, so the arrow is happily restored.

Map 3A   **ANGOVILLE-SUR-AY** 50430 Manche. 5 km N of Lessay

Take the D 306 off the D 906 south of La Haye to find this hamlet, strategically sited, a convenient drive from the ferry on the way south and only four miles from the sea.

Mme Danièle Boulland
(C)S *'Semilly'* 33.46.04.84

Mme Boulland has two guest rooms, in her farmhouse, for which she charges 130f for two people or 210f for four in a family room.

'Our "chambre famille" was clean and comfortable and with a very pleasant breakfast – two types of home-made jam, all for £20 for the four of us. If the children had woken early enough, they could have watched her husband do the milking. It was well sign-posted off the main road, certainly off the beaten track. You would have to go looking for an evening meal, but for us it was a very good first-night stop after arriving off the ferry in the early evening.' – Mrs. Andy Edgecombe.

Map 4E   **ANNEBAULT** 14430 Dozulé, Calvados.   9 km W of Pont l'Evêque. On the N 175

Le Cardinal
(HR)M   *31.64.81.96   Open year round   All cards*

A very useful address indeed. La patronne, Mme Légentil, doesn't cash in on her strategic position – on a crossroads so near the autoroute – to offer take-it-or-leave-it food. The Cardinal would merit a detour, not just a convenience stop.

Inside all is mock-rustic, with black and white tiled floors, copper pans, rush-seated chairs and a healthy fire to combat winter chills. The cooking is traditional – veal kidneys Normande, duck with wild mushrooms, fish in cider sauce – copious and good, on a recommended 85f menu. We were made most welcome and given complimentary appetisers even after we had placed an extremely modest lunch order.

Five bedrooms were in course of being refurbished when I was there, prices not yet established. I would guess, judging by the pristine efficiency of the rest of Mme Légentil's domaine, that they would be good news. They could of course be noisy, but the hotel is set back from the main road behind a garden. Reports welcome.

Map 2B   **ANSE-DU-BRICK** Manche. 10 km E of Cherbourg

Take the coast road D 116 east of Cherbourg, signposted not very clearly from the terminal 'Anse du Brick', to get away from the town almost immediately, dodging all the other ferry passengers' cars and starting your holiday at least 15 minutes before them. The ride is a peaceful and attractive one, with sea views to left and the rolling Norman countryside to right. Michelin calls it 'the Fermanville-Bretteville Corniche', which, it says, 'should be taken slowly to be appreciated.'

On the way you could visit the lighthouse at Cap Lévy, where 113 steps to the top will reward you with a spectacular view of the port and as far west as Cap la Hague. There's a good crêperie on the road, on the site of an old windmill; in fact the valley in which it stands is called the Valley of the Windmills and is well worth exploring.

Above a bay that is beautiful out of season, but has too many bodies on it in July and August, stands:

➤ Auberge du Maison Rouge
(R)M   *33.54.33.50   Cl. Mon*

The 'rouge' theme used to be carried through in tablecloths, walls, and general decor, but nowadays it is uncompromisingly blue. I wonder why. It is also smarter than it used to be, with menus starting at 95f; but the view over the water is still as spectacular and this is still recommended as a good stop within easy reach of the port.

Lobsters caught on the rocks below feature on the carte, with a selection of other fresh fish. At the rear there is a new choice, the more rustic Le Pressoir, where you get a choice of entrée thrown in with main dish, averaging about 55f.

This F.E.3 recommendation has won universal praise from readers:
'A superb meal in a superb setting, with excellent service' –James Sandys-Renton.
'It's very smart, the lady in charge very friendly and the food is wonderful. My 85f menu was rillette of duck, salmon, two quail, cheese, pud and coffee. Really excellent value.' – Steve Grainger.
An arrow for position, and good food.

Map 1G   **ARQUES-LA-BATAILLE** 76880 Seine-Mar. 7 km SE of Dieppe

---

From Dieppe I suggest you head for St-Aubin on the D 1 and the Manoir is on your right, near Martigny. If you get lost, it's no great hardship, since the forest of Arques is delightful, with narrow lanes cutting through the beeches, and the D 56 to St Nicholas is pleasure all the way.

Manoir d'Archelles
(HR)S   *31.85.50.16   Cl. Sun. p.m.; 28/7–13/8   AE, EC, V*

A delightful small manor-house which has been restored and modernised, with a bright and cheerful interior. It had a bad patch for a while, and did not live up to its enormous potential (accommodation drastically short in this area), but it seems things are looking up:
'The room was very cheap and the food was delicious – lovely

Manoir d'Archelles

vegetables out of the garden. The people were friendly and if the room was a bit damp and basic, the wonderful atmosphere of the 16th-century building compensated amply. We would certainly go back there.' – Penny Cleminson.

A certain amount of thought must obviously go into deciding whether the Manoir would suit – not everyone is prepared to put up with damp and basic rooms at any price – but bearing in mind its position and value, it would at least make a possible first and last night stop. Rooms 130 – 220f. Menus from 60f.

Map 3D   **ARROMANCHES** 14117 Calvados

Ⓣ *r. Mar-Joffre Summer only 31.21.47.56* Ⓜ *Every day from June to September*

They say that this little town is a tourist trap in the summer, or more particularly around the time of the D-Day landings in June; I have only been there out of season, when I found it unexpectedly delightful. Admittedly the D-Day museum does dominate the seafront, but the rest of the town retains a lot of its old character and there is a very pleasant little beach.

A visit to the excellent museum is a must, not only for the veterans who remember, but for subsequent generations who cannot fail to be moved by this unique slice of history vividly recaptured. Climb the hill above the town and look down upon the caissons that formed part of the astonishing Mulberry Harbour. A substantial portion of the original 8 km stretch still remains. The *table d'orientation* clarifies the different landings and the tourists seem strangely quiet, as the impact of just how it must have been hits them.

> **Marine**
(HR)S   *33.22.34.19   Cl. 14/11–1/3   AE, EC, V*

How pleasant, how unusual, to have a steady stream of praise for a modest little hotel like this, over a considerable number of years. Set on the quayside, with a splendid view over the port, it would be very easy to cash in on easy trade, but M. Verdier has never allowed this to happen. The rooms are clean, smallish, comfortable, many with sea views, and cost from 230–300f. Menus from 70f.

'*This one is outstanding. It can be recommended to anyone for its cuisine, especially to those who like superbly cooked seafood. Rooms are good and the staff efficient and friendly, particularly M. Verdier and his wife. When he heard that, as a young officer, I had landed almost on his doorstep, he prepared a special Normandy dinner for our party. He played a considerble part in organising the anniversary celebrations.*' – G. Kearn.

Well, you can't say fairer than that. An arrow for consistent good value.

Map 4D   **AUDRIEU** 14250 Calvados. 13 km SW of Bayeux

Clearly marked to the south of the N 13 between Caen and Bayeux.

> **Château d'Audrieu**
(HR)L   *31.80.21.52   Rest. cl. Thurs. lunch; Wed.; both hotel and rest. cl. 30/11–28/2*

A stunningly beautiful 18C château, perfectly symmetrical. It is set in immense grounds, surrounded by ancient trees and flower gardens that always seem ablaze with colour no matter the season. There is a heated swimming-pool.

This treasure was nearly destroyed during the Normandy landings. For six weeks it was in no man's land, attacked by British and Canadians from one side and by Germans from the other. 27 shells landed on the building. But the golden Caen stone resisted most of the blast and there is little trace today of the horrors and destruction.

In its reincarnation it is an elegant hotel, a member of the Relais et Châteaux chain, which not only offers exceedingly comfortable bedrooms – from 400–1,650f – but outstanding cooking. Usually I counsel going for the best rooms or bank on disappointment, but here the 400f version, newly converted in the old attics, are probably the best value.

The cooking of Alain Cornet, trained at Senderens, has gone from strength to strength and a second Michelin star may be on its way. He uses local ingredients with originality – a croustade d'Isigny, overflowing with oysters, set in a bed of spinach, and the best

Château d'Audrieu.

andouille in this land of andouilles. If you remember blancmange from schooldays, make sure you taste the Audrieu version, just to lay the ghost. Laced with Calvados, it is highly unsuitable for the under-ages.

Catch the weekday menu if you can. At 130f it's the bargain of the week. If not, it will be a well-spent 250f. Arrowed for accessible luxury, if you can afford it, and sublime cooking, whether you can afford it or not.

Map 2H **AUMALE** 76390 Seine-Mar. 45 km SW of Amiens; 22 km E of Neufchatel

---

Ⓣ *Hotel de Ville (summer)* Ⓜ *Sat. p.m.*

Right on the Normandy border, where the D 316 crosses the N 29. An important dairy-farming centre, but of little other interest.

Le Mouton Gras
(HR)S *2 r. de Verdun* *35.93.41.32* *Cl. Mon. p.m. and Tues.; 20/12–6/1* *DC, EC, V*

Definitely a 'restaurant with rooms' rather than a hotel with food, so staying here means sorting out priorities.

It's an attractive old Norman building, heavily beamed, with a local reputation for excellent food and a good welcome from the entire Gauthier family. The six rooms are simple, but cost only 150f.

'Dinner was superb, with Madame Gauthier coping cheerfully, quite unperturbed, with a three-minute power cut in the middle. The dining room was full, and we met some customers who had been coming here for over ten years.' –T. Lamb.

'Rooms in barn annexe across courtyard, not cheap at 250f per night, but high standard of comfort, equipment and cleanliness. The 110f three-course meal in restaurant excellent, but wine prices astronomical.' – M. R. Cooper Cocks.

Map 5D   **AUNAY-SUR-ODON** 14260 Calvados. 29 km SW of Caen

(T) *pl. Hotel de Ville 31.77.60.32* (M) *Sat.*

I cannot claim that Aunay is a lovable little town in its post-war reconstruction, at the hub of six D roads. Do not make a detour, but just in case:

Le St. Michel
(HR)S *r. Caen 31.77.63.16 Cl. Sun. p.m. and Mon. o.o.s.; 15/1–30/11 EC, V*

'A delight. It has just been refurbished and for 130f. we had a warm comfortable double room with shower. We had an excellent meal for 82f, from which I can particularly recommend the feuilleté de saumon and truite de mer. Also the impressive cheeseboard. Madame was welcoming and helpful and can speak English.' – Ann Mellor.
   Rooms 140–170f; menus from 60f.

Map 2G   **AUZOUVILLE-SUR-SAANE** 76730 Bacqueville-en-Caux, Seine-Mar. 25 km SW of Dieppe

One of the prettiest roads in the Caux area is the little D 2, which follows through leggy poplar avenues the valley of the Saane to the village of the same name – Val de Saane. This is neat, prosperous organised countryside, with glimpses of well-tended formal gardens surrounding elegant châteaux – weekend retreats for Parisien aristocracy. The farms are tidier than usual, too, with white-picket fences, timbered homesteads, flowers all the way, clean white chickens and Norman cows spoiled by the abundance of rich pasture.

There used to be two excellent restaurants to justify a visit to this little village, but both of them have fallen by the wayside. I was therefore delighted to have another excuse to renew acquaintance.

Mme Rémy Mortier
(C)S *35.83.74.43*

> Double room, sharing shower costs 145f, including a good breakfast.
> *'We agree that this is a very attractive village in a delightful area. We discovered Madame Mortier, who has just made available two rooms in her attractive house, each with shower and WC and washbasin. She herself is very cheerful and we feel it could be thoroughly recommended.'* – Dennis Greig.

Map 6B   **AVRANCHES** 50300 Manche. 125 km S of Cherbourg

Ⓣ *r. Gén. de Gaulle 33.58.00.22* Ⓜ *Sat.*

> A lively and colourful town, sited on the main approaches to Brittany and Mont St-Michel and therefore popular for overnight stops; well served with hotels.
> In 1944 General Patton launched his victorious 3rd Army attack from Avranches, which got off the mark so quickly that the town escaped extensive damage. American soil and trees were flown over to form a square for the Patton Memorial, which thereby stands on American territory.
> On the site of the former cathedral is 'La Plate-Forme', where Henry II knelt to do penance for the murder of Thomas à Becket, which resulted from his exasperated plea for someone to rid him of this insolent priest. Having viewed the little square, walk to the end of the terrace to get a good panorama of Mont St-Michel.
> Another good viewing point of the Mont and surrounding countryside, river Sélune threading through, is from the Jardins Publiques above the town. From there you can train a telescope on the distant island and, like a James Bond film, watch unsuspecting figures walking round the ramparts.
> The gardens themselves are a blaze of all the unflower-like flowers so dear to French gardeners' hearts. Cannas, cacti, begonias, tortured into unnatural cohabitation, dazzle the eye with their strident orange, purple and fuchsia-pink. Gertrude Jekyll would have turned in her grave at the vulgarity, but the gardens are certainly a cheerful, cool retreat, and the Avranchins are extremely proud of them.
> For connoisseurs of the bizarre, a visit to the basilica of St-Gervais might prove interesting. There in the Treasury rests the skull of St-Aubert, holed by the reproachful finger of St-Michel, grown impatient at Aubert's dilatoriness in building the usual tribute to the saint on the summit of Mont Tombe, later Mont St-Michel.

La Croix d'Or
(HR)M-S *83 r. Constitution 33.58.04.88 Cl. mid Nov.–mid Mar. EC, V*

> A pleasant old building on the outskirts of the town, with beamy rustic dining room and attractively decorated bedrooms in a peaceful chalet annexe, from 100–400f.

The only hiccup in the past has been the uninterested attitude of the staff, but recent reports are encouraging, and the food has been particularly praised. Dinner is obligatory for hotel guests. Menus from 90f.

Du Jardin des Plantes
(HR)S   *10 pl. Carnot   33.58.03.68   Cl. Sun. p.m. o.o.s., 20/12–5/1   EC, V*

Several readers have commended this simple hotel on the pl. Carnot:
'We had an excellent meal here and the 39f menu contained a splendid couscous as the plat du jour. The service was slow (it was packed with Frenchmen) but the food was so good that it seemed very good value for money. We were able to buy a carafe of house wine instead of the usual bottles of overpriced wines in the other establishments you recommend.'(!) – J. L. Humphreys.
Rooms: 140–280f, menus from 52f. Carafe wine.

Mme. Suzanne Couëtil
(C)M   *8 pl. Carnot   33.68.29.88*

I was pleased to have this comprehensive report from a reader:
'The house is in a terrace and is immaculate. The furniture is beautiful and 'real'. The four of us had the top floor to ourselves – 2 bedrooms, each with cabine de toilette and on the landing there was a separate shower and toilet. We ate our breakfast in a delightful conservatory, which looked out onto a secluded walled garden. Mme Couëtil does not speak much English but she is so very kind and goes out of her way to help.' – Mrs. A. Small.
120f for a double room makes this seem a real bargain, in the centre of the town and yet quiet.

Map 7D   **BAGNOLES-DE-L'ORNE** 61140 Orne. 39 km SW of Argentan; 96 km S of Caen

---

(T) *pl. République, summer only 33.37.85.66*   (M) *Tues., Sat.*

A town of many moods; an impression formed on a warm summer's day would be very different from one out of season; at weekends the atmosphere is nothing like that on a Monday afternoon. It has been interesting to note the date of readers' letters and to verify that those who agree with me have visited more than once, at varying times of the year.
This is a spa town, very green, very tidy, very manicured, not very French. Its season is extremely short and most of its numerous hotels close firmly for at least three months of the year, but are booked well ahead for the summer. You can hardly go wrong in selecting one, if cleanliness and rectitude is all you seek.
On a recent summer's visit I liked it better than previously – I'm getting older – but would suggest that it only shakes off its lethargy at

the weekends, when all the cafés are full and the families strolling round the lively central lake contribute to a general sense of well-being and restrained animation. The Norman-style mock towers and terraces, chequered bricks, balconies and beams all add a touch of whimsical eccentricity, accentuating its unreality. Without doubt Bagnoles provides the perfect antidote to motorist's stress. Frenetic it is not.

> ## Hotel Lutétia
(HR)M   *bvd. Paul Chalvet   33.37.94.66   Cl. Oct.–April   AE, DC, EC, V*

Perhaps my softening attitude to Bagnoles has something to do with discovering the Lutétia. Those readers – and they are many – who have loved the Moulin du Vey at Clécy would do well to consider an overnight stop here, under the same direction, presided over by the kind and efficient Mme. Tramontana.

The rooms are gradually being restored; they are all quiet and look out over soothing greenery. In the annex they may be brand new, but they still have lots of character, tastefully decorated, with luxurious bathrooms, good value at 195f. Those in the older main house are quite rightly more traditional in style, and cost a very reasonable 420f.

A new addition is a lovely glassed-in terrace where, on a hot summer evening, the windows – looking out on to the garden, dotted with expensive loungers – slide back, and the feeling is of eating al fresco, without the midges.

The menus are 100f and 160f. On the latter I ate terrine of duck with pistachios, assorted fish in Vouvray sauce, noisette of lamb and a terrine of fresh fruit.

Arrowed for excellent value and sympathetic management.

Ermitage
(H)M   *24 bvd. P. Chalvet   33.37.96.22   Cl. 30/9–1/5   EC, V*

One reader, who came across Bagnoles on a stiflingly hot day, and found its coolness and calm utterly delightful, had no reservations:

'A pleasant-looking hotel with balconies to the rooms. Ours was one of the nicest we have had, with shower and separate lavatory. The management is very pleasant and courteous. Price 195f.

We do not agree with your opinion of the town. There were plenty of people about, some watching the football semi-final on TV in a bar. Nothing could look more French than the restaurant of the Gayot Hotel' (pl. République, 33.37.90.22) *'where we had dinner. It could be used, untouched, in any film where a typical French restaurant was required.'* – Mrs. A. Vause.

Hotel Capricorne
(HR)M   *Allée Montjoie   33.37.96.99   Cl. October-Easter   AE, DC, EC, V*

'Following a visit in January we would agree wholeheartedly with your statement on its moods. However in 1989 the town played host to the UK Military Vehicles Trust, who were in France to celebrate the 45th anniversary of the D-Day landings, and from 30th May to 3rd June Bagnoles was ALIVE.

We spent three nights at the Hotel Capricorne, and can thoroughly recommend it as a place to stay, although we cannot comment on the food. The rooms were comfortable, airy and quiet.' – Mrs. M. A. Cole.
Rooms are 270–400f. Menus from 95f.

Le Manoir du Lys
(HR)M   *Rte de Juvigny   33.37.80.69   Cl. Sun. p.m. o.o.s; Mon.; 1/1–4/3   CB, AE*

In the middle of the forest, just 3 km out of town on the D 335, is this turn-of-the-century manor-house, which would be an excellent choice for a peaceful base. Patron Paul Quinton is head chef and loves to cook local produce, including wild mushrooms he so diligently searches out in the neighbouring grounds. His wife Marie-France offers smiling welcome. The rooms are luxurious and good value at 290–470f and Paul's excellent cooking features on menus from 95f (weekdays), or 170f at weekends.
Tennis, golf, and extensive grounds.
There is such a choice of hotels that it seems invidious to make a selection, but others that have been hightly recommended are Albert Ier and the Beaumont (both in a more inexpensive category).

Map 5B   **LA BALEINE** 50650 Hambye, Manche. 3 km SW of Hambye; 22 km SE of Coutances

---

In a maze of country lanes due west of the Abbey of Hambye. You could try turning west off the D 38 from St. Denis le Gast and taking the D 238, but I recommend getting lost – it's all so pretty you will not consider the time wasted.

➤ l'Auberge de la Baleine
(R)S   *33.61.76.77   Cl. Sun. p.m. and Mon.; open every day in July and Aug.*

Is it possible? Yet another rural treasure so near Hambye? It seems it is.
The old village school has been transformed into a delightful country inn run by young anthusiastic Jean-Charles Vézin and his wife. His pedigree is impressive – he has worked at the great Rostang in Paris amongst others, and it shows.
Baleine is well known for the production of local ham and andouilles smoked over charcoal fires, and the complimentary amuse-bouche is, sure enough, a piece of delicious andouille on toast. From then on it gets surprisingly sophisticated, but always with a great respect for local ingredients – and I count the sea as local (this is France, not Britain!). Menus at the moment are from 55f (and 75, 95, 135, 160f!), but it can only be a short while before Michelin gets wise, and then the sky's the limit, so catch this one soon. I have not inspected the rooms yet, so all reports particularly welcome.
The first sighting of the Auberge came in 1987, with this report:
'We remembered seeing the Auberge last year and it was then in a

state of dilapidation. The present proprietors have only been there four months and have done the place up very nicely. We had a really lovely large room at the front, looking out across the courtyard to trees and fields. All spotlessly clean. A big attractive dining room had a log fire. We think that we were the first English people to stay there.' – Mary Kerridge.

Since then a steady stream of readers have confirmed that this is a winner:

'Tranquil surroundings, superb food, slightly nouvelle cuisine and reasonably priced, and the owners are very attentive and eager to please. I had warm skate salad to start with and it was superb. For the main course I also chose excellent fish; the dessert which was from a choice of eight was an amazing concoction of apple with an unusual sauce. Quite fabulous. Although we did not stay there, we asked to see the rooms, which were all quite large, all facing south and very clean indeed. Prices about 80f per room. Would recommend.' – Jennifer and Noel Ashton.

So would I. An arrow for exceptional cooking in lovely surroundings, at modest cost.

Map 4C   **BALLEROY** 14490 Calvados. 80 km SE of Cherbourg; 16 km SW of Bayeux

---

An enchanting village, like a stage set, with one wide main street of grey stone houses, all of a period, leading down to the focal point, the Château de Balleroy, built in the 17C by Mansart for Jean de Choisy, whose descendant, the Marquis of Balleroy, sold the château to the late Malcolm Forbes, the American publishing tycoon.

One of Forbes's many passions was hot-air ballooning and every June a great festival was held here, when balloonists from all over the world assembled in the grounds and took off over the Calvados countryside. The grounds were open to the public then for Norman country dancing, brass bands, and discreet funfairs, with much eating and drinking throughout. What will happen now that the Lord of the Manor has died remains to be seen.

At other times the château is open from mid-April to late October, except Weds. and 1/5. Admission 12f. There is a hot-air balloon museum in the stables which is open at the same times.

The interior of the château is unexpectedly richly furnished with impressive portraits, silk wall hangings and panellings; the gardens are by Le Nôtre.

► **Manoir de la Drôme**
(R)M   *31.21.60.94   Cl. Sun. p.m. and Mon.; 15/1–15/2   AE, DC, V*

A welcome newcomer to the Calvados gastronomic scene. Many readers have enthused about the food in this nice old stone house, just outside the village, and it gets the coveted red Michelin R for a commendable good-value menu at 98f.

Château de Balleroy.

The cooking is a happy compromise between traditional Norman and modern lightness, the service comes with a smile and the ambiance is quite delightful, meriting a new arrow.

'Service was superb. We had the 98f menu, with five different sorts of bread, including wholemeal, onion, etc. A small helping of smoked duck came with the chef's compliments. Whelks in lemon sauce on rice and caviar, olive tart wrapped in smoked salmon, chicken in ginger, calves liver were all superb. The cheeseboard was easily the best of the holiday. The puddings were lemon mousse in a raspberry coulis or three sorbets in a brandy snap nutty tulipe. Will the prices escalate when it receives the acclaim it deserves?' – Stephen Hayes.

'M. Leclerc cooks (equipped with his Grande Diplome d'Honneur de la Poële d'Or) while she welcomes. The dining rooms are stylish and the setting rather formal but the white-jacketed waiters are very friendly. We chose the 94f Menu Terroir and were not disappointed. The meal got off to a good start with complimentary slices of terrine de poison. Tarte aux poireaux and marinaded trout followed, the latter superb, garnished with avocado. Then pintadeau au vinaigre du cidre and Émincé de Boeuf. A vast cheeseboard preceded the dessert – 5 boules of refreshingly flavoured sorbets and a delicious charlotte. Presentation was full of nice touches, from a choice of bread to bitter chocolates with the coffee.' – Peter and Sue MacDonald.

▶ Hotel des Biards
(HR)S *1 pl. du Marché 31.21.62.05 Cl. Mon.; Jan.; Feb.*

Six years ago I hesitated to include Les Biards in case the lack of paint and carpet should bring down a hail of protests from readers. Now I recognise that this is one of the best-loved entries in F.E.3. I should have given readers credit for looking behind outward appearances to the warmth of the Briards' welcome (the name incidentally is an incredible coincidence), the excellent value for money, and the general ambiance of exceptional French bonhomie.

The bedrooms are about as basic as they could be, but clean, at 75f; Madame Briard hinted that there would be another seven ready for next year, but her husband told her to wait and see. They are approached by steepish uncarpeted wooden stairs, and not recommended for the infirm; the loo is reached through the frenetic kitchens, the dining rooms are decorated with minimum decor, maximum clientèle.

You can easily get away with the 42f menu, which offers good honest copious nosh, but for a real blow-out go for the four-course 68f version.

Arrowed for its consistent popularity, good value and charming proprietors.

'The welcome from both Michel and Madame Briard was both warm and sincere. The cost for five of us for a week at half pension, including all drinks and most excellent food was £357, which I think you will agree is amazing value.' – J. Chappell.

'But what a joy we found at the Hotel des Biards. Notwithstanding the plain exterior the warmth of welcome from Mme Briard and Jacques, the waiter, was quite overwhelming. The genuine friendliness of the couple and the staff and the superb cooking left us quite astonished. We decided to stay there for three days and nights. The menu at 40f is exceptional value though we ventured big and had the 60f bonanza! We met several couples who had returned there for a second time. All were equally enthusiastic. What other hotelier would go out on the green and play football with his sons after cooking a superb supper for his guests?' – Alan and Jane Parkinson.

Map 2B   **BARFLEUR** 50760 Manche. 28 km E of Cherbourg

(T) *Rond point G. le Conquérant 33.54.02.48.* (M) *Sat.*

I sense a revival in the air. For years Barfleur held promise and little more. Its wide main street of granite houses looked important but lacked animation; its port, with sizeable fishing fleet, was always colourful, but without any good restaurant and only one indifferent bar. Once one had looked at the plaque commemorating the departure of William the Conqueror to England (from this very spot) and mugged up the Richard Lionheart story (also embarking from Barfleur, on his way to be crowned King of England), there was not much incentive to linger. Most folk called it a day and drove on to the Pointe de Barfleur to see the 71 m high lighthouse and climb the 365 steps to the panorama, covering the whole of the east coast down to the cliffs of Grandcamp and stretching over the vicious rocks that guard the entrance to the harbour.

But nowadays, I feel there is progress about to be made. A new marina is planned, which will certainly bring more trade to the town, and with it shops and restaurants to bring this sleeping beauty back to life.

There used to be no recommendable hotel, but now:

➤ **Hotel Le Conquérant**
(H)M   *16 r. St. Thomas-Becket   33.54.00.82   Cl. 15/11–15/12; Jan.*

A dignified 17C manor-house in the main street, with the unusual advantage of a large and leafy garden at the rear, in which it is most agreeable to sit and sup. M. and Mme Démore have converted the interior to provide 17 comfortable bedrooms, with mod. cons. like English TV. Calm, peaceful, more like a private house than most hotels, and a very welcome addition to the Barfleur scene. It's good value at 120–300f and arrowed accordingly.

The only problem here might be that it has no restaurant, involving a drive to Quettehou or St. Vaast perhaps. The alternative is to eat at the newly smartened-up Hotel Moderne, where the cooking is said to be very good:

'The most remarkable transformation has been to the Hotel Moderne. It has been taken over by M. and Mme Roulier and refurbished. M. Roulier presides in the kitchen. His standard menus are above average in range and quality, but his specialities are very good indeed, far better than anything else for miles around. Tried and recommended are: Marmite Barfleuraise, a copious and delicious marmite of seafood topped with puff pastry, feuilleté de bar à l'estragon, huitres chaudes en verdurettes and feuillantines de framboises.' – Theo Dampney.

Map 3E   **BARNEVILLE** 14600 Honfleur, Calvados. 6 km SW of Honfleur

Even if you have no intention of staying in Barneville, do yourself a
favour by taking a drive along the Côte de Grace, then swinging inland
on the D 62 and D 279 amid deeply rural and very green countryside.

Auberge de la Source
(HR)S   *31.89.25.02   Hotel cl. Wed.; 15/11-1/2; Rest. cl. Wed., 1/9-1/6, except
weekends in Sept. and May*

There are few inexpensive simple hotels in the Honfleur area, and
those in the town itself are often noisy. For those who value total calm
and peaceful surroundings, the Auberge is a blessing. New rooms in
the single-storey Norman-style annexe are cheerful, bright, all with
bathrooms; in the main house they are older, some with shower.

Less convenient is that demi-pension is insisted on, at 220–250f per
person, which is why there is no arrow in my book. Not that the food is
bad – far from it. (Menus for outsiders are 78f and 140f), but it does
seem a shame that all Honfleur's evening eating alternatives should be
denied to the pensionnaires. That said, I know there are many people
who do not want the hassle of driving out again, and for them the
Auberge is ideal, with a pretty garden and a feature made of the spring
that gives the hotel its name.

Map 3A   **BARNEVILLE-CARTERET** 50270 Manche

Ⓣ *r. des Ecoles 33.04.90.58* Ⓜ *Sat.*

The name is confusing. There is the lively little port and seaside resort
of Carteret, there is the inland market town of Barneville-Carteret, and
there is Barneville Plage, which is more residential and up-market. In
the town is a typically French hotel that pleased many readers under its
former name, the Hotel de Paris:-

Les Embruns
pl. de l'Eglise   33.04.90.02   Cl. Mon. o.o.s

I don't like changes when they involve old favourites, so it was with
some doubt that I re-inspected here. I needn't have worried, since M.
Appaire is every bit as friendly and helpful as his predecessor and,
apart from putting in a new bar, has done little to change the
unassuming character of the place.

There is still the same choice of accommodation – some very simple
rooms with shower at 90f, some with bath at 230f, some in the annexe
that are suitable for disabled, and all variations on single and double
beds.

Menus are from 50–150f. One reader enjoyed his dinner but found
the breakfast 'mediocre'.

Le Gohan
(R)S *r. au Lait* 33.04.95.33

On the way to the beach, signposted from the road.

Gohan is patois for the earthenware pot in which Norman housewives used to take the midday meal out to their menfolk working in the fields. Its deliberately rustic image was chosen to represent this little restaurant crêperie/grill, with bags of atmosphere, friendly owner and a dedication to offering simple well-cooked food at honest prices. Menus from 60f.

Les Isles
(HR)M 33.04.90.75 *Cl. 22/11–1/2* AE, EC, V

Overlooking the beach, a modern hotel, with a nice garden, that readers have found comfortable and efficient.

Rooms are 145–275f, with menus from 75–222f.

Map 4E **BAVENT** 14860 Ranville, Calvados. 7 km SW of Cabourg by D 513 and D 95A

Hostellerie du Moulin du Pré
(H)M R(L) *Rte de Gonneville-en-Auge* 31.78.83.68 *Cl. Sun. p.m.; Mon.; Oct.; 1/3-15.3* AE, DC

This picture-book little hotel, all freshly painted white, set in a flowery garden with a stream running through, beamed interior, comforting log fires in winter, is all that one could ask of a Norman country inn, except in one respect. The prices, which have always been on the high side, are now ridiculous. One is lulled by the room tariff – 230f (but these are very tiny rooms) – and shocked by the bill; the dining room so attractive that the prospect of driving away from it to find an alternative (even if that were encouraged, which it is not), seems unthinkable. The food is so good that it is not until the hour of reckoning comes that you realise that the cheapest menu is 225f and a meal à la carte can cost double that, with wine included. It's lovely if you can afford it.

'A charming place and a bon accueil'. I would describe the food as good not sensational. The huge fire in a low timbered room, made the dining room rather hot, but I liked the place very much and was interested to hear from M. Marion (see Merville-Franceville Plage) that it was his favourite local restaurant.' – R. Furber.

Map 3C   **BAYEUX** 14400 Calvados. 28 km W of Caen

Ⓣ *1 r. Cuisiniers 31.92.16.26* Ⓜ *Sat., Tues. (animals)*

Thanks to its unique treasures – the tapestry and the cathedral – Bayeux has always been special, but I find it a town that actually improves at each visit. Now that the main street has been pedestrianised and you no longer have to walk Indian file on the narrow pavements, a gentle stroll over the cobblestones, admiring the restoration work that is constantly in progress, is most agreeable. The shabby old patricians' houses and smaller dwellings have been spruced up: iron balconies gleam with fresh paint, creamy Caen stone glows grimeless. What is more, it is not just a tourist honeypot. Its hotels and restaurants stay open all year round, and it would be top choice for a winter break.

Try not to rush Bayeux. Its quiet tree-lined side streets, vast squares, river walks and elegant old buildings deserve time to be discovered, just as much as the more obvious tourist attractions. The city had the good luck to escape the devastation that removed so much character from other less fortunate Norman centres, by virtue of serving as a hospital town during the 1944 fighting and by being the first French town to be liberated.

The Tapestry of Queen Mathilde:
About three years ago the city fathers obviously realised that their biggest and unique asset, the tapestry, was not being seen to advantage. At that time it was housed in the Maison du Doyen beside the cathedral and it was almost impossible to see it without peering over burly German shoulders or shuffling round in a slow gaggle of Japanese. A huge amount of restoration has since developed a 'cultural centre' in an old seminary and signs all over the city persuade you in that direction. 17f now to get in, but you get an awful lot for your money. Don't think of trying to fit it in in less than two hours, and that's pushing it.

On the first floor is a mock-up of every detail of the work and a clear description in English and French of what is going on. The critical scenes – Harold's oath, Edward's death, Harold's coronation, the Norman invasion, William's bravery, Harold's death – are all emphasised to make identification easier when you do eventually get to see the actual tapestry. Then there's a 15-minute film, regrettably americanised, and here I would advise a preliminary check of the times of the English version – you could just miss the last showing of the day, or have a very long wait. And then at last into the dark passage where this priceless account of the customs, clothing, food, events of 900 years ago, recorded so unforgettably vividly, awaits you. Don't miss the English moustaches!

Open all day from mid-May to mid-Sept.; the rest of the year from 9–12, 2–5. Admission 17f. 31.92.05.48.

Hotel Lion d'Or
(HR)M   *71 r. St.-Jean   31.92.06.90   Cl. 21/12–21/1   AE, DC, EC, V*

The approach to this old coaching inn, recessed in a courtyard, is much improved by the pedestrianisation of the rue St. Jean, and the atmosphere is calmer than one would expect of a central town hotel. has for generations been a favourite with English tourists, and the changes over that time have been very gradual indeed. It is hard to be hard on an old faithful – like kicking a family dog – but it has to be said that the place has long been due for a renaissance. The Michelin star still hangs on, but only just, one suspects, and there have been several disenchanted grumbles about the service and accueil. Now I am pretty sure that things are looking up. Another generation of Jouvin-Bessières is involved, and the welcome from the patron's daughter is encouraging. Most of the rooms have been refurbished (320–350f) although the downstairs reception area is still incongruously 1960s 'modern'.

Here are some recent experiences:

'Everyone recommends it, so we went there for my birthday. We had the 145f menu. The terrine was boring and plasticky, the chicken vallée d'Auge was boring, with no apple flavour and the pudding was Black Forest gâteau or meringue (no other choice). Service wasn't good, with mistakes in the orders. We rate this B-, taking into account the expense involved.'

'When I phoned it was obvious that we were expected to have dinner. We found the hotel transformed to its advantage. The courtyward now has striped blinds and geraniums on every window sill. Bedrooms cheerfully and attractively decorated. We did not mind having to dine here, as we had a very good meal.' – Miss J. A. Kirby.

My own last meal here was better than previously; there is now a worthy 100f two-course meal, or 140, 190, 270f menu and a wonderful wine list. I hope that the improvements will continue.

Hotel du Luxembourg
(HR)M   *25 r. des Bouchers*   31.92.00.04   *Open every day*   AE, DC, EC, V

A new and grander Hotel de Luxembourg has risen from the flames. It is now the top-rated (on the national star system) hotel in the town and priced accordingly – 450f for a double room with bath. Its rooms are large, and furnishings border on the luxurious. Its restaurant, Les Quatre Saisons, aims at plushness, with its Louis XIII decor, and there is a disco for those who complain that there is no life after 9 p.m. in French provincial towns. The chef uses prime products and the wine list is impressive and expensive. Menus from 90f (weekdays), otherwise 135–280f.

'We thought it good. The rooms were more international in style rather than typique français, but remarkably comfortable and they persuaded us to take their special b. and b. and dinner rate of 290f per person. The first night the set menu was very 'nouve' – beautifully cooked but short of main course! The second was my idea of good French cuisine and more than made up for the previous famine. Staff young, very attentive and friendly.' – Robert Blayney.

Hotel de Brunville
(HR)M   *31.21.18.00*   AE, DC, EC, V

Under the same management as the Luxembourg, but rating only two stars on the national system. Predictably the rooms are smaller and cheaper – 200–250f, but well fitted and comfortable, if somewhat characterless. A practical choice for an overnight stop. It has a restaurant, La Marmite, and the same group owns La Taverne des Ducs in the rue St. Patrice, but I would choose to eat at La Rapière.

Hotel d'Argouges
(H)M   *21 r. St. Patrice   31.92.88.86*

Contrived out of a nice old 18C 'hotel particulier', the Argouges is approached through an archway inthe place St. Patrice. The rooms, with their high dormer windows, are simply furnished; the bathrooms work; all is blissfully quiet, and parking is free. 230–320. No restaurant, but that is no problem in Bayeux, with a choice in easy walking distance.

Churchill Hotel
(HR)M   *14–16 r. St.-Jean   31.21.31.80   Cl. 15/11–15/3   AE, DC, EC*

Recently renovated, in the centre of the town, the Churchill is a stylish hotel, with thirty-two rooms, all with bathroom, for 250–350f. The rooms are not large, but are comfortable, with plenty of accessories. It now has its own restaurant, claiming to use regional ingredients in 'family cuisine' but I have not yet put it to the test, so reports would be welcome.

Hotel Mogador
(H)S   *20 r. Alain Chartier   31.92.24.58*

Continue westwards from the town centre, along the main rue St. Martin to find this little hotel, uninspected by me so far, but sounding good news:-
'Found a little treasure just opening, paint still wet, just off the main square but overlooking it. Entrance just a door between shops. Very friendly proprietor, rooms with showers or baths; own fridge and cooking facilities in some rooms. Very pretty. Excellent breakfast complete with orange juice – real – not ordered.' – Mrs. M. Cannell.
Rooms approximately 150f. More reports please.

La Rapière
(R)S-M   *53 r. St.-Jean   31.92.94.79   Cl. Tues. p.m.; Wed.; 20/12–31/1*

Especially useful on a Monday, when, in common with so many other French towns, Bayeux dies, with no concern for the hungry. But La Rapière is recommendable on many other accounts – it is in an attractive courtyard just off the main pedestrianised area and has been converted into a very pretty little restaurant, with stone walls, lace table-cloths, pink napkins, open fire, all very spruce and agreeable. Equally agreeable are the prices, starting from 65f. The arrow remains.
'We have been here twice, excellent each time, with wine reasonably priced and very friendly staff.' – Louise Scott.
'On the 85f menu we had oysters, skate in hazelnut butter, local cheeses and prunes in an orange sauce. Quite delicious.' – Pat Nappin.

Bayeux is a good choice for an out-of-season break, but with less-than-perfect winter weather and early darkness the idea of a pleasant tea interval becomes even more appealing. I am often asked for recommendations for a good tea-shop and in Bayeux there is certainly one such: *Le Garde-Manger*, 49 rue St.-Jean, is one of those essentiall French salons de thé, where you sit on spindly chairs, sip delicate China tea from delicate china cups and watch the locals dropping in to spend a surprising amount of money on pâtisseries and chocs. A hot chocolate and an indulgent cake make the inclemency outside seem less important.

➤ **Family Home**
(C)S   *39 r. Général de Dais   31.92.15.22*

Never closes! Readers have chalked this one up as an interesting experience! Invariably they have loved the unique atmosphere, with Madame Lefèvre dishing up copious meals, to be eaten by the assembled company at a long table in the old beamed dining room.

It is a nice, faded 16C house set sideways on to a quiet street leading from the main r. St. Mâlo to the Place Charles de Gaulle, i.e. very central. The name is somewhat unfortunate, but it really is the family home for the Lefères, who now let out 28 rooms, some with cooking facilities, all with washbasins, some with twin beds, some family rooms. Those in the older part are nicest, but all are irreproachably clean, if decidedly modest.

Unfortunately, the establishment is sometimes used as a youth hostel. Foreign students use it while 'doing Europe'; they sleep in mixed dormitories in one of the old houses and pay 69f for b. and b. Everyone eats together. This state of affairs only applies at odd times, during school holidays, but it is something to be aware of, since gaggles of schoolchildren can be extremely noisy: it is always best to check before committing yourself.

150–180f buys a room for two or a family, with breakfast included. I think the arrow is still well deserved, for a cheap base in the heart of a fascinating city, in quiet pleasant surroundings, with a good deal of flexibility for accommodation.

'Breakfast was excellent – unlimited butter and coffee, with cheese and preserves; we had one evening meal only, on our last evening. Our mistake! The value was superb – a really excellent meal, with unlimited red wine, all for 55f. For the young in heart, with appetites, I can recommend the Family Home.' – Frank Etherington.

Map 6B   **BEAUCHAMPS** 50320 La Haye Pesnel, Manche. 11 km W of Villedieu-les-Poëles

On a crossroads where the Coutances-Avranches road, the D 7, crosse the Villedieu-Granville road, the D 924.

Les Quatre Saisons
(R)M   *33.61.30.47 Cl. Tues. o.o.s.   EC, V*

A very pretty old building, inside and out, with interesting menus and friendly proprietors. It makes a useful en route stop and is popular locally, particularly at weekends, so a phone booking is not a bad idea at busy times.

'It is run by M. and Mme Muret and was very good, little changed in eight years. The cheapest menu was 45f – four courses and not all andouillettes or tripes or whatever.' – Alastair Wilson, 'very much aided by Jill Wilson'.

Map 4F   **LE BEC-HELLOUIN** 27800 Brionne, Eure. 24 km SE of Pont Audemer

 Fri.

Follow the river Risle, on the D 130, 2 km from Pont Audemer, through the Montfort Forest, to Bec Hellouin, whose great ruined abbey gives the hamlet a cathedral-close atmosphere. Founded in 1034, the abbey has strong links with England through Duke William's friend and counsellor, Lanfranc, who was instructor at Le Bec and subsequently Archbishop of Canterbury. His secretary, Gundulf, became Bishop of Rochester and architect of the Tower of London. A profitable way to work up an appetite for lunch at the Auberge is to climb the 210 steps up St. Nicholas' Tower for a fine view over the Bec valley.

Auberge de l'Abbaye
(HR)L   *32.44.86.02   Cl. Mon. p.m.; Tues. o.o.s.; 8/1–23/2*

Well known to generations of Brits, and perhaps suffering from a surfeit of popularity because of its superb site, and picture-book appearance. It really is a gem visually – black and white and beamy and very very old. The furniture is ancient oak and the fire in the great hearth glows from dawn to dusk and later.

The rooms are too simple – basic plumbing, modest comforts – for the price tag of 350f per person, obligatory demi-pension, but the peace is absolute. Meals are concocted from family recipes and none the worse for that, but again the prices are for tourists – from 175f.

Map 4D   **BÉNOUVILLE** 14970 Calvados. 10 km NE of Caen

Manoir d'Hastings
(HR)L   *18 av. de la Cote de Nacre   31.44.62.43   Open every day   CB, AE, DC*

A hard one to assess, having been around a long time (20 years now since Claude Scaviner took over), and having had more than its shares

Auberge de L'Abbaye

of misfortunes (illness, losing a second Michelin rosette and a chef who left to make fame and fortune at La Bourride in Caen). A couple of years ago people were saying that the Manoir had had its day. Now it's time for a completely unprejudiced re-assessment.

It is a 17C priory surrounded by an apple orchard, setting itself the highest standards for service and accoutrements. Its restaurant is famous, but recently it has a new accessory – eleven bedrooms in an annexe, La Pommeraie. Again standards are high, as are the prices – 570–850f. Breakfasts are exceptionally good.

Claude and Aline Scaviner are aided and abetted nowadays by a young and enthusiastic family team – Hélène their daughter-in-law and Yves, their son, who works with his father in the kitchen. Yves has brought new ideas to the traditional Norman cuisine for which the Manoir was known, but the best tarte Normande for miles around is still to be found on the menu. The 198f menu is a bargain and the wine list an education. I am confident that things are going to continue to look up here and so have taken the decision to retain the arrow, in spite of some dissension among readers.

'We were not disappointed. It lived up to everything you say about it. We chose the 'menu suggestion' at 270f, but were surprised and delighted when the head waiter volunteered to substitute for the set dessert one we had admired on the next table – a wonderful concoction of apple and pancake flambéed in Calvados with lashings of Normandy cream. The petits fours were particularly spectacular and

the presentation of the home-made truffles was unique! (Chilled, set in foaming ice! – P.F.) *Our total bill with two kirs, a bottle of Fleurie at 100f and some Calvados came to 830f. For those who enjoy good food, not one franc of this was to be regretted.'* – John and Georgie Roberts.

Le Mycène
(R)S   *Pont de Bénouville   31.44.62.00   Cl. Mon.*

Good for averaging-out after an extravagant meal at the Manoir. This little restaurant near the Pegasus Bridge offers excellent value. Menus, prepared by Michel Harivel, are way above average at the price (55f), and service by his wife Brigitte comes with a smile.

La Glycine
(HR)S   *31.93.30.02   Cl. Wed.*

Just across the road from the Manoire, a nice young couple have done up this little bar/hotel, all covered in wisteria. At 90f for a double room you could save on bed, Glycine-style, what you had lavished on dinner, chez Scaviner.

A recent bulletin from M. and Mme Decker tells me that they have made several improvements to their little hotel, raising their standard to two stars. They now have sound-proofing, one smart room with marble 'from floor to ceiling' (!), a family room with two double beds, and an extended brasserie menu. More reports particularly welcome.

'To compensate for our gastronomic extravagance we stayed opposite at La Glycine, where the welcome was friendly and the room clean and comfortable, even though small and basic. The bill came to 85f, but we were warned not to expect breakfast on the Wednesday morning, the jour de fermeture – but after that divine dinner, who cared?' – J. and G. Roberts.

Map 5E   **BERNIÈRES D'AILLY** 14170 St. Pierre-sur-Dives, Calvados. 8 km SW of St. Pierre-sur-Dives; 12 km NE of Falaise

---

Madame Vermes
(C)S   *31.90.73.58*

Turn S of the D 511 on to the D 271. The farm is 2 km past the village.

Arlette and André Vermes have converted four rooms in their old stone farmhouse into guest bedrooms of different styles. You can sleep 'retro' – with fin-de-siècle lamps and beading, 'romantique' – with a small draped four-poster, 'Campagnard' – Laura Ashleyesque, or .... Oh dear I forget. But you get the idea. Anyway they're all comfortable, one has a private shower, one has three beds, for 160f. The other three are from 90–130f for two people.

The Livre d'Or down in the old beamed sitting room is full of praise from families of all nationalities, who have enjoyed the Vermes' hospitality in such peaceful surroundings.

Map 4E   **BEUVRON-en-AUGE** 14430 Dozulé, Calvados. 30 km E of Caen; 15 km S of Cabourg

Ⓜ *Sat., Fri. (animals)*

If Beuvron seems familiar, it might well be because it is the archetypal pays d'Auge village, recognisable from many a poster and postcard. It centres round an ancient beamed and crooked market hall, and takes pride in its picturesqueness, with a flurry of flowers in cottage gardens and village window-boxes.

Le Pavé d'Auge
(R)M   *pl. du Village   31.79.26.71   Cl. Mon. p.m.; Tues.   EC, V*

A Norman institution, under the ownership of the Engels and with Madame Engel's far-famed Michelin-starred Norman cooking; it seems incredible that things at Le Pavé could ever change. But now I hear that M. and Mme Bansard, who ran La Terrasse at Javron-les-Chapelles so successfully, have taken the place over; although it will undoubtedly be different, I am confident that it will very soon be as well installed on every tourist's 'must' list as the old Pavé.

They have certainly inherited a treasure. The building is part of the magnificent old wooden halles, the focal point of the village, and is as interesting inside as out. The Bansards tell me that there will be two menus, at 140f for four courses and 250f for five. I look forward to hearing more about them, and to restoring the arrow to one of the most attractive restaurants in Normandy.

Map 3F   **BEUZEVILLE** 27210 Eure. 15 km E of Honfleur; 14 km N of Pont l'Evêque

Ⓜ *Tues.*

An ideal staging post, on the N 175, just off the autoroute. We often use the Cochon d'Or for a breakfast stop. From then on everything looks distinctly brighter, especially if it happens to be a Tuesday and legs can be stretched strolling round the market just outside, for that magical first sight and smell of France.

➤ **Auberge du Cochon d'Or**
(HR)S   *32.57.70.46   Cl. 15/12–15/1   EC, V*

A steady history of good unpretentious value, with excellent food meriting a red R in Michelin, majoring on simple substantial Norman fare. Menus from 70f.

'Never fails to amaze me by the quality and quantity for the price.' – Keith R. Whettam.

'By turning the erstwhile bar into a dining room, they have gained extra dining space but lost themselves an erstwhile bar! Which wouldn't matter except that every other bar in town seems to close down around 9 p.m. Beuzeville is no place for night owls.'

Long a favourite with the Brits, en route further south, but good enough in its own right for a Normandy base. The rooms here (140–200f) are simple, clean, perfectly adequate, but only one has a bath, so if this is high priority, best cross the road to another, slightly more up-market hotel, under the same management:

▶ **Le Petit Castel**
(H)M   *32.57.70.46   Cl. Mon. 15/12–15/1   EC, V*

Smarter altogether, with a little garden; all rooms have baths, loo and TV. Rooms from 250–300f.
The combination shares an arrow, as before.

Map 3H   **BÉZANCOURT** 76220 Gournay en Bray, Seine-Mar. 16 km NE of Lyôns-la-Forêt

---

Deep in the forest of Lyôns. Take the D 132 and the D 141 out of Lyôns for a delightful prelude to:

▶ **Château du Landel**
(HR)M   *35.90.16.01   Cl. 15/11–15/3   Rest. cl. Sun. p.m.; Mon.   CB*

Once a resting place for pilgrims on their way to Santiago de Compostela, this lovely 17C manor-house now offers modern travellers comfort and peaceful repose. Both public rooms and bedrooms are spacious and light and beautifully furnished.
The food, cooked by the son of the house, is in keeping: à la carte only, from 180 to 250f. Demi-pension only: 400–450f per person.

'Lovely 17C château, miles from anywhere. The bedrooms look out over park and forest. You really feel this is the family's home – which it is. Not a place for an overnight stay; it's for the short break for complete rest and relaxation in civilised surroundings, with civilised people. The Cardons turned this, their inherited home, into a hotel 10 years ago. Madame C. is very likeable, with excellent taste and no pretentiousness. The first-floor rooms are furnished in compatibility with the 17C. The second floor has been done up in a modern way, and she has had fun doing every one differently. The suite for 480f would cost a lot more than double that in England. Period furniture (bed on dais), views in both directions and salon.

Son is chef, à la carte only is good and unpretentious, and they don't mind whether you eat there or not. Go there Pat – and I'll be broken-hearted if my impressions are mistaken in any way.' – Robin Totton.
Well, I did, and they weren't, and the arrow proves it.

Map 4D BIEVILLE-BEUVILLE 14112 Calvados. 6 km N of Caen on the D 60

Just a hamlet, straggling bucolically along the road.

Mme Annei Barthassot
(C)M *4 r. Haute   31.44.34.99*

So much depends on the welcome with a chambre d'hôte, and here we were unlucky. Arriving on a miserably damp day, weary after many hours at the wheel, we turned into the muddy courtyard of this nice old stone farmhouse and were greeted with blank stares from our host and his fellow tractor-drivers. Although I was hobbling with the aid of a stick, after a tennis accident, he let us carry our own suitcases up a painfully steep and hazardous flight of stairs to an icy bedroom.

I report all this sob stuff because it emphasises how extra important in an establishment like this are the details that cost very little. To be fair, Madame Barthassot almost made up for her husband's shortcomings; when we returned from an essential sortie to find a refreshing cuppa, she was making up the bed and quite happy to chat. She has five guest-rooms, three of which have private bathrooms, all of which are perfectly comfortable (once the heat has been turned on). The cost is 185f. for two, and breakfast, included in the price, is a good one, with home-made jams. A quiet and convenient stop near Caen in fact. Especially in warm weather.

Map 4E LA BOISSIÈRE 14340 Cambremer, Calvados. 5 km W of Lisieux, N off the N 13

Le Manoir
(C)M *31.32.20.81*

Look for a water tower on the right, just after the hamlet of La Bosquetterie. Take the D 103 on your left, opposite tower. 1 km to the drive on right.

An ancient unspoiled 16C typical Auge farmhouse, but no longer a farm. Madame Délort is the farmer's widow, and now takes in guests from Easter till All Saints Day; she has two guest rooms, both with private bathrooms, capable of sleeping four and five people respectively. She charges 165f for two, 210f for three or 245f for four or five bodies. It's a lovely place to be and Mme Délort is a kind and smiling hostess, but she only serves breakfast, so it would mean searching out a suitable evening eatery.

Map 7B BOUCÉEL 50240 St. James, Manche. 10 km S of Avranches

The D 308 runs between the D 40 and the D 998 and there is the hamlet of Boucéel. Pleasant countryside, conveniently situated for Mont St-Michel, 18 km away.

La Ferme de l'Etang
(C)S   *33.48.34.68*

A reader who had chanced upon the Ferme de l'Etang originally recommended it to me, and since then there have been a steady stream of followers who have all loved it.

It's a charming old stone farmhouse, white-shuttered, creeper-covered, geranium window-boxed, run by Brigitte and Jean-Paul Gavard, dairy farmers who speak good English. The optional evening meal includes produce from their farm..

'The first night was so good, we stayed another. On our floor was accommodation for twelve people, with one bathroom, lav and shower room. As we were the only guests it was fine, but might be pushed if it were full. The food was plentiful and most appetising, well served with wine, cider and a Calvados with a large pot of coffee after dinner, now 50f for four courses.' – Audrey Barritt.

Sounds like a perfect family spot to me, especially as no matter how many children you pile into one room the price stays the same – 100f. The arrow remains, for position, friendly patrons and good value.

Boucéel is not easy to find – I was funking trying to describe how to get there, since we have only succeeded by asking the way every time. Here is some help, both for directions and as an alternative to the now very popular Ferme de l'Etang.

'If you get to Vergoncey you will have to come back. We stayed with a friend of Madame Gavard's in La Croix-Avranchin, which is the key to finding both villages. It is at the crossroads between the D 30 and the D 40 Avranches road. The b. and b. signs are 2 km north towards Avranches. We cannot recommend our stop too highly: **Mme Gerard Meslin**, *Mouraine, La Croix Avranchin, 33.48.35.69.'* – Mr. and Mrs. L. Watson.

Map 3G   **LA BOUILLE** 76530 Gd. Couronne, Seine-Mar. 75 km E of Le Havre; 20 km W of Rouen

---

Ⓜ *Thurs. a.m.*

Turn off the autoroute at La Maison Brulée, follow the signs down the steeply winding hill to La Bouille and enter another world. Tucked under the lofty white escarpment, heedless of the traffic thundering by just three km away, lies this peaceful little Norman town, curving along the very banks of the Seine. It is set in a loop of the wide river, lined with cliffs, woods, villas on one side and apple orchards on the other. It's a lovely drive on the south bank to follow the course of the river all the way to Duclair, via the ferry.

Rouen's proximity is hard to believe, but it is only a very short drive away, either by autoroute or by following the river through Moulineaux and the oil refineries of La Grande Couronne; thus making La Bouille an ideal place to return to after exploring the big city.

This year I noticed distinct signs of up-marketing. The good news is that the village looks prettier than ever, all newly painted and pedestrianised, with flowers everywhere; the bad news is that prices have rocketed, and La Bouille, always understandably popular as an escape for the rouennais looks like being fully booked whenever good weather appears.

➤ Le St. Pierre
(H)M(R)L   35.23.80.10   Cl. Tues. p.m.; Wed.; 1/11–31/3   V

The closing times indicate how dependent the St. Pierre is on good weather. Not surprising in view of its site – the best in La Bouille, and that's really saying a lot, right on the banks of the river, with lavishly-furnished and flower-decked terrace always full when the sun shines, sadly deserted when the river mists overflow. It's a big white modern building, dominating the little town, with two additional dining rooms on the ground floor, and a green and white latticed overflow for busy times and parties; but it's the terrace that is so special.

This short season means that the patrons, Bernard and Giselle Huet, and Patrice and Thérèse Kikurudz, have to get their living while the sun shines; consequently prices in the restaurant are undoubtedly high, and there have been grumbles about the wine charges in particular. if you have to watch the sous, forget it; if you can afford it, don't miss it.

Patrice translates the freshest of ingredients into a cuisine that is as rich or as 'moderne' as you like to choose from the carte. Fish dishes are particularly good. On weekdays there is a 120f menu, which I consider very good value. At weekends, 240f. Most people can't resist the carte, which will involve a bill of at least 350f. Bernard's message is clear and unrepentant. If you want Parisian standards of quality, service, elegance, you must expect to pay.

The bedrooms are delightful and good value at 300–450f, but this is primarily a restaurant with rooms, rather than a hotel, and Bernard likes to reserve them for his restaurant customers. It is worth paying for the more expensive ones, since the view, with the elongated barges passing seemingly at arm's length, is unique. All are extremely comfortable, with Japanese-style furnishings and good bathrooms.

Arrowed for good food in exceptional surroundings.

➤ Hotel de la Poste
(HR)M   6 pl. du Bâteau   35.23.83.07   Cl. Mon. p.m.; Tues.; 24/12–21/1

The little Hotel de la Poste has been the focal point of Le Bouille ever since its 18C coaching inn days. It is looking very fresh and smart at the moment, with its fresh cream paint and brown beams. Readers have been well pleased with the good value offered by the 95f menu, cooked and served by a family team headed by 'Tante' Denise.

This year they should be equally pleased with the two bedrooms, refurbished in cheerful chintzes. One has twin beds and bath, at 250f, the other a 'lit matrimoniale' and shower, for 230f. Both have amazing views over the Seine.

An inexpensive and agreeable base in this special place, and arrowed accordingly.

Maison Blanche
(R)M   *35.23.80.53   Cl. Sun. p.m.; Mon.; 17/7–4/8   EC, V*

As you might expect, a white house. In this case a pretty, balconied
one, with first and second-floor windows profiting from probably the

La Maison Blanche

best view in town of the sweep of the river. The dining rooms are most attractively furnished in rustic elegance and there are tables outside for drinks.

Food is steadily reliable, high quality; no fireworks, but variations on traditional cooking from a practiced chef, who has been a Meilleur Ouvrier de France finalist. Menu at 100f, except Suns and fêtes when it's 150f. Always full at weekends, so do book.

Arrowed because, like its rivals in La Bouille, it is of very high standard in an outstanding setting.

Les Gastronomes
(R)M   *35.23.80.72   Cl. Wed. p.m.; Thurs. in Jul. and Aug.; 1/2–20/2   AE, DC, V*

The only recommended restaurant without That View, but very pretty nevertheless, and in any other town outstandingly so. Small and warm and intimate in winter, flowery and cool on the green shaded terrace in summer.

Menus start at 135f and use only fresh ingredients of high quality. This could well be another arrow for the town, except that I have not eaten there recently and neither, it would appear, have any of my readers. Reports welcome.

Le Bellevue
(HR)M   *35.23.80.57Cl. 24/12–31/12   EC, V*

A newcomer to the La Bouille scene, and to French Entrée, having arrived in 1987. Yet to be investigated beyond a single visit, but promising well, with comfortable modern rooms at 220–310f and menus from 95f.

Map 5D   **BOULON** 14220 Thury-Harcourt, Calvados. 17 km S of Caen

---

A hamlet east off the Thury-Harcourt road, the D 562.

La Bonne Auberge
(R)S-M   *31.79.37.60   Cl. Mon. lunch; Tues; 3 weeks in September*

I am disappointed in French Entrée readers. How can it be that *no-one* has discovered (or perhaps bothered to write about) this inexpensive gem? The general rule is: no comments, no inclusion, but in this case I refuse to drop an unusually good find. That's if you like simple well-cooked traditional Norman food of the ilk of chicken with cream, apple tart, and, yes, tripes à la mode de Caen, and a bill of 55f (other highly recommended menus at 82 and 100f.) M. Gouget is too good a cook to ignore, so come on somebody. Reports essential to merit what I think should be an arrow.

Come to think of it, perhaps no-one has been able to get a table. There are only seven, and the locals like to keep them to themselves. You should book at least three days ahead.

Map 5D   **BRETTREVILLE-SUR-LAIZE** 14680 Calvados. 15 km S of Caen

Ⓜ *Thurs.*

Turn W off the N 158 on to the D41 towards Fontenay-le-Marmion and
the Château is signposted, doubling back towards Brettreville.

Les Gastronomes

Château des Riffets
(C)M   *31.23.53.21, 31.95.62.14*

It's an imposing pile, approached by an appetite-whetting drive, and perhaps the first impression of grandeur initially militates against it. My first reaction was disappointment that the inside didn't come up to expectations. But remember that this is a family house, where the charming M. et Mme Cantel bring up their children, and it is easy to accept that the furnishings are modern and not château-esque.

I called at a terrible time – earlyish on Jan. 1st, when they had not had time to clear up after the St. Sylvestre celebrations, and they still made me very welcome with lots of offers of refreshment. Madame Cantel has lived in England and speaks perfect English; she and her husband are friendly, helpful hosts.

The bedrooms, at 130–230f, are spacious and light, as are all the rooms, with wonderful views down to the village and the roofs and towers of another château. Their own grounds are extensive, but suffered badly in the 'tempête' of 1988. Lots of clearing up still for poor M. Cantel.

The position is ideal – so near Caen, yet deeply peaceful. A recommended stop, on which more reports would be welcome.

Map 4E   **BREUIL-EN-AUGE** 14130 Pont l'Evêque, Calvados. 20 km S of Deauville

---

The D 48 from Pont l'Evêque to Lisieux is much the more scenic route, but Breuil, it has to be said, is not a particularly attractive village.

➤ **Le Dauphin**
(R)M   *31.65.08.11   Cl. Sun. p.m.; Mon; 17/1–10/2   CB*

In the centre of the village, bang on the road, is a solid white building, giving little indication of the pleasures within. Once inside all is warm, and intimate (a bit too much so sometimes for perfect comfort) and beamy, with a large fireplace, most welcome in winter months. The bistro style comes as a relief after the chichi of Deauville, from whence cometh many a customer sneaking away from the glitz to the cosiness of the Dauphin.

Chef patron Régis Lecomte cooks divinely, and his 160f menu is a bargain. He loves to use local ingredients in new ways – a 'flan' of Honfleur shrimps with a shellfish sauce, Isigny oysters deep-fried in batter, apples in flaky pastry with honey.

Oddly enough I have no reports from readers, but since local gourmets have repeatedly confirmed my own experiences, Michelin has awarded a rosette and the Queen has had lunch there, I think it must be all right. Arrow for outstanding cooking.

Map 3C   **Le BREUIL-EN-BESSIN** 14330 Le Molay, Calvados. 10 km SW of
Bayeux on the D 5

➤ **Le Château de Goville**
(HR)M   *Rte de Bayeux   31.22.19.28 or 31.22.90.80   Cl. Tues; Wed. lunch;
15/11-30/11; 10/1-31/1   CB, V, AE, DC*

> Jean-Jacques Vallé used to escape from his busy career as a couturier
> on the Faubourg St. Honoré to spend peaceful weekends here in the
> family château. Gradually he came to realise its potential as a hotel and
> now has nine guest rooms and a restaurant, La Carité. Next door is his
> antique shop, which he raids to furnish the château in a highly
> individual style. His partner and equally artistic friend, Gilles Michot,
> aids and abets him in the daring decorative schemes that, thanks to
> their professional eye, come off. It would certainly not have occurred to
> me to paint the walls forest green, shocking pink or amethyst, or to
> drape fanciful swathes of exotic fabrics over curtain poles, pelmets and
> canopies. My room had royal blue panelling, curtains and drapes in
> black and rose voile, blue Bristol glass, black lacquered furniture, and I
> loved it.
>
> Loving or hating I suspect will be the reaction to this definitely over
> the top, definitely different, new Calvados possibility. Not for the
> cautious or hide-bound; something special for the adventurous.
>
> Rooms, obviously all different, all with bath, cost from 385–495f.
> Menus from 99–160f.
>
> Arrowed for convenient position, lovely house, warm welcome,
> unusual experience!

Map 5A   **BRÉVILLE-sur-Mer** 50290 Bréhal, Manche. 5 km N of Granville
on the D 971, the Coutances road out of town

La Mougine des Moulins à Vent
(H)M   *33.50.22.41   EC, DC, V*

> A modern building set well back from the main road in its own
> immaculately manicured gronds. Nobody seemed very interested in
> the Mougine when I wrote about it before, but now I have confirmation
> of my own impressions – that this would be an unusually comfortable
> base from which to explore the region. It has only seven bedrooms,
> costing a reasonable 270–360f, and no restaurant.
>
> *'We have yet to find such luxurious comfort, plus the little things that
> make a holiday. Balcony, sea view, bathroom etc., beautifully
> presented breakfast in wicker baskets, with lots of fresh rolls and
> croissants.'* Anne Bates.

Map 2A   **BRICQUEBEC** 50260 Manche. 22 km S of Cherbourg

 Mon.

An obvious and ideal stopping place in a nice old town, with an ancient castle keep and a Monday market that takes over the vast market square.

Le Vieux Chateau
(HR)S   *33.52.24.49   Cl. 20/12–1/1*

A lovely old building, built into the ramparts, and for many years a favourite of mine, F.E. readers and many other compats. Alas, little favour has been found here of recent years and I only include it in the persistent (perhaps foolish) hope that such a potential gem must one day get its act together again. Any reports to that effect most welcome. Rooms 115–355f. Menus from 65f.

Map 4F   **BRIONNE** 27800 Eure. 28 km S of Pont Audemer; 76 km SW of Le Havre

Ⓣ *pl. Eglise (July-August) 32.45.70.51* Ⓜ *Thurs., Sun.*

A delightful 28 km drive from Pont Audemer, following the river Risle and skirting the Montfort forest, leads to Brionne, where the river's streams divide to form the islets on which the pleasant little town, crowned with its imposing Norman keep, is built.

The D 137 leads to two châteaux owned by the Harcourts, one of the oldest families in the French aristocracy. When the town of Thury-Harcourt was devastated in 1944, the 17C **Champ du Bataille** was returned to them in part-compensation for their loss. Now it is open to the public from March to September (not Tues. or Wed.) and its glorious paintings, furniture and architecture make it a very worthwhile excursion. The gardens of the château bearing the family name, a few km away, are equally rewarding (open mid-Mar. to mid-Oct.), planted with rare and mightily impressive trees. Back to the town for refreshment:

➤ **Auberge Vieux Donjon**
(HR)S   *r. Soie   32.44.80.62   Cl. Sun. p.m. o.o.s.; Mon.; 15/11–6/12   EC, V*

Never a cross word for this little timbered restaurant in the main street. Eat by the log fire in winter, admire the flowery courtyard in summer, be cheered by Serge Chavigny's welcome, relish the value of the good and imaginative food, and count the change in your pockets. Menus from 70f.

There are eight simple rooms, again representing a bargain at 110–200f. How I wish there were more little French inns like this one, continuing the tradition of hospitality and honest value.

'Our room was particularly good value, being very well appointed, at

175f, including an excellent modern shower.' – Andrew Chyba.

'Spotlessly clean rooms overlooking the flower-filled courtyard. Excellent dinner and a very nice breakfast. With the car parked off the road in the courtyard, what more could anyone wish?' – Jean Fairhurst.

A caution: *'Our room overlooked the road, which was exceedingly noisy all night. Well worth insisting on a room over the courtyard. Food exceptionally good – rabbit and hazelnut terrine quite delicious and the moules the best we've had. Highly recommended.'* – Susan Leyland.

Arrowed for good value.

Map 3D   **CABOURG** 14390 Calvados. 24 km NE of Caen

(T) *Jardins du Casino 31.91.01.09* (M) *Wed.*

Once a fashionable seaside resort, Cabourg still retains a grandeur now sadly beyond its station. Particularly out of season it has a ghost town quality. One ghost in particular dominates the names of the streets and hotels – Marcel Proust. Proust used to stay here in the Grand Hotel for a month every summer (having booked four surrounding rooms to ensure silence), and wrote here *Within a Budding Grove.* His heroine Albertine could still play on the breakwater – the magnificent beach and promenade have changed very little. Very few English people seem to have discovered the town and its surroundings.

Pullman Grand Hotel
(H)L *Promenade M. Proust   31.91.01.79*   Open every day   *CB, AE, DC, EC*

A must for Proustians. This vast building dominates the prom, and the rooms are exactly what one would expect – palatial. Just have a look inside the marble entrance hall if you do not fancy staying in one of them for 460–2500f.

Le Balbec
(R)M

The restaurant is more affordable (menu at 180f). Proust called it the aquarium because of its enveloping glass windows; it would certainly provide a taste of temps perdu.

Here is a description I cannot better:

'We lunched there on a Sunday and found it charming and rather touching. An aged Head Waiter in smart blazer and dark grey flannels, attentive waitresses and, surprisingly, the food served by a busy little man in a tartan jacket! The children were welcomed and my request for a quiet corner (quickly rendered unquiet) was observed. The meal was good – rather what one would expect at Claridges or the Ritz – slightly impersonal and not exorbitantly expensive. A bottle of Veuve Clicquot as apéritif seemed appropriate in that ornate room, reeking of past glories.' – R. Furber.

Map 4D   **CAEN** 14000 Calvados. 107 km W of Le Havre; 119 km SE of
Cherbourg

(T) *pl. St. Pierre 31.86.27.65*   (M) *Tues.–Sun.*

Sad though it undoubtedly is to imagine how Caen must have looked
before three quarters of its heart was torn out by wartime devastation,
there remains enough of the old city to make a visit here enjoyable in
its own right. Below the castle in the paved Vaugueux area there is
more atmosphere of the fifteenth than of the twentieth century. Sit
there by the fountain at one of the several pavement cafés and study
the crazy angle of La Poterne's gables, like a Disneyland pastiche,
enjoy the colour of the windowboxes, potter round the antique shops.

To the north of the rue St. Jean lies another preserved area of
dignified patricians' houses, medieval beams and plaster, winding
alleyways and a great leafy square, where old ladies calmly sit and
watch the children playing. The Bassin extends right into the heart of
the town, so that yacht masts and fishing boats add interest to the
urban scene. The market along the quays and in the Place Cortonne is
a particularly good one and makes Caen an ideal base for a winter
weekend break, when Sunday can otherwise be a difficult day to fill.

Shops are good here too, with a variety of large stores and
boutiques in the pedestrianised area, and the best food shops in the
north. The rue St. Jean is particularly well endowed with charcutiers,
pâtisseries and chocolatiers, some of which stay open on a Sunday for
inspired picnic-purchases.

But, for all its reincarnations since the eleventh century, Caen is still
first and foremost William's town. References to that great Duke of
Normandy and his Queen, Matilda, crop up repeatedly in street names,
shops, and of course in the two great abbey churches. His castle, built
in 1060, is still the focal point of the city. Its wartime damage has been
repaired and the grounds are a pleasant base from which to stroll,
picnic, and visit the Normandy Museum. Students from one of France'
most prestigious universities, rebuilt just behind the castle, sprawl on
the grassy slopes looking down on St. Jean, lending a casual laid-back
feeling to this important commercial centre.

The **Abbaye aux Hommes** was William's outward sign of repentance
at having married a blood relation against the Pope's wishes. Matilda
was his cousin and she took some persuading that the marriage to a
bastard was a good idea. To convince her, William had to drag her
round her chambre by her hair; convincing the Pope he left to his
Secretary, Lanfranc (see Bec Helloüin), who talked the Pontiff into
rescinding his prohibition of the match. it was a nice touch for the
happy pair to build their spiritual memorials at opposite sides of the
city, with the great fortified castle protecting them from their worldly
enemies in the centre.

The Abbaye aux Hommes protected the citizens of Caen during the
bombardment of 1944; many thousands of them took refuge inside it,
and the abbey and the church of St. Étienne within it were
miraculously saved (as indeed was Matilda's Abbey, though somewhat
battered).

Caen - Abbaye aux Hommes

William was buried there, but now only a slab before the high altar marks the spot: the tomb was ravaged once when the Huguenots sacked the church in the 16th century and again during the Revolution, when his remains were thrown into the river. No doubt about priorities: 'Duke of Normandy, King of England' reads the dedication. The abbey started off in 1077, Romanesque, and was finished two centuries later, Gothic. Marvellous contrast of styles within and without. Recently cleaned, the glowing Caen stone illuminated by lots of light flooding through the three layers of windows, framed in graceful Norman arches, makes the abbey a warm, not solemn, place in which to linger.

Outside too, all is bright and cheerful. The former abbey buildings that flank St Étienne are now part of the Town Hall and are approached through a blaze of well-groomed gardens.

Matilda's church is less colourful, but impressive, as is her mausoleum inside. Don't do as I did, though, and puff the considerable distance between the two abbeys, to arrive on the threshold at 11.55, when the adamant curator was locking up for lunch.

As though some inspired history master had arranged Caen, St. Pierre provides the perfect contrast to the austere simplicity of the two abbeys. The rich merchants of Caen vied with each other to contribute decoration upon decoration. Its famous 12C belfry was destroyed during the battle of Caen, when a shell from HMS *Rodney* hit the spire, but it has since been restored exactly as it was and the king of all Norman belfries rules once more.

A not-to-be-missed-on-any-account addition to the attractions of Caen is the 'Mémorial', a museum dedicated to Peace. And if that sounds less than attractive, especially for those not especially interested in all the other war memorials in the area, it's time to think again. A morning is not long enough to experience this unique concept – we nearly missed our afternoon ferry home because I needed longer.

It makes use of the very latest technology to display the build-up to, the duration of, and the after-effects of the last World War. Three wraparound screens show contemporary films taken by both sides, skilful representations of both points of view, with powerful sound effects. Prepare to find some of the photographs harrowing, particularly those of the youthful Norman freedom fighters about to be hanged; prepare to be enlightened and inspired.

Mémorial Caen Normandie
Esplanade Dwight Eisenhower 14066 Caen   Open every day except 1/1–14/1; from 1/9–31/5 from 9.30–7.30, and until 10 p.m. from 1/6–31/8   31.06.06.44

Services include a pleasant restaurant, tea room, day-care centre, tourist office, exchange bureau, bus connection with Caen city centre. It is well signposted to the north of the city off the Ouistreham road.

Quatrans
(H)M   *17 r. Gémare 31.86.25.57   EC, V*

I have been very pleased with this find, in a side-street near the castle. It actually has 36 rooms, but gives the impression of intimacy and is family-run, always a good pointer. The rooms have recently been decorated in pleasant pastel shades, and are surprisingly spacious for a central hotel. Their price is another pleasant surprise – 190–220f. Breakfast in a bright and cheerful downstairs room.

'Room 24 – grand lit, extra bed, separate bathroom – 209f. Room 16 – grand lit, extra bed, bath and shower, toilet and bidet – 218f. We found the beds comfortable and clean and the lift was very handy. Petit défjeuner 16.50 – plenty to eat. Madame was very helpful, struggling hard with my inadequate French.' – Patricia Keane.

Central
(H)S   *23 pl. J. Letellier   31.86.18.52   EC, V*

Michelin used to give the Central a rocking chair for its peacefulness, but it has wisely now withdrawn it. The fact that it is set in a square, not a thoroughfare, does not guarantee that traffic will not pass by and my experience has been a noisy one. Not smart but small, friendly, central and cheap, with rooms at 190–220.

Malherbe
(H)M   *pl. Foch   31.86.04.23   AE, DC, EC, V*

Caen's grandest hotel, overlooking the green Hippodrome. First impressions are of somewhat faded grandeur, but most of the rooms have been recently 'done up' and are spacious and quiet, thoroughly meriting the price of 420f. Cheaper ones at 290f.

Moderne
(H)M   *116 bvd. du Mal-Le clerc   31.86.04.23   CB, AE, DC, EC*

The fact that the Moderne is the most central hotel (in the midst of the pedestrianised area) is good news and bad news. The good part is that there is little traffic disturbance and you can dash back for your umbrella if it rains; the bad is that it is almost impossible to locate by car. Letter after letter testify to the frustration of seeing the front door and being prevented from getting there by an impenetrable one-way system. Even on our third visit, armed with the map I had cannily asked the hotel to send me, we couldn't crack it, until the penny dropped that we were being too frightfully British and law-abiding, observing No-Entry signs. The only way to the Moderne's front door is to turn right off the rue St. Jean, ignoring the 'Buses only' sign, down the pedestrianised rue Bellivet, and voilá. You can stop long enough to unload and get directions to the hotel car park, which has an exit to bring you up directly into the reception area. This once-favourite hotel was beginning to look distinctly down-at-heel on our last visit and I am relieved that something has now been done about it. It has been sold, and all the rooms have been completely renovated and equipped with greatly improved bathrooms. You now take breakfast on the fifth floor, with a lovely panoramic view of the city, but it's a pity that the restaurant, which was such asset, has had to go. Rooms are now 310–610f.

Le Dauphin
(HR)M *29 r. Gémare 31.86.22.26 Rest. cl. Sat.; both closed 17/7–6/8 AE, DC, EC*

Once an old priory but now unrecognisable as such in its heavily-restored reincarnation. The double rooms with bath are in the new wing which overlooks the road and could be noisy (380f). If you don't mind a shower, the ones in the older building are calm, nicer and 100f cheaper. The main reason for staying here would be the excellent food.

M. Chabredier makes good use of local ingredients and his up-market rustic dining room, with warm and friendly atmosphere, is one of the most agreeable places to eat in Caen. His weekday 85f menu is a bargain, but more exciting items are to be found on the 150 (or 195, 280f) versions.

Le Relais des Gourmet
(HR)L *15 r. de Geôle 31.86.06.01 Rest. cl. Sun. p.m. and 1/5 AE, DC, EC*

Caen's only luxury hotel, small and elegant, with superb service. Rooms cost 230–420f, apartments 600–800f. The restaurant is delightfully airy and light, opening out on to a little garden. One guide describes its clientele as being 'bon-chic-bon-genre', which approximates to Sloane Ranger. I would have thought these Sloane Rangers were on the elderly side but they were certainly enjoying their smart meal. Mid-week menu is 130f, otherwise it's 210f including wine, which is not expensive for these standards of cooking and, particularly, service.

➤ La Bourride
(R)L *15–17 r. Vagueux 31.93.50.76 Cl. Sun.; Mon.; 3/1–24/1, 16/8–3/9 CB, AE, DC*

Michel Bruneau has come a long way since I first wrote about him, fresh from Le Manoir d'Hastings, tucked away in this most charming street in old Caen. The first Michelin star followed swiftly, and now the second ensures that his tables are always full.

The interior of the tiny galleried restaurant is as delightful as the venerable exterior. Beams, copper pans, fresh flowers, stone walls make for a warm and intimate atmosphere, and how I appreciate being given the option of going straight to the table, in a top restaurant like this, where a sometimes unwanted spell in the bar is so often obligatoire.

It was a dark and dirty night, probably the lowest time of the year in fact – New Year's Day, when restaurants close their doors and sweep up from the night before, when the Bourride took us in. The raised fire in the lower room made us feel welcome, gentle classical music set the scene and spirits rose. Along with the bottle of wine, ordered to help us make decisions, arrived the kind of amuse-gueules that indicated the quality of the food to come – miniscule strips of duck arranged over quails' eggs in a Cassis sauce. A change from Twiglets.

Menus are 319–447f, with a Petit Normandy menu at 217f (170f at lunchtime), suggesting regional specialities. If ever there were a chance to enjoy tripes à la mode de Caen, chicken vallée d'Auge or oysters with Pommeau, it would be here, but so far I've always allowed myself to be seduced by the carte (and never regretted it).

After all the Christmas excesses something fresh was indicated and I put myself in the capable hands of Mme Bruneau to suggest it. She explained that the Bourride version of soupe de langoustines was not at all rich and filling as I had imagined, but a cluster of crayfish, barely poached, served just warm in a pool of clear fresh tomato consommé, with the crunch of shredded baby leeks and chervil. A treat for eye and tastebuds.

I have never cared much for pigeon, so in the spirit of possible sacrifice in the good cause of research, I ordered it next, challenging Mr. Bruneau to make me change my mind. He did – by presenting the whole bird in a case of sea salt, so that all the juices were preserved and the flavour intensified. But the touch of genius came with the sauce, flavoured with my favourite spice – vanilla. Inspired.

An assortment of desserts revealed mini-masterpieces – bitter chocolate terrine studded with black cherries, a millefeuille filled with cream flavoured with you'll-never-credit-it-but-it-was-sensational liquorice, and exotic sorbets in a peach sauce.

How after that lot one could even contemplate petits fours is a mystery, but how could one turn away the ultimate in chocolate truffles enclosed in a bitter chocolate flaky case, nor the little fruit tartlets of fraises des bois (in *Jan*)? Perhaps the micro bûches-de-Noël were left-overs, but I ate them too.

When you consider that behind the plate glass wall of this tiny restaurant no less than seven be-toqued chefs and three white-capped dogsbodies could be seen beavering away, there can be no surprise that the bill was high. When you consider what the same would cost in England, there can be no question that the Bourride is a bargain. It worked out at 280f each, including wine.

Arrowed as probably the best restaurant in Normandy.

Daniel Tuboeuf
(R)M-L   *8 r. Buquet   31.43.64.48   Cl. Sun. p.m.; Mon.*

In a side-street just north of the Place Courtonne, from whose rather dingy aspect it is a particular surprise to arrive in this deliberately shocking decor, startlingly 'modern', with lots of steel, plaster casts, and, to my mind, garish aquamarine fountain. The tables are so far apart (business secrets? hanky-panky?) that the atmosphere never gets animated or warm. So far, so bad.

But I can forgive a lot if the food is as well conceived and cooked as it is by 'M. Tuboeuf, Restaurateur', a man who clearly loves his métier. The carte 'suggestions' run into funny money – Scallops with fresh girolles – 180f, turbot with leeks and truffles – 178f – but that makes the menus look even more attractive good value. On the 168f version, for example, I happily ate a chicken liver salad, rich in gently-cooked baby livers and designer lettuces, then a fresh salmon with a red pepper sauce, then wonderful cheeses and a gratin of fresh raspberries. Mid-week menus at 95f are even better value: 155f for dinner, 168f including wine for lunch. If you feel like pushing the boat out, go for the menu dégustation at 280f.

I forecast a Michelin star here before long, and a serious rival to La Bourride, but personally I prefer my decor less smart.

l'Écaille
(R)M-L   *13 r. de Geole   31.86.49.10   Cl. Sat. lunch   CB, AE, DC, EC*

Under the same management as Les Gourmets next door, with the same excellent service but specialising in fish, with a vivier full of lobsters and crayfish, and a takeaway service. Run by Michel Legras, son of Les Gourmets' patron.

You can't go wrong – it's all wonderfully fresh and classically cooked, from the vivier-ed lobster to the very model of a perfect platter de fruits de mer. There are two good menus. The one at 130f inclusive of wine is fine and an excellent lunch choice; the 250f 'Gourmet' would give you a crack at the lobster. The same extensive wine list as next door, with a range of 50,000 bottles.

Le Chalut
R(M)   *3 r. Vaucelles   31.52.01.06   Cl. Sun. p.m.; Mon.   V*

If you're not particularly bon-chic, nor bon-genre, there is a more than adequate, more modest alternative just across the river. A fishing boat and nets form part of the decor, just in case you haven't got the message. This nice little restaurant may not be as smart as l'Ecaille but its fish is undeniably ultra-fresh and well cooked too. And you can eat on a 92f menu.

La Petite Cale
(R)M   *18 Quai Vendeuvre   31.86.29.15   Cl. Sun.; 2/8–23/8   V*

Another fishy scene, somewhere between the two preceding suggestions in price. Don't be deceived on entry – it's tiny, but not that tiny. A mezzanine floor takes the overflow. Good straightforward cooking on menus from 130f.

St. Andrews
(R)M   *9 quai de Juillet   31.86.26.80   Cl. Sun.   AE*

An intimate little restaurant on the quayside, whose stained glass windows, imposing front door and panelled walls generate a club-like atmosphere. Inside is lighter and brigher, with a good welcome. For 75f you can eat the 'formula' – feuilleté of snails, dish of the day like grilled steak, duck, or sea trout, and dessert. Otherwise it's 120f.

Relais Normandy
(R)M   *Buffet de la Gare   31.82.24.58   Usefully open every day year round*

Another station winner, with daily-changing menu. Try asking for a Surrey speciality on Guildford station! Here traditional regional dishes are served in style. Menus from 60f.

Le Pressoir

(R)S   *3 av. Henry Cheron (near the stade Malherbe)   31.73.32.71 Cl. Sun.; 15/8–1/9*

A newish most attractive little restaurant, whose patronne Denise
Barbier is trying hard to please. Its decor includes an ancient cider
press to justify its name, old copper utensils and authentically worm-
eaten furniture. Cooking is honest and unfussy; menus start at 62f,
with items like cassoulette of mussels, black sausage with apples,
grilled beef.

Chantegrill

(R)S   *17 pl. de la République   31.85.23.52   Open seven days a week*

Chantegrill is a chain of brasseries in big towns throughout France,
quite unlike anything we have at home, in that they offer well-cooked
interesting food and a daily-changing menu, in very pleasant
surroundings, at around £6 a head. The Caen example is in the
spacious Place de la République, where there is a large underground
parking area, and part of a new complex still being developed,
comprising lots of boutiques and eateries – a saladerie, pizzerie,
crêperies, etc. Many readers have found it a useful standby since it was
first mentioned in F.E.3, and although the Stégosaure part has gone,
amalgamated into one restaurant on three floors now, I feel sure it will
still be a popular choice, especially for family eating.

The formula is that you kick off with as much you can eat from a
huge buffet, of high-quality ingredients. Or you can have daily-
changing starters, like a fish mousseline or chicken liver terrine. If you
halt at this stage it will cost you 46f. But for 59.50f you go on to a
choice of grills, like a rumpsteak béarnaise or lamb chops or 'l'idée du
jour' – fresh salmon béarnaise in this case.

A similar exercise is the 'buffet des douceurs'. For another 25f you
can gourmandise your excess-calorie way through tarts, gâteau and
ices galore, which should nicely fill in the gap until teatime.

Le Boeuf Ferré

(R)S-M   *10 r. Froide   31.85.36.40*

Turn up the rue des Croisiers and take a right to find this attractive
hideaway in one of the oldest quartiers in Caen. The original Boeuf
Ferré was so successful that it has overflowed into a satellite next door.
Different entrance, same menu. Both have raftered ceilings and stone
walls; both are highly popular with the locals, particularly at lunchtime.
The only black mark that I can think of is the piped pop – regrettable
but less intrusive than most.

It is easy to see why the place is so well patronised. Both menus at
65f and 90f respectively offer amazing value. We had one of each.
From the cheaper menu I chose a terrine of sea trout, served with a
chive cream sauce, then fresh salmon with sorrel, topped up with three
generous chocolate profiteroles. Husband's 90f version included a Kir
apéritif. If oysters are on the menu he will always choose them, and
here he got nine beauties for starters, then a beef fillet with morilles.
Not bad for a light lunch, with the prospect of a trencherman's dinner

on the cards, so he rejected a raspberry charlotte and caramel bavaro
and settled for a variety of house sorbets with a peach coulis. A quart
bottle of red wine set us back 8f each. What would that lot have cost
back home?

You should book or get there early (our 1.30 reservation was grante
reluctantly, but honoured.) Arrowed for exceptional value.

*'Our evening was made by Le Boeuf Ferré. By 7.30 it was full and ju
got in – they were queuing all the evening.'* – Pauline Bennett.

L'Assiette

(R)S *pl. Fontenne 31.85.29.16 Cl. Sun.*

A cheap and cheerful bistro, usefully situated near the Abbaye aux
Hommes, and well recommended locally. I take it as a good sign that
they change the menus every day 'selon le Marché'. Good value at 60
80f for three courses.

Alcide

(R)M *1 pl. Courtonne 31.93.58.29 Cl. Sat; July; 25/12–31/1 V*

Easy to find, in the town centre, and approved of by several readers:-
*'Excellent moules marinières and the best coq au vin ever eaten. I
think they quite properly had used the blood to thicken the sauce.'* –
Steve Grainger.

*'Very busy with lots of locals – very professional and not at all chi –
honest-to-goodness French eating. Huge bowls of moules, grilled lott
tournedos, crêpes, Muscadet-sur-lie 39f and excellent Bordeaux 63f.
Cracking good meal for two for about 300f, including a rather steep
13% service charge.'* – W. Williamson Jones.

Menus 80–150f.

l'Ambroisie

(R)S *11 r. des Croisiers 31.50.30.32*

Because I like Le Boeuf Ferré so much, I'm afraid that I hardly gave a
glance at this other little restaurant just across the road, which always
seem to have been empty when I have been around. Next time I will.

*'Le Boeuf Ferré being full, we sadly crossed the road – and
discovered what must be the best value menu in all Normandy. A six-
course meal for 80f combined nouvelle cuisine with substantial
portions. My choice was: rabbit pât', snails in a cèpe sauce, lotte in
lobster sauce, local veal, a generous cheeseboard and raspberry cake.
Amazing'.* – Bob Smyth.

I should add that Mr. Smyth has a house in France and knows a thin
or two about French restaurant bargains.

La Poterne

20 r. Porte au Berger 31.93.57.46

It is strange how difficult it is to find an agreeable bar in many French
towns, in which to take an apéritif before dinner, or a digestif or coffe
later. No problem in Caen. La Poterne has a splendid atmosphere, par

engendered no doubt by its position in the enchanting Vaugueux quarter. Inside it's all old bricks, stone, huge fireplaces; in summer you sit outside on the cobbles, watching the world pass by. It's a cross between a night club and an English pub, with live piano music and cabarets in the evenings. It does have a restaurant, Le Ménéstrel, but I would only advise a snack here – there are so many other wiser choices nearby for a full meal.

Hotel de l'Espérance
(HR)S   *512 r. Abben Alix, Hérouville-Bourg   31.44.97.10   Cl. Mon. and Aug.*

For those allergic to city hassle, needing a cheap overnight stop a few km outside Caen. The best way to find it is to take the Ouistreham road out of Caen, turn right towards Colombelles, and right again before the Pont de la Saviem on the rue Vasse. The position of the l'Espérance on the water's edge sounds better than proves to be the case, since the view is of wharves and bunkers rather than willows and swans, but it is always agreeable to be near a river – and here huge ships edge their way past the very terrace of the hotel.

It is extremely modest – 104–130f – but well thought of locally, with menus from 50f.

'From the time I stepped into the hotel I was treated like one of the family, especially when I showed M. and Mme Paire what you had written and her son translated it for them. The staff too were warm and friendly and so organised and helpful. For the price I was more than pleased.' – Colin Holloway.

Map 6D   **CAHAN** 61340 Les Planches, Orne. 3 km SW of Pont d'Ouilly

The D 511 out of Pont d'Ouilly is a very pretty route to take to Flers, taking advantage of the picturesqueness of the Suisse Normande. Cahan is a hamlet along the way.

Au Rendez-vous des Pêcheurs
(R)S   *31.69.80.49*

The French pêcheurs seem a discriminating lot. The restaurants where they rendezvous are legion and frequently good-value. Here is no exception, with menus from 60f.

'The patron was as amusing and warm as the meal was first-rate – the whole thing was a festivity. He had no half bottles of my choice, so

just produced a new bottle and invited me to drink what I wanted. With such cooking and such good humour it was not surprising that his dining-room was full of locals and returning visitors. We shall certainly return.' – Mary Shannock.

Map 3E   **CANAPVILLE** 14800 Deauville, Calvados. 6 km S of Deauville on the N 117

L'Auberge du Vieux Tour
(R)M   *31.65.21.80   Cl. Mon.; Tues.; 15/11–15/3*

A pretty little Norman-style restaurant, serving honest Norman cooking in most attractive surroundings, particularly the garden. On a hot summer's day, when the beaches are crowded and the chi-chi Deauville fails to appeal, it is a very good idea to sit in the shade of a parasol here and enjoy M. Jarrasse's cooking. Both the 127f and the 200f menus include wine.

Map 5B   **CANISY** 50750 Manche. 8 km SW of St. Lo, on the D 38

Au Pichet d'Etain
(HR)S   *33.56.61.13   Cl. Sun. p.m.; Mon.; 2/1–10/1; 28/6–11/7   CB, EB, V*

A reader who had suffered grievously from a Canisy recommendation that had changed hands found considerable compensation in this little Logis de France run by M. Leseine.
'Friendly couple – he paints – beautifully clean, fine dinner for 60f. Rooms from 85f.' –R. L. Hewson. The cheapest meal is still only 60f; rooms are 90–205f, so this would seem to be extremely good value for an en route stop.

Map 5E   **CANON** 14270 Mézidon, Calvados. 20 km SE of Caen on the D 47; 6 km S of Méry-Corbon off the N 13

Deep in the Calvados countryside, on the old coach route from Lisieux to Falaise, the château and, particularly, the gardens of Canon make a delightful diversion from the main tourist attractions of the region. Essential, though, to pick a fine day, when a stroll around the magnificent lakes, following the many streams and springs and admiring the rose gardens, set out in the 'English' style, can be best appreciated.

Around the 18C château (not open to the public) are the Chartreuses, a succession of flower gardens, surrounded by ancient walls, on which apricots, figs and peaches flourish. Wander deep into the woods following the streams (bluebell time especially rewarding) and you will stumple upon neo-classical ruins, a Chinese 'kiosk', and a temple.

The house and gardens were designed by an 18C lawyer who instigated the feast of the Bonnes Gens. Once a year the villagers chose from among their numbers a Bonne Mère, a Bon Vieillard (Good Old Man) and a Bon Chef de Famille and rewarded their virtues by a feast in their honour. Bonnes Gens is still the alternative name for Canon.

Open weekends and holidays from Easter to 30/6 from 2 p.m.–7 p.m. and every afternoon, except Tues., from 1/7–30/9.

Map 2F　**CANY-BARVILLE** 76450 Seine-Mar. 20 km E of Fécamp on the D 925

Ⓜ *Mon. a.m.*

Not a very interesting village, but the countryside is green and peaceful and the peaceful and the position, just 30 minutes W of Dieppe, makes this a useful place to know.

Manoir de Caniel
(C)L　*35.97.88.43　Cl. Mon. p.m.; Sun.*

A 17C manor-house in the centre of the village, with six well-furnished room to let. The furnishings are traditional 'vieille-France', but the comforts are modern. We had room number 4, for 350f, which had a grand canopied blue bed and a fabulous art deco bath; the other rooms are much smaller, but correspondingly cheaper, from 270–350f, and there is a suite for three people for 450f.

Unusually for a château chambre d'hôte, there is a restaurant here, serving four good courses for 110f, or a modest range for 75f – Terrine de Manoir, truite aux amandes, cheese and dessert.

This is good value for a stylish stop, and Anyk and Francois Monnier are keen to welcome English guests.

Map 3B　**CARENTAN** 50500 Manche. 50 km SE of Cherbourg; 69 km NW of Caen

---

Ⓣ *Mairie 33.42.33.54*　Ⓜ *Mon., Fri.*

For years I have always always rushed through this dairy farming centre, on the way to pastures new, with only a short diversion to its Monday market or a meal at one of the recommended restaurants. Recently, with time to kill before catching the ferry home, I decided to follow the signs to 'Port de Plaisance' and came upon an unsuspected whole new world. There, dominating the flat marshy countryside of the estuary of the Douves, rose a forest of masts. The marina here is the shelter for hundreds of boats during the winter. It's all an interesting new slant on the Cotentin peninsula, with the option of a gulp of sea air by taking a walk along the banks of the canal.

Hotel du Commerce et de la Gare
(HR)S

A delightfully old-fashioned inexpensive hotel, prominent on the corner of the ring road, with friendly management and a consistent record of good value. Now that L'Auberge Normand has gone (see Honfleur), the Commerce may well go upmarket, but at the moment it is simple honest fare with copious portions. The rooms are distinctly basic, as one would expect from the price.

'Very good value – breakfast 18f, dinner 60f and the room (without shower or loo) only 99f. A vegetable soup was delicious, a generous helping in a very large bowl, and the slice of apple tart was also large and very good. Ditto the cheese, but the steak was a bit leathery.' – N. Fixsen. At 60f, I'm not surprised.

Map 6A   **CAROLLES** 50740 Manche. 10 km S of Granville

A little old-fashioned family holiday resort.

Le Relais de la Diligence
(R)S   *33.61.86.42   Cl. Sun. p.m.; Mon. o.o.s.; Oct.*

This used to be my absolute favourite in this area, partly I suppose because it was such a surprise to find superb cooking in such a shabby, faded, totally unpretentious family hotel, at prices that were a gift. To my amazement Gault-Millau cottoned on and included it in their très snob guide. But then the letters of disappointment started arriving; the management had changed and I thought all was lost.

Now it appears there has been a renaissance:

'We found it to be superb and have visited it for the last 3–4 years. Still excellent food in lovely clean surroundings. Don't know what the rooms are like but would recommend the restaurant highly.' – Jennifer and Noel Ashton.

Well, the rooms never were any great shakes, so I would't get excited about them, but it's good news to know that the Diligence is alive and well again.

Map 3A   **CARTERET** 50270 Barneville-Carteret, Manche. 37 km SW of Cherbourg

---

I am constantly being asked which is my favourite place in Normandy.

Carteret

An almost impossible question, except that I have no doubt about my favourite seaside resort. It is certainly Carteret.

Perhaps it is the variety that appeals. There are fine dry sands and firm wet sands, and rivulets and pools, and rocks and cliffs, and sand dunes, and the drama of the impulsive tides that rush out so far, so hastily, only to turn around and bring in with them the brightly-painted fishing fleet. There are the old-fashioned bathing huts, haphazardly piled above the beach, and a lighthouse, a corniche road with glorious views along the coast and out to Jersey, and a river that curves between little picturesque Carteret and the residential Barneville, where yachts all need fin keels to stop them leaning over when the tide leaves them high and dry. Walks are wonderful, on the sands, around the rocks at low tides, up to the lighthouse, or best of all perhaps across the estuary on the dunes at Barneville, with the bonus of a photogenic view of Carteret. If all this palls there's always the boat to Jersey for a change of mood.

In the prime position, halfway up the river, looking out to sea, is:

► La Marine
(H)M(R)M-L   *11 r. de Paris   33.53.83.31   Cl. 15/11–1/2 Rest. cl. Sun. p.m. and Mon. from Oct. to March, and Tues. lunch o.o.s.   DC, EC, V*

Gone are the Marine's bucket and spade days, when the likes of us used to bring the brood here for a modest family fortnight. Nowadays, though still as popular with the Brits, it has gone decidedly up-market, with the fifth generation of famille Cesne taking over the management.

Laurent, fresh from 'stages' with some very classy chefs – Taillevent to name but one – has changed the style of cuisine from familiale to très distinguée, and won a Michelin star. That is not to say that faithful clients (and the Marine is the kind of place that nurtures its regulars) are now obliged to pay hugely to eat unwanted chi-chi cooking. There is a 99f menu on weekdays only which is a model of restraint and value for money. A June example feature a terrine of chicken livers, pork noisettes, hot goats cheese and salad, and chocolate pavé with pistachio sauce. Cooked by a Michellin-starred chef, I reckon this superb value.

For serious eaters, who might perhaps wish to indulge in just one prime dish, the carte offers a supreme salmon steak gently cooked in a casing of crunchy gros sel with a julienne of young vegetables. Then a pigeon 'aux cérises' – an almost raw breast of baby pigeon (how do they gauge that the pigeon will be so reliably tender?) in a richly-reduced sauce, wild mushrooms accompanying.

Rooms are on the small side perhaps and the walls are thin, but all are newly decorated and comfortable and most have a splendid view. 250–420f in old building and 550f in new annexe across the road.

An evening drink on the west-facing terrace, overlooking the flooding water of the estuary as the sun goes down, must be one of the high spots of a holiday in the Cotentin.

Recommended for superb site, family concern, some of the best food in the peninsula, long-term reliability – and Carteret.

L'Hermitage
(R)M *Prom. Abbé Lebouteiller 33.04.96.29 Cl. Mon. p.m.; Wed.; 10/1–25/1; 12/11–20/12 CB, DC, EC*

Stick to seafood at this hotel-restaurant overlooking the water, and you can't go wrong. The assiette de fruits de mer beats many a so-called platter. Good menu at 70f.

'L'Hermitage has got its act together. We had an excellent lunch, very untouristy. Place full of people, mainly locals tucking into vast plates of shellfish.' – Ian Anderson.

La Flambée
(HR)S *24 av. de la République 33.04.92.80 Open all year*

It's good news to be able to include a simple hotel in this popular seaside area. Not, alas, that La Flambée has sea views – the Avenue de la République is the main approach road to the town, and it is a fair step to the beach – but when you consider that its comfortable if modest bedrooms cost a mere 85–160f, other shortcomings can be overlooked.

There aren't many shortcomings, since the little creeper-covered house is set well back from the road, which in itself is not exactly a nationale, so that noise should not be a problem; the owner, M. Gallet, is charming, and anxious to get his venture well established with a faithful clientele. There's a pleasant rustic dining room, where he serves simple meals – crêpes and galettes a speciality – and white tables and chairs outside on the terrace. Reports please.

Map 3F   **CAUDEBEC-EN-CAUX** 76490 Seine-Mar. 51 km E of Le Havre; 36 km W of Rouen

---

(T) *pl. Ch. de Gaulle 35.96.20.65*   (M) *Sat. a.m.*

Only three medieval houses and the Church of Our Lady survived the fire that destroyed the old town in 1940. The hint they give of its former character is a sad one, since now, in its concrete reincarnation, the town has little to recommend it apart from its happy situation on the banks of the Seine and of course the very fine 15C Flamboyant Gothic church, which Henry IV described as 'the most beautiful chapel in the kingdom'.

That is not to say that Caudebec is not a good stopping place, because it makes an excellent base to explore the Caux area and especially the bosky banks of the Seine. It also has a good market in the Place on Saturdays.

Normandie
(HR)M   *Quai Guilbaud   35.96.25.11   Cl. Feb. Rest. cl. Sun. p.m. except fêtes   AE, EC, V*

An old favourite with the Brits, and good value, especially as it shares the same marvellous view over the river as its more up-market (and no longer recommended) neighbour, the Marine. Rooms are 200–275f. Menus from 55f.

'Our second visit confirmed the first impressions. We were immediately welcomed and Madame showed us to our room, treating our children like her own. The room was immaculate and included TV, shower, WC en suite. The 55f menu was excellent. My only minor criticism is that there is no reasonably priced wine to go with this menu. We paid 64f for the cheapest wine, which was a Muscadet-sur-Lie.' – David Felton.

The wine grumble is a common one, I'm afraid, and well justified. Other readers have not been so pleased with the food and fear that the cost of putting the waiters in pretentious black jackets and ties left fewer francs to be devoted to the chef.

Mme. Villamaux
(C)S   *Cavée St. Leger   35.96.10.15*

Christiane Villamaux has two double rooms (shared shower) and one for four people, with private shower and WC, in her pleasant b. and b., and charges a modest 145–185f for two people, 240f for three and 278f for four, including a good breakfast, so this would make a splendid family stop. I am glad to have a personal confirmation:

'Croissants for breakfast! Madame Villamaux was very helpful and sat with us to practise our French. 270f for three middle-aged ladies!' – Patricia Cook.

Map 6A   **CHAMPEAUX** 50530 Sartilly, Manche. 14 km S of Granville on the D 911

Between Carolles and St Jean-le-Thomas, on what is claimed to be 'le plus beau kilomètre de France'. I wouldn't know about that, but the coast road is certainly spectacular, with its unique view of Mont St. Michel rising out of the watery mists; even in high season it never seems to get overrun with tourists – probably because there's a much faster inland road from Granville to Avranches. On the cliff edge is:

➤ **Au Marquis de Tombelaine**
(R)M   *33.61.85.94   Cl. Tues. p.m. and Wed. o.o.s; 26/9–1/10; 5/1–30/1*   V

A star. To find such an attractive restaurant – low-beamed ceiling, flagstones, flowers, in such a romantic setting, that takes the trouble to add good cooking to its attributes, is unusual. I loved it when I first found it by chance years ago, but never suspected that it would rise and rise. Readers all agree that the food is the best for miles around, but that the accommodation is simple to the point of disaster.

'Our second visit; the food gets better if anything. It was a good job we had booked in advance. Accommodation is certainly primitive, albeit clean. We had the top(!) price last year and were very happy. The lower-priced rooms are very small and our bed dipped in the middle.'
'Huge grilled langoustines – absolutely magnificent and good value.' – Jennifer and Noel Ashton.

Menus now start at 70f, and the wine list is both reasonably priced and well-chosen. The combination of all these virtues merits a new arrow for the restaurant.

Map 3H   **CHARLEVAL** 27380 Fleury sur Andelle, Eure. 10 km SW of Lyons-la-Forêt

---

Ⓜ *Sat.*

Turn off the N14 from Rouen on to the D 1, or take the pleasantly green drive through the forest from Lyons, via the D 321 and D 11. The village looks more interesting from its map location than proves to be the case, but is nevertheless a usefully situated stop.

Charles IX
(R)M   *32.49.01.51   No credit cards*

> *'A good Sunday lunch attractively served by well-trained Norman wenches. Mme Boutron welcoming and friendly, plenty of French customers. I had a panaché de poissons, lotte in ginger, delicious Livarot and an apricot bavarois for 120f. All very pleasant and good value without going overboard. They're nice people and obviously trying hard.'* Robin Totton.

L'Ecurie
(HR)S   *16 Grande Rue   32.49.30.73   Cl. Sun. p.m.; Mon.*

> Traditional country menus in a little restaurant, popular with locals, not least because of its modest prices (menus from 50f). No fireworks, but the place to stop if you fancy a straightforward filet with pommes frites, or trout meunière. Madame Robin also has some rooms upstairs, which are spotlessly clean, but basic, for 110–195f.

Map 5A   **ÎLES CHAUSEY** 50400 Granville, Manche. Island off the Brittany/Normandy border, 9 km from Granville

---

A daily ferry runs from Granville from 1 May to 30 September

Firm though my intentions were, I fear I have not managed to visit these delightful-sounding islands, known to few British visitors. I still intend to do so, but meanwhile I cannot do better than quote the letter received from Bernard Pichard, the patron of the hotel there, the **Hotel du Fort**. He sent me photographs of his hotel – white, modern, panoramic restaurant, tables outside, overlooking a seemingly idyllic scene – hundreds of reefs and islets in a Mediterranean blue sea, dotted with little sailing boats. If any reader does venture thus far, I should very much like to hear of the experience.

> *'You have forgotten the existence of our islands – the only Channel Islands not under the rule of Brittania. There are no motor cars in Chausey except two vans and two tractors. It is a bird sanctuary and a preserved area, the building of new houses forbidden. The main island is 2½ km long, but at low tide it is possible to walk for miles.*
>
> *British yachtsmen know Chausey well and say it is like the Scillies, but ordinary tourists ignore us because we do not appear on most charts. The Hotel du Fort et des Îles, on a family estate nearly one hundred years old, is built on a garden along the shore. Our eight rooms have private showers and some of them private loos. Our main activity is the restaurant, visitors landing from ferries on day trips or yachtsmen. Our specialities are lobster, crab, oysters, mussels, all from Chausey, and fish of course. We have been honoured to have had the late Duke of Windsor and President Mitterand as patrons. From July 14th–August 31st our hotel is always fully booked; in other months we have Parisian guests at weekends but nobody during the week, so we*

would be particularly glad to see British tourists at these times.'
95f for the menu and 400f for demi-pension, with a three-night minumum in July and August. Closed Mon.

Map 3B   **CHEF-DU-PONT** 50360 Picauville, Manche. 4 km SW of Ste-Mère-Eglise on the D 67

Hotel Normandie
(HR)S *pl. Gare 33.41.32.06 Cl. Sun.*

Francophiles will be well aware that in France some of the treasures hotel-wise do not lie on the surface. An unlikely exterior often hides a gem within. Such is the case with the Hotel Normandie, no beauty from the outside, or inside for that matter, but a gem for the bargain-hunter. It does have nine rooms, very cheap, but these are uninspected; it is the food that draws the customers. No wonder when three courses cost around a fiver.

'We are indebted to French Entrée for finding this one – the 55f menu started with a whole crab and moved on to a wide range of fish and meat. The ultimate in family-run French restaurants, where service and quality are pre-eminent.' – David Campbell and Vicki McLean.

Map 2A   **CHERBOURG** 50100 Manche

(T) *2 quai Alexandre 111 33.93.52.02; Gare Maritime afternoons in summer only.* (M) *Mon., Thurs.*

One of the more agreeable ferry ports. Cherbourg is small enough to be visited on foot, and the ferry docks within easy walking distance of the town, so it is a good choice for foot-passengers and car-drivers alike. Parking in the town centre is not easy, so I would recommend leaving the car on the quayside and walking over the bridge, or using the Continent car park. If you have to negotiate the town, it's best to drive round the harbour to the Hotel de Ville area.

The Continent is in scale with the rest of the town – not so mammoth that it requires half a day to do it justice, but perfectly adequate and user-friendly. If you have left your French shopping – duty-free and all – until the last day, you need have no qualms about short-comings here. Good for petrol fill-ups too, and the restaurant is better than average.

However Cherbourg deserves more than a last-minute scramble. It still retains much of its character as a fishing port, with the colourful

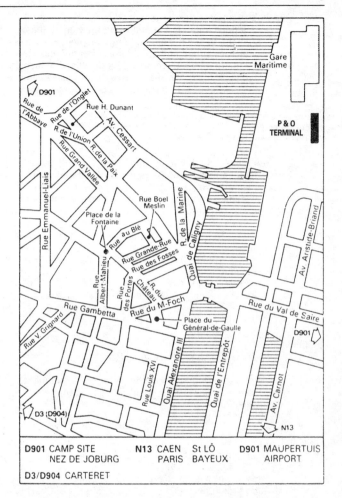

Gare Maritime 50101 — Cherbourg Tel: (33) 44 20 13

old boats and attendant screaming gulls animating the harbour and the fish being sold to sharp-eyed housewives on the quays. The port de plaisance provides an alternative vista of masts and marine activity.

Pedestrianisation of several central streets has been a great success. Turn up by the tourist office into the main square, the Place Général de Gaulle, with its splashing fountain, flower-stalls and voluptuous theatre, and on the right, by the Printemps department store, is a network of precincts where strolling, shopping, sitting is a pleasure. There are several pavement cafés for refreshment.

Renovation of the area around the Rue au Blé continues, and it is a pleasure to see the old buildings resplendently face-lifted, with their stone de-grimed and paintwork shining. This is the region to make for if you are interested in small foodie shops, which, in the delightful haphazard manner of all French towns, alternate with hat shops, umbrella shops, ironmongers, boutiques and bars.

Hotel Mercure
(HR)M   *Gare Maritime   33.44.01.11   AE, DC, E, V*

Averse generally to modern chain hotels I might be, but there's no denying that the Mercure has easily the best site in Cherbourg, that it's quiet and functional (open every day year round, near the ferry terminal), and as there are few attractive alternatives in the town I can but recommend it.

Avert your eyes from the virulent orange of the bedroom decor, and just look out of the window at the sailing boats and the sea. Rooms 240–490f.

The restaurant, Le Clipper, is also way above usual hotel standards, with fair enough menu at 98f and a very good one at 130f. The young Norman chef uses fresh local produce and lots of fish. What's more it doesn't despise carafe wine. You can have drinks first on the only terrace in town that has a sea view (shame on Cherbourg).

Le Louvre
(H)M   *2 r. H.-Dunant   33.53.02.28   Cl. 24/12–1-/1 CB*

A reliable and practical choice for an overnight stop near the port. Rooms are now double-glazed against traffic and pedestrian noise. 155–280f.

Chez Pain (Le Plouc)
(R)M-L   *59 r. au Blé   33.53.67.64   Cl. Sat lunch and Sun.*

My my how times have changed! I never dreamt when I came across the first little Le Plouc in the backstreets of Cherbourg some eight years ago that the day would dawn when Jacky Pain felt confident enough to name his restaurant after himself, nor that its status and prices would ever rise to the L category.

Its new(ish) up-market quarters are in the pleasantly restored quarter near the market halls, an easy walk from the ferry. It's rustic, cool, stone-walled, log-fired. Jacky Pain still cooks, but with several assistants now; Mme Pain still greets, more confidently than of yore, and takes the orders. Maddeningly, its closing days now make it useless for Saturdays and Sundays, when we weekenders need it most. Local businessmen like it for lunch, so it is prudent to book or sit down by midday. Menus from 130f.

Le Fait-Tout
H(M)   r. Tour Carrée

>Under the same management as Le Plouc, but nearer to the original Le
>Plouc in character and prices. Jacky Pain here supervises the cooking
>of traditional family dishes, like cassoulet or coq au vin, at much more
>modest prices (100f upwards).

▶ **Le Grandgousier**
(R)M   21 r. Abbaye   33.53.19.43   Cl. 26/3–2/4; 13/8–3/9; 24/12–1/1; Sat. lunch, Sun.
and fêtes   EC, V

>The best bistro in Cherbourg, according to many readers, who like the
>style, ambiance and prices here.
>   I certainly found it even better than I had remembered it, with a
>wider variety of cooking on menus that commendably had not
>rocketed in price since I first wrote about it and since it has gained
>Michelin recognition. There is now a new room at the rear to take the
>overflow that popularity has brought. I call 89f a bargain, when it
>includes, for example, an assiette de coquillages, salmon trout with
>almond cream, and a gratin of fruits. I took the next price up, at 110f,
>and enjoyed my mussels, escalope of salmon with sorrel, excellent
>cheeseboard, which included expensive cheeses like Roquefort, and
>interesting desserts (soupe de kiwis à la crème de menthe).
>   The décor is still pink and pretty, the service is still friendly and
>helpful, with beautiful fresh fishy specimens being presented before
>choices are made, and I consider the whole set-up well arrow-worthy.

L'Ancre Dorée
(R)M   27 r. Abbaye   33.93.98.38   Cl. Sat. lunch and Mon.; 15/7–31/8;
10/2–27/2   EC, V

>Almost next door to the Grandgousier, M. et Mme Albert Jeanne run
>this attractive alternative. Fish is the speciality here and it is probably
>the best place in Cherbourg to sample substantial and fresh fruits de
>mer, or a hunk of sea bass with good beurre blanc. What is more, it is,
>mercifully, open on Sunday evenings. Menus from 88f.

La Raclette
(R)S   9 pl. de la Révolution   33.04.09.99   Cl. Sun. p.m.

>Another new discovery in the attractive little Place de la Révolution,
>usefully open on Monday.
>   Madame Lamache runs the tiny restaurant, and specialises in Swiss
>dishes, as the name would suggest. The raclette is good for a cold
>winter day, when the spirits and the stomach both need warming up.
>Allow 65f.

La Marmite
(R)S   5 bis pl. des Moulins   33.94.71.58   Cl. Sun.; Mon.

>The Place des Moulins is a quiet paved square, just off the
>pedestrianised area, surrounded by newly restored houses, a very

pleasant addition to the Cherbourg scene. So is La Marmite, a tiny atmospheric restaurant usually overflowing with satisfied customers (so book). It specialises in seafood and its 65f fruits de mer is rightly popular. Go soon while it's still trying hard.

'The food was excellent and good value for money; service and presentation first class. We shall not hesitate to use it again.' – David and Elizabeth Handscomb.

Map 5D   **CLÉCY** 14570 Calvados. 37 km S of Caen

 Sun.

The 1188 inhabitants of Clécy claim that it is the 'Capital of the Suisse Normande', a particularly attractive area of Normandy that (truth to tell) bears little relation to Switzerland. It does not even claim to include Normandy's highest peaks, but it does have a distinctive landscape of green hills and greener valleys. The river Orne winds peacefully through rich pastureland or dramatically cuts into the rocky escarpment of the Armoricain massif.

The whole area is very well organised for tourists, but even in July I did not find it unduly crowded. Paths and excursions are well indicated and brochures are readily available from tourist offices and cafés. The two most popular outings are south to La Faverie Cross and to Le Pain de Sucre, both of which offer spectacular views of the rocks, river and the La Lande Viaduct. Varying levels of exertion are all catered for – rock-climbing for those who like to get to the top the hard way, hiking, canoeing, fishing, bicycling, riding. All the scenic routes are well signed and the day's activity need be no more taxing than to follow the arrows. An impressive example is the road to the Oëtre Rock overlooking the Rouvre gorge.

At Vey, 1 km east of Clecy on the D 133A, an imposing old bridge crosses the wide fast-flowing river and a scattering of restaurants and cafés make the most of the setting. Their balconies overhang the river and here the inactive can sit and sup, watching the fit get fitter in their pedalos or canoes.

➤ Le Moulin du Vey
(HR)M *31.69.71.08 Cl. 30/11–28/12; rest. cl. Fri. lunch o.o.s. E, DC, V*

If Monet didn't paint here, he should have done. Here is the hotel with the most perfect setting imaginable. Willows droop into the diamanté ripples, water-lilies beg to be immortalised, in paint or photography, the river bends obligingly to frame the mellow old bridge, and the hotel's flower-filled terrace is the perfect vantage point from which to appreciate the chocolate-box tranquility. If you feel like packing a long muslin dress, straw hat and parasol, this is the place to wear it.

Readers have been satisfyingly bowled over and enthusiasm for the site and the creeper-clad old water mill hotel has been unanimous. Less so for the food, with which two judgements I entirely concur.

Moulin du Vey

The rooms are delightful and not expensive, at 350–500f. It's worth going for the more expensive ones, with that soothing unique view. Meals are served in a separate building and have been disappointing, and nothing like the bargain of the hotel. Cheapest menu is 125f.

There is an annexe (the Moulin is understandably often full) 3 km away, the Relais de Surosne, which is okay, but definitely second-best, and a new venture, the Manoir de Placy.

Undoubtedly an arrow, especially for those who don't mind eating outside their hotel.

To be fair, although the above is the consensus, there have been several differences of opinion:

'We need not have worried about the annexe. A superb little château in its own peaceful grounds. Our room (no. 3) was so beautiful and the windows open onto the balcony overlooking the grounds. Off to the Moulin for our second superb meal – the 104f menu, four courses of wonderful food in this magnificent setting.' – Philip Mitchell.

'We were assured that the comfort in the annexe was the same as in the main hotel, but were extremely disappointed. The beds were soft and lumpy and badly lit. The meal was a great disappointment – luke-warm fish soup which cost 60f, with no rouille, and 110f for a small portion of kidneys with rice. We thought the restaurant very expensive for what they serve.' – Claude Landes.

'We stayed at the Manoir du Placey, where our room 26 was like a small apartment, with patio doors to a lawn. Most unusual and excellent.' – Elsa Taylor.

➤ Auberge du Châlet de Cantepie
(R)M   *31.69.71.10   Cl. Sun. lunch   CB, AE, DC, EC*

A short distance from the charming little town, towards the river, is this little black-and-white timbered chalet-type restaurant. It's a delightful place in a delightful setting, with tables set outside under the trees in the garden and a folksy intimate interior, with lace curtains and brass and knick-knackery. The waitresses wear Norman costume.

Maryse and Patrick Charpentier have proved popular hosts and various readers testify to the welcome they received and the quality of the food. My last meal there was certainly perfection and good value at 85f (weekdays only) for such a popular tourist-orientated spot. The next price up is 135f and offers greater variety, but I was more than happy with my crudités, fresh trout from the Orne, and Norman cheese. Time for an arrow here, I do believe.

Le Site Normand
(HR)S   *31.69.71.05   Cl. Mon. o.o.s.; 1/1–7/3   AE, EC, V*

It is good to have a range of hotels in all price brackets for such a charming location, and this little hotel has pleased more than once:

'Attractive and comfortable and the staff both friendly and helpful. The food was unimaginative but well prepared.'

'We were disappointed with the dinner at the Moulin, which compared unfavourably with those we had at the Site Normand, which had more atmosphere and infinitely more character.' – Pat Priday.

Rooms 180f; menus from 65f.

Mme Leboucher
(C)M *Le Vey* 31.69.71.02

> Yet another attractive alternative, even more modestly priced at 150–
> 180f. Mme Leboucher has five comfortable guest rooms in an
> independent building in her husband's farm. Three have private
> showers, two share a bathroom and they have their own sitting-room
> with fireplace. I have a reader's confirmation that they are clean and
> wholesome and that Mme Leboucher is a kind and attentive hostess.
> The farm is very near the Moulin and shares its unbeatable location.

Map 5H   **COCHEREL** 27120 Pacy-sur-Eure, Eure. 6 km N of Pacy

---

> The D 836 from Pacy follows the river Eure, a green and pleasant drive.

La Ferme de Cocherel
(HR)M *32.36.68.27 Cl. Wed.; Tues.; 2/1–24/1   AE, DC, EC, V*

> There are only three rooms attached to the farm, but they are spacious
> and peaceful, in maisonettes in the flowery garden. Their cost of 350–
> 400f represents good value when you think of the absolute peace and
> comfort guaranteed.
>
> Pierre Delton cooks lavishly from seasonal produce – dishes like
> stuffed morilles with sweetbreads and roast beef flavoured with truffle
> juice. There is a 150f midweek lunch menu, but otherwise it's going to
> be 200f including wine.

Map 3B   **COIGNY** 50250 La Haye du Puits, Manche. 14 km E of La Haye-
du-Puits

> Turn north off the D 903 half-way between La Haye and Carentan.

Château de Coigny
(C)L *33.42.10.79 Cl. 1/11–1/6. Open o.o.s. on request*

> When Madame Ionckheere was widowed in 1989, she was left alone in
> an 18C château set romantically in deeply rural isolation. Her solution
> to the loneliness and mortgage problems is to take in paying guests.
> The château, unlike many a crumbling stately pile, is maintained in
> spanking order, with ordered flower beds and not a sign of peeling
> paint inside or out.
>
> The two bedrooms set aside for her guests' use are exactly as they
> were when the Ionckheeres entertained their own friends – luxurious
> and extremely comfortable, with antique furniture, expensive curtains,
> glossy bathrooms. Use of the salon, with its astonishing pink
> Renaissance fireplace, classed as a Monument Historique, is part of the
> deal.

A lovely peaceful place to stay, half way between Carentan and La Haye but a million miles away in time and character from 20C hassle. Rooms are 450f. Breakfast 50f.

Map 3D   **COLLEVILLE-MONTGOMERY** 14880 Hermanville sur Mer, Calvados. 4.5 km W of Ouistreham by the D 45A

La Ferme St.-Hubert
(R)M   *3 r. de la Mer   31.96.35.41   Cl. Sun. p.m.; Mon. o.o.s.   E, DC, EC, V*

Don't go expecting a farm. It may have been once, but its rustic origins have long since been forgotten. Nowadays it's a modern châlet-like building, set in the middle of nowhere, with never a snort nor a grunt to be heard.

It's more rustique inside, with plenty of beams and an open fire, so that the atmosphere is warm and cosy. Henry Famin, the chef, trained at the hotel school in Paris, so his dishes are more sophisticated than you might expect, with home-made foie gras and suprême de turbot featuring on the carte. There is a cheap weekday menu – 80f, which is good value (terrine, fish of the day, cheese or fruit) – or menus at 123f or 240f for those who can manage five courses. The fish is always good and fresh. Good news if you fancy a fairly smart meal, near the coast, without the hassle of parking in Caen.

Map 4D   **COLOMBELLES** 14460 Calvados. 6 km NE of Caen by D 513

(M) *Fri. p.m.*

Virtually a suburb of Caen, and an unlikely place to find a good restaurant, in this case in a shopping parade.

Du Parc
(HR)M   *44 r. Jules Guesde   Cl. Fri.; Sept.; 21/12–6/1*

The mention of M. Artur's cooking brings much lip-smacking to the local gastronomes – and to the residents of Caen itself – who like to eat well without paying over the top. The Parc is a modern logis in the middle of a row of shops. We had to stop and ask the way, but there was no shortage of advice, culminating in the experience, often encountered in France when the matter of eating is concerned, of a driver saying 'Follow me' and going out of his way to lead us to the shrine. The importance of getting to a good restaurant is clearly recognised.

Anyway, when you do arrive you start by wondering what all the fuss is about (very ordinary exterior) and end up by congratulating yourself on making the effort. Menus are 85, 150, 280f, offering dishes like a soufflé of smoked salmon, terrine of hare, grilled bass with tarragon, calves-liver with Cassis. Fish particularly recommended.

Map 5G **CONCHES-EN-OUCHE** 27190 Eure. 18 km W of Evreux

 Thurs.

A smashing little town, set on a spur encircled by the little river Rouloir. It forms the hub of three forests, Conche, Breteuil and Evreux, which radiate from its crossroads, and is therefore a centre for 'la chasse', an obsession with the French, who cannot see anything flying, creeping, running, swimming, without visualising it on the table. Every little town hereabouts has at least one huntin' shootin' fishin' shop prominently in the main street and in the autumn the butchers are draped with gamey loot. The most impressive of these corpses is the marcassin or wild boar, bristly fierce and still looking very angry at the indignity of being suspended upside down.

The good townsfolk of Conches had such respect for their game that they decided to honour it in the form of a statue. There in the gardens behind the lovely old church of Ste-Foy (famed for its stained glass windows), on a plinth commanding the best view of the whole valley, they erected a (very bad) statue of the boar. I long to know what Clochemerle-like deliberations, arguments, claims and counter-claims must have been put forward to result in the glorification of the swine. Did the town band parade in his honour? Was the mayor inspired to recite his virtues? Was he a special boar with a story I have yet to hear?

Auberge du Donjon
(HR)S   *55 r. Ste Foy   32.30.04.75   Cl. Tues. p.m. o.o.s.; Wed.; 20/10–15/11   E, C, V*

The worst news I have to pass on to readers is that M. Guille has had to leave Conches. Le Donjon has been one of the most consistently popular of all F.E.3's recommendations, and I hate to lose it or have it changed in any way. The new owner has a hard act to follow.

For the benefit of his many loyal fans, I can pass on the news that M. Guille has now opened up a little rustic restaurant in Le Mans – La Marmite, 95 r. du Bourg Bélé, 72000 Le Mans, 43.24.97.89 – and he tells me he would be delighted to see any of his old friends.

Let us think positive and describe things as they are:- Le Donjon is a timbered cheerful little restaurant in the main street, with a bar entrance and colourful red-checked table-cloths, gleaming copper. The three bedrooms are all good-sized doubles with washbasins, one overlooking the courtyard garden, where tables are set in summer, and they have all been recently redecorated. 110–130f. Menus from 70f.

Hotel Grand'Mare
(HR)S   *13 av. Croix de Fer   32.30.23.30   Cl. Sun. p.m.; Mon. o.o.s.; 24/1–7/2   V*

A perfect site for this highly attractive little black and white auberge. It overlooks the expansive park, lake and fountain on the other side of the main road from the church, and is perfectly peaceful. For several years past, its potential has not been fully realised, but at last there is new management to exploit it:

'The young couple who have recently taken over the hotel are obviously working hard to upgrade the restaurant. The hotel is quite delightful. We had a room on the top floor overlooking the cathedral and the donjon. It was very spacious with the most wonderfully comfortable firm double bed. With shower and cabinet – spotlessly clean – it cost 85f. The setting of course is perfect and Conches is a delightful little town. We were devoted to the boar, staring out across the valley and forest .... Presentation of the food was first class. A beautifully sculptured mound of melon and salad, followed by fish in cream sauce and then the speciality – blueberry sorbet set in a tulip-shaped biscuit shell.' – Susan Leyden.

The rooms are now 85–145f and the menus (dining-room full of French tucking in) start at 80f, but all this is excellent value and an arrow will soon be appropriate.

La Toque Blanche
(R)M   *18 pl. Carnot   32.30.01.54   Cl. Tues. p.m.; Mon.; 16/8–10/9; 15/12–1/1   CB, AE, EC*

There is yet another option in this well-blessed little town, which anywhere else would be a star turn in its own right. La Toque Blanche is perhaps more popular with the French than the British, and I do not have a catalogue of praise to report on this one, probably because the alternatives are so good. However, with a few days spent here – and I can think of few more agreeable spots to linger – a meal in the pretty little dining-room of La Toque Blanche would be an excellent idea. Its chef patron, Bernard Bachet, is devoted to his region and dedicated to serving regional specialities. His fish dishes are especially to be recommended, along with the cheeseboard. Prices are higher than at the other two establishments, but the ingredients are absolutely prime. Mid-week lunch is a bargain 60f and there is a 98f mid-week dinner menu. Otherwise it's 147f. A pleasant touch is the waitresses dressed in local costume and the complimentary trous normands and Calvados sorbets.

Map 6D   **CONDÉ-SUR-NOIREAU** 14110 Calvados. 12 km N of Flers

Ⓜ *Thurs., Sat.*

Hotel du Cerf
(HR)S   *18 r. du Chêne   31.69.40.55   Cl. Sun. p.m. and school holidays   EC, V*

Just nine rooms in this little logis: they cost from 148–215f and M. Malgrey feeds his guests well on menus starting at 60f. Very popular with several readers.

'After two nights at the Moulin du Vey we moved down-market to Le Cerf, where we have stayed previously. Can only reiterate our complete satisfaction. We were recognised, made to feel instantly at home, and nothing was too much trouble, even though la patronne was away skiing. Attention to minor details – such as the half-finished bottle of mineral water from lunch being represented at dinner time with room number written on bottle. I know it was only coppers, but such actions instil a certain amount of confidence. However do not expect Homes and Gardens interior design.'

'Double room with bath etc. at 185f and excellent food at 103f for four courses. Very hard to thread large car through coaching arch to car park, not much room for pre-prandials, but accueil excellent. Nothing too much trouble. 49 candles produced from nowhere for a surprise birthday cake, complimentary bottle of bubbly, complimentary tasters for unknown dishes. An excellent feeding and watering hole.' – Michael Cooper Cocks.

Map 3F   **CONTEVILLE** 27210 Beuzeville, Eure. 13 km NW of Pont Audemer; 42 km SW of Le Havre

---

To find the village of Conteville, head east from Honfleur on the coast road, D 312; it's a pleasant route all the way, very rural with glimpses of the Seine along the way. From here you can rest assured that Le Havre is only about 45 minutes away, so a last stop before catching the night boat might be at:

➤ **Auberge du Vieux Logis**
(R)L   *32.57.60.16   Cl. Wed. p.m.; Thurs.; 20/9–20/10   AE, DC, EC, V*

The only thing that has changed in this hyper-Norman village inn, in all the years I have known it and Yves Louet has been cooking there, is that he now has two sons, Guillaume and Antoine, to help him in the kitchen. They have brought a touch of sophistication to the highly traditional cooking of their father, but this is still *the* place to taste such homely fare as pigs' trotters and wonderfully fresh locally-caught fish. The cheeseboard is reason alone for paying a visit. Here you will find cheeses almost impossible to locate elsewhere, and certainly not in other restaurants.

It's a lovely warm atmosphere in the little beamed restaurant, with a collection of old plates and copper utensils on the walls, and the welcome from Madame Louet matches the feeling. The only snag is the price – you should allow at least 300f per head now, since there is no menu. But you won't regret it. An arrow for some of the best cooking in Normandy.

Conteville, in peaceful countryside, near the ferry, and the joys of

Auberge du Vieux Logis

Honfleur, is also popular as a convenient overnight stopover. Several houses in the neighbourhood have opened their doors as chambres d'hôte:-

Le Clos Potier
(C)M *32.57.60.79   Open year round*

Mme Anfrey has two guest rooms in an immaculate house, with a picturesque farmyard and duckpond as a setting. One has a private bathroom and the other a shared shower, for 155f for 2 people. Evening meal is 75f, using home-grown produce.

Les Pierres
(C)M *32.57.60.57   Open year round*

Mme Jeannine Larcie also has two guest rooms in her village house, one for three people, with private bathroom, and the other with private shower and loo. 145f for two; 180f for three.

'Not as picturesque as Le Clos Potier but quiet and very private, with good mod cons and an unfussy hostess.' Robin Totton.

Map 3F   **CORNEVILLE-SUR-RISLE** 27500 Pont-Audemer, Seine-Mar.
6 km SE of Pont Audemer

A crossroads, formed by the junction of the N 175 and the D 130, in pleasant hilly countryside.

Les Cloches de Corneville
(HR)M   *32.57.01.04   Cl. Wed.; 20/11–15/12; 20/2–2/3   AE, DC, EC, V*

There's a legend about the bells in the carillon above this little eccentric gothicky hotel. Or rather there are several, but here's the favourite. The wicked English, during the Hundred Years War, stole the bells from the Abbey of Corneville and made off with them in a boat down the river Risle. But they hadn't allowed for the considerable weight: one bell was dropped and still rests at the bottom of the river. The legend was that if the bells should ever ring again from the abbey, the one in the water would chime in unison. The abbey was destroyed in the Revolution, and a composer Roger Planquette, inspired by the legend, composed his operetta *Les Cloches de Corneville*. By doing so money was raised to subscribe for the new set of bells now installed. Some there are who say they can hear the lost chimes whenever the Corneville bells ring out.

It's an eccentric, fairy-tale kind of hotel, to fit well with flights of imagination. All in miniature, the rooms are far from spacious, but very well fitted out and comfortable, at 245–325f. The food in the similarly-scaled dining-room or on the very pleasant glassed-in terrace is way above small-hotel average. The menu at 135f is an excellent choice.

A useful, imaginative alternative to the Pont Audemer hotels.

Map 1B   **COSQUEVILLE** 50330 St. Pierre Eglise, Manche. 15 km E of Cherbourg

---

The north-east corner of the Cotentin peninsula is not very interesting between Cap Levy and Gatteville, unless utter seclusion is of prime consideration. The sandy beaches are deserted for ten months of the year and most of them have a sad and desolate air. Cosqueville is the most attractive of the villages in this area.

➤ **Au Bouquet de Cosqueville**
(HR)S   *33.54.32.81   Cl. Wed. o.o.s.*

This used to be called the Hotel de la Plage. It is wisely re-named, sinc
it is five minutes' walk away from the Plage du Vicq, with fine sand an
a dozen fishing boats in a little natural harbour. It always had vast
potential, with views across the flat countryside to the sea, but was,
truth to tell, always a little sad, if not run-down. Happily it's a different
story now.

New owners have smartened the place up in every way, and all is
light and bright and cheerful and thoroughly to be recommended.
Locals love it too. Here is a recent experience:

'Gorgeous spot. Pretty beflowered dining-room. Predominantly fish
menus. The cheapest at 72f is superb, with lovely sauces. Delicious
Gros Plant at 40f puts many a Muscadet to shame. Nothing too much
trouble for kindly patronne, including loan of alarm for early morning
sailing.' – Tony Bishop.

So far prices have remained amazingly modest, no doubt to
encourage a regular clientele, but I worry that they might rise when th
obvious virtues of the place become better known. So go soon, paying
100–170f for a good double room. The excellent menu at 76f wins a re
R in Michelin. A new arrow for value and position.

Map 3C   **COTTUN** 14400 Bayeux, Calvados. 5 km W of Bayeux

Take the D 5, direction Molay-Littry, out of Bayeux and follow the signs
after 5 km for Cottun.

Château de Cottun
(C)L   *31.92.41.55* and *33.20.45.33*

M. and Mme Francis Lenormand opened their manor-house home
three years ago, and several readers have been pleased with their
hospitality; the consensus is that it is worth paying the 250f for a
double room in the house, rather than 150f for a room with shower in
the annexe.

'A real find. It was super – spacious, quiet and very comfortable. We
had a large room with separate bathroom, but there were cheaper
rooms in the annexe. We also ate here, and although the service was
painfully slow (the family seemed very new to it all), the food was very
good.' – Dr. Hugh G. Davies.

Map 5B   **COUDEVILLE** 50290 Bréhal, Manche. 9 km N of Granville; 2 km
S of Bréhal

Mme Lechevallier
(C)M   *Le Hébert   33.61.67.87*

Four guest rooms, each with private shower, and a bathroom reserved
for guests' use in this comfortable 'French bourgeois' house quietly set
in the countryside. 134f for two people, including breakfast.

*'2 km down a quiet lane towards the sea, an old-fashioned French
villa, with large rooms furnished in bourgeois style. Lots of good
towels and a large bathroom with copious hot water. Breakfast
comprised orange juice, three sorts of home-made jam and honey,
with no less than eleven different breads: croissants, ficelle, baguette,
crispbread, baps, madeleines and toast ... Oh and honey savarin,
naturally home-made. A truly gentil welcome from Mme Lechavalier
who greeted us with a tray of tea and fresh-baked buns. All this for
100f a couple!' – J. Belafield.*

Map 3D   **COURSEULLES-SUR-MER** 14470 Calvados. 18 km W of Caen

(T) *r. Mer   31.37.46.80* (M) *Tues., Fri.*

A sizeable modern fishing town, which to my mind lacks the kind of
scruffy charm that goes with an older port and its surroundings.
However it is always pleasant to look at yachts and fishing boats and
stalls selling oysters and fish.

La Crémaillière
(HR)M and **Annexe Gytan**   (H)M   *31.37.46.73 and 31.37.95.96   DC, EC, V*

Pleasant well-furnished rooms at 138–495f, overlooking the sea in the
case of the Crémaillère and a garden for its annexe Le Gytan. The
former does have a restaurant, good value at 125–400f, but it would
probably be more interesting to eat at the restaurant under the same
management:-

La Pêcherie
(R)M   *pl. du 6 Juin   31.97.45.84   DE, EC, V*

Very popular for Sunday excursions, when fish is fancied. It's a
largeish, smartish restaurant on the quay, with awnings and umbrellas
shading tables outside. Menus from 80f include the freshest fish, well
cooked and presented.

Map 7B **COURTILS** 50220 Ducey, Manche. 8 km E of Mont St. Michel

 Thurs.

· On the D 75 from Pontabault to Mont St. Michel.

Le Manoir de la Roche Torin
(HR)M *Rte du Mont St. Michel* *33.70.96.55* *Cl. 15/11–15/3* *CB, AE, DC, EC*

> The Gothic-style country house is well signposted down a lane off the main road. It offers exactly what its brochure claims – 'calme, confort, espace', situated as it is in the midst of leafy, traffic-free countryside. A its best in high season, when the Mont St. Michel tourists fill the hotels and a restful stop is hard to find. The youthful proprietors have furnished it attractively so that the price of 320–600f is probably justified. Cooking is mostly grills in panoramic rustic restaurant. Demi-pension at 360–400f per person obligatory in high season.

Map 5A **COUTAINVILLE** 50230 Agon-Coutainville, Manche. 77 km S of Cherbourg; 13 km W of Coutances

> M. Hulot would have been very much at home here in this unsophisticated little seaside resort, smattered with a couple of souvenir shops and several hotels de la plage. Like a king salmon swimming in this pool of tiddlers is the newly-smartened:

Hotel Hardy
(HR)M-L *pl. du 28 Juillet* *33.47.04.11* *Cl. Mon. o.o.s.; 5/1–5/2* *CB, AE, DC, EC*

> The fifth generation of Hardys are now in charge here and Emile has upped the standards of food in both quality and price. This is now far from being the family beach hotel, with plentiful simple cooking that used to make it a local landmark. At lunchtime the restaurant is full of serious dark-suited eaters – not a pair of shorts or plimsolls in sight – and the prices are expense-account (though there is a 100f mid-week menu that is good value for this quality). The food is very good – lots of fish, simply cooked, well presented in a charming dining-room.
>
> The rooms have all been improved too and are now very pretty, especially in the new annexe next door, and good value at 200–380f. Demi-pension at 280–350 p.p. obligatory in high season.

> A new and unexpected delight in this year's research was the discovery of the *Pointe d'Agon* just south of Coutainville. Finding the Hardys' menu too rich and rare for my simple lunchtime needs, on a beautiful June day, I set out to look for a picnic spot and succeeded beyond wildest hopes.
>
> Follow the signs to the lighthouse and be spoiled for choice. To the left is the estuary, approached by peaceful salt marshes, where sheep

crop and rare birds shelter; lovely walks here. To the seaward side are dunes and a spectacular beach, with only one picknicking family along its entire considerable length. Drive on to the point; look at the gorgeous views surrounding it; see the toy lighthouse set atop a doll's house.

Map 5B   **COUTANCES** 50200 Manche. 75 km S of Cherbourg

(T) *Hôtel de Ville (in season) 33.45.17.79*   (M) *Thurs.*

Miraculously having survived the battering of the 1944 bombardment, the largest cathedral in the Cotentin, Notre Dame de Coutances, still dominates the city, as it has done for over seven centuries. The towers of its façade have stood there, in the market-place on the hill, for even longer – they were salvaged from the Romanesque original when it was burned in 1218. In complete contrast, just a step down the r. Geoffroy de Montbray, is the Renaissance St. Pierre, with its striking lantern tower.

The public gardens here are particularly pleasant, with Son et Lumière in summer on Thursdays, Saturdays and Sundays. For hotels and restaurants, it's a disappointing town.

Hotel du Commerce et da la Gare
(HR)S   *28 r. Dr. Caillard   33.42.02.00   Cl. Fri.; 22/12–5/1   AC, DC, EC*

A puzzle. This old-fashioned family hotel, with a local reputation for copious and good-value meals, was drawing regular compliments:
'This turned out to be the favourite of the trip. Large light airy room in this charming old-fashioned hotel. Excellent meal, but the major plus is the very friendly patrons and staff.' – William Bennett.
Suddenly the flow has dried up, with no changes in the management or attitude that I know of. I recommend this therefore with some reservations. Rooms 120f; menus from 60f.

Le Relais du Viaduc
(HR)S   *25 av. du Verdun   33.45.02.68   Cl. 10/9–10/10*

A very superior Relais Routier 'one of the very best in France' says a well-travelled reader. No good complaining about its prominent, traffic-encircled position – relais routiers were after all designed to suit the needs of the lorry-drivers and if we choose to avail ourselves of their huge portions and low prices, we must accept the shortcomings. Think of it as a French Happy Eater and you will be delighted.

You can still tuck into five courses here for around 65f, and there are more expensive options if you're in the lobster and duck league. It's spotless and fast and excellent for family feasts. The rooms are cheap – 110f – but I don't know about the noise.

Map 3D   **CRÉPON** 14480 Creully, Calvados. 12 km NE of Bayeux by D 12 and D 112

A hamlet in the middle of farming country, just 7 km from the coast at Arromanches.

Ferme de la Rançonnière
(C)L   *31.22.21.73   Open year round*

A decidedly upwardly mobile b. and b. When a friend of mine first discovered it some eight years ago, it was a straightforward working farm just beginning to realise the potential of taking in a few guests. It was lovely then:-

'This place is a treat – beautiful old farmhouse with huge courtyard,

LA Rançonnière

all lovingly restored – antique furniture, good ambiance. It has been in the same family for years and the present owner was born there.' – Judy Wright.

And it's even lovelier now.

There can't be many farmhouse b. and b.s that make it to inclusion in the très chic, très snob Gault-et-Millau, but La Rançonnière has broken new ground and is there along with the greatest in the land. The 13C and 15C farmhouse has been restored with a grant from the Beaux Arts and now has 22 rooms available, from 145–260f, with mod. cons. It is still a working farm, however, and the ambiance hasn't changed.

Readers have thoroughly approved, with only one grumble – cold tiled floor and small bath.

'Definite thumbs up! We can only echo what you have said about the rooms and ambiance. We had a spacious room with shower and loo, for 190f. The farm has now opened a restaurant, where we ate good fresh country food, in pleasant surroundings. Menus were 65f, 88f and 130f. All the staff were friendly and we thoroughly enjoyed our stay.'

'Breakfast at 20f, included fromage blanc, cream and two boiled eggs if you wanted them. There was no choice for dinner and we were asked to sit down between 7.30 and 8 p.m. in the large attractive dining-room, with a blazing log fire although it was early July. The cost, including liberal jugs of wine was 80f for six courses – soup, quiche lorraine, lotte cooked in cider with rice, salad, cheese, and a choice of desserts.' – R. F. Hayward.

I hope it's all not going to get too grand and expensive, but for the time being a definite arrow for a delightfully different experience.

Map 3D **CRESSERONS** 14440 Douvres la Délivrande, Calvados. 16 km N of Caen; 3 km SW of Lion sur Mer

---

At the crossroads of the D 271 and the D 35, a hamlet in deep countryside.

La Valise Gourmande
(R)M   *7 route de Lion sur Mer   31.37.39.10   Cl. Tues. and Wed. lunch*

A welcome new addition to the gastronomic scene, within an easy drive from Caen. La Valise is an intensely pretty old stone house set behind a high wall, in a green and peaceful garden.

It was the family home of Jean-Jacques Hélie, who in 1986 decided to deposit his suitcase here permanently (hence the name) and open up a restaurant. He has retained the atmosphere of a private house, with lovely old furniture, lots of flowers, and the effect is warm and convivial.

His specialities include Assiette de la Valise Gourmande, which is an assortment of meats, fowl, and fish smoked on the premises, and he likes to include old-fashioned regional recipes like teurgoule and clafoutis, and lovely fresh fish from down the road. Menus at 95, 170 and 250f.

An arrow, I suspect, after a few more favourable reports.

Map 3D   **CREULLY** 14480 Calvados. 15 km NW of Caen

Ⓜ *Wed. a.m.*

On the D22, off the D12 from Bayeux to Courseulles.

St. Martin
(HR)S   *6 pl. Edmond Paillaud   31.80.10.11   Cl. Sun. p.m.; Mon. lunch; school hols   CB, EC, V*

This little Logis de France, with only eight rooms, is strategically situated in a village only a few km from the tourist attractions at Arromanches and the coast and would certainly make a comfortable first or last night stop after a Caen ferry crossing.

The rooms cost from 125–165f and menus start at 55f.

'This little hotel, centrally situated in the village, is kept absolutely spotless and is beautifully adorned with masses of geraniums in window boxes. We occupied a family room, double plus single bed, with plenty of room to spare and bathroom and toilet en suite for 190f.' – John L. Anderson.

Map 2G   **CROIX-MARE** 76190 Yvetot, Seine-Mar. 8 km S of Yvetot by N 15

Auberge de la Forge
(R)M   *35.91.25.94   Cl. Tues. p.m.; Wed.   CB, AE, DC*

A useful stop in an area not well served for good eating places. The Auberge is a timbered and very old little Norman house, where the chef-patron Mr. Truttmann serves excellent menus based on traditional recipes. The 138f version includes wine, but the 90 and the 118f versions are equally good value, offering dishes like rabbit terrine, with an interesting sauce made from prunes and hazelnuts, and a fruit brioche overflowing with poached fruit.

Map 4G **LES DAMPS** 27340 Pont de l'Arche, Eure. 1.5 km E of Pont de l'Arche; 22 km S of Rouen

Head east on the little road that follows the river from Pont de l'Arche

La Pomme
(R)M *35.23.00.46 Cl. Mon. p.m. o.o.s.; Sun. p.m.; Tues. p.m. and Wed. V*

On the river road, set back a little, an unpretentious restaurant, that I first discovered for F.E.2. When I had no feed-back and was unable to re-check for myself, I had to drop it for F.E.3, but now I am pleased to be able to re-introduce a very attractive possibility in this generally built-up spaghetti junction area. I would suggest doing a preliminary recce in daylight, as it is not easy to find in the dark, away as it mercifully is from the bright lights.

The food is interesting and well cooked by the chef-patron, on menus from 98f.

Map 4H **DANGU** 27720 Eure. 8 km SW of Gisors

Take the 181, then the D 146, or, for a more rural ride, the D 10 all the way deep into the little-known Vexin country.

Les Ombelles
(C)M *4 r. du Gué 32.55.04.95 or 45.22.18.07*

Nicole de St. Père keeps her two guest rooms, in a nice old restored house in the village, open all year round. Both have private loos and showers (190f for two), and her garden runs along the river Epte.

'The garden by the stream is pleasant and the room and bathroom are fine, but it is really for Nicole that you should arrow Les Ombelles She is actively interested in the tourism of this little-known area, and speaks fluent English.

She serves an evening meal, if so requested with due warning. I hadn't realised this was the form with b. and b.s, so arrived lateish, tired and hungry. No nonsense – I was tacked on to the family and he son barbecued a large piece of beef. We sank a good Burgundy, ate mirabelles from the garden and chatted and laughed our way into the darkness.' – Robin Totton.

Map 3E **DEAUVILLE** 14800 Calvados. 74 km SW of Le Havre; 47 km E Caen

Ⓣ *pl. Mairie 31.88.21.43* Ⓜ *Tues., Fri. o.o.s.; daily at Easter and Pentecost and July–15 September*

Deauville has two faces. For a few brief summer weeks it glitters like a courtesan; for the rest of the year it subsides, passée and querulous, into a fantasy, not enticing enough to please the Top People, not cheap enough for the hoi-polloi. That's not to say I don't like it, because I do. I admire its eccentricity, without wishing to become too involved in anything quite so artificial, and I always enjoy an excursion into its elegant never-never-land, knowing that the real world of Trouville is (incredibly) just across the bridge.

In high season a stroll along les Planches, the wooden walkway between the cafés, boutiques, restaurants, and the 'cabines' bizarrely facing inland towards the sun, not the sea, might well reveal a famous face or two. The glitterati, here for the Grand Prix and its attendant fuss, still like to be seen at Ciro's, the ultimate in beach cafés, and the least one can do is to gawp obligingly.

Out of season I find the place depressingly shuttered, unless the weather happens to be fine, when at weekends there are usually to be seen those prosperous, well-wrapped, stout French couples, arm in arm, walking their well-groomed poodles along the well-groomed prom. The most exclusive shops are closed then, owners migrated with their summer flock, but a few chic boutiques sell out-of-season bargains, and the market still functions on Tuesdays.

Readers have greeted my feeble attempts to find hotel and restaurant gems in this extraordinary town, with distinct lack of enthusiasm. I can hardly blame them – I would not choose to stay here myself if I were footing the bill. The severely limited opening times – packed in July and August, closed for much of the rest of the year – compound the problem. However, I persist in recommending Deauville as an excursion from some nearby base, if only for the contrast, and assuming that a meal here is required, you could not do better than:-

Le Spinnaker
(R)M-L   *52 r. Mirabeau   31.88.24.40   Cl. Thurs. o.o.s.; Wed.; 15/11–15/12   CB*

The opening times are encouraging – here is a restaurant that is not geared entirely to the summer no-expense-spared clientele. For Deauville, Le Spinnaker is modest in concept – minuscule dining-rooms on two levels, blue and white decor – and its menu at 150f is excellent value. You can go mad on the carte if you feel inclined and will be delighted with the imaginative and delicious results.

Map 2A   **DIÉLETTE** 50830 Flamanville, Manche. 20 km SW of Cherbourg on the coast

---

The coast between Joburg and Carteret, little known to tourists, is a green timewarp of narrow lanes and old stone cottages. It is well worth the curious traveller's time to potter down from the sensational Cape to the enchanting but well-discovered Carteret via the contrast of the road from Beaumont, the D 138, for example, and then making another loop further south off the D 37 towards the coast, through Diélette, until time or patience runs out.

Diélette is not a particularly attractive port, especially now that the nuclear power depot has taken over part of it, but it is appreciated by those looking for a complete lack of sophistication, in an area of natural beauty. And there are beaches to explore, cliffs to walk upon, and fishing boats to watch.

Hotel de la Falaise
(H)S   *33.04.08.40   Cl. Sun. p.m.*

M. and Mme Poard took over this formerly gloomy pile overlooking the sea in 1987, and have transformed it into an attractive and welcoming hotel. Comfortable bedrooms, with sea views, cost from 180–230f and menus, featuring lots of local fish, from 60f, though one reader found the cooking unimaginative and pointed out that the out-of-date diplomas on the walls were for cooking on French railways (not nearly so bad as that sounds, by the way). Another reader was happier:

'Diélette is just like Cornwall used to be, absolutely unspoilt and underdeveloped. The hotel received us warmly and managed to fit us in in spite of being busy (not another English tourist in sight). Lovely room and bathroom overlooking the sea, and nothing too much trouble. Our two evening meals were well cooked, but the menu was limited, so we could have had a problem had we been staying longer, unless all we wanted was fruits de mer. We paid 180f a day and 120f each for dinner (there was a cheaper menu). Please don't overlook this delightful place and hotel in future editions.' – Mike and Mary Butler.

Sound like a good-value family base, open year round, which is unusual in this area.

Map 1G   **DIEPPE** 76200 Seine-Mar. 58 km NE of Rouen; 103 km NE of Le Havre

---

(T) *bvd. Gén-de-Gaulle 35.84.11.77; Rotonde plage (July-August) 35.84.28.70* (M) *Tues., Wed., Thurs. a.m., Sat.*

Dieppe gets on with its business of being a real French port, with real French fishermen and real French housewives going about their really French lives.

Into the very heart of the town probes the deep water, so that ships are part of the urban scenery, to be walked round and remarked upon, with all their evocative accessories of screeching gulls snatching at fish, engine thud, constant animation, a sense of the importance of the sea's moods.

No surprise to find many fishy restaurants lining the quays, no surprise to find them good value – when the tourists have gone, they must stake their claim for stalwart local appetites. Not so with hotels – the Dieppois don't use 'em and don't seem concerned that they are generally a sorry lot, spoiled with too easy custom; but eating ... that's another story.

So Dieppe is first a port – and a lively, colourful, absorbing first it is – but then a market town. As easy to shop well here as to eat. And, logically enough, the Grand' Rue leads straight from one focal point, the harbour, to another, the Place de Puits Salé, the obvious conclusion to a gentle stroll through the pedestrianised shopping area being the **Café des Tribunaux**. Always lively, best in the evening when the pavement tables catch the last slant of sun; a hundred years ago it was the meeting place of revolutionary young artists, fascinated by the clarity of the coastal light – Pissaro, Renoir, Monet, Sickert, Whistler, all gathered here. The Café still attracts youthful customers, hot in debate over a 'pression'. The ghost of Oscar Wilde, exiled, disgraced, the imbiber of many a sad drink at the Tribunaux, troubles them not at all.

Opposite the Café, in the r. de la Barre, is probably the best pâtisserie in Dieppe, though it is hard to be definitive because there is an exceptionally high standard here. This one is named after the dashing Duchess of Berry who 'invented' sea-bathing. Thirty different flavours of ice-cream on offer too, so not a bad idea to sit in the Tribunaux to contemplate and decide between, say, a fraise du bois, or guava, or caramel. Not easy.

Dieppe.

A little further up the r. de la Barre is the kitchen shop which is not only my favourite but that of most local chefs – **La Magdalene**. For serious cooking **Tout Pour La Maison** in the Grand' Rue has a good range too.

Zigzag back to the harbour between other Grand' Rue temptations, gastronomic (good charcuteries – **La Rôtisserie Parisienne** – boulangeries, épiceries), sartorial (upmarket labels at B.D.T. and Le Roy-Délépouille, lots of shoe and jeans outlets) and two good teashops (Divernet/Grisch and Aux Fins Gourmets), and finish with a quick nip round the department stores, Le Printemps and Prisunic. If you're homeward bound, the final fruitier, 'Royal Fruit', sells good-value fruit and veg; if there's a seasonal glut of, say, peaches, strawberries or tomatoes, this is the place to pick up a cheap kilo from the brimming stalls outside.

That is, of course, unless it's Saturday, when it would be a crime to miss the market. Hard to miss it in fact, since it takes up the whole of the pl. Nationale and spills over into the adjoining streets. It's one of the best in Normandy, exploiting to the full the regional products. If you think all butter and cream taste the same, just try some from one of the farmers' stalls there and relish the difference.

Dieppe's fishing fleet unloads its catch on the quayside. If you get up early enough you'll catch the auction, but it's always a pleasure to buy fish anywhere in Dieppe. All kinds of shellfish, including oysters, are wonderful value and there is a huge range of prime white fish, alive and kicking; on the stalls by the harbour, in the market, from shops like 'À la Marée du Jour' in the Grand' Rue, or from the fish restaurant, L'Armorique, on the quay.

What's in a name? Quite a lot, apparently, if it's Olivier. In Boulogne the fromagier Phillippe is a phenomenon; here in the r. St-Jacques, his father, Claude, provides another essential shopping experience. This is where I always stock up on cheeses in guaranteed prime condition – just tell him on which day you wish to eat them – and cheap wines. You can trust his special offers or play safe with Nicolas. Usefully open on Sunday a.m.

If you're hell-bent on a hypermarket, the nearest is **Mammouth** on the Rouen road. Allow plenty of time, though – the checkout queues can be diabolical. So is the parking in the town during July and August; because it is one of the nearest beaches to Paris, you can expect more crowds here than in other ports.

Dominating the promenade, with its wide stretches of grass dotted with picnickers, is the 15C castle, complete with maritime museum, displaying not only all things nautical but a fine array of ivory (closed Tues. o.o.s.). In the castle's shadow is a plaque commemorating the controversial Operation Jubilee, the costly Anglo–Canadian raid on Dieppe in 1942.

You can't stay in Dieppe for long without being reminded, by road and café names, of one of her most famous sons, Jean Ango. He was the maritime counsellor to Francis 1. In the 16th century he took on the Portuguese fleet off the coast of Africa, with notable success, and became Governor of Dieppe. He is buried in the chapel he built in the church of St-Jacques, especially worth a visit when the evening sun floods its rose window.

Dieppe has many virtues, but hotels are not among them. Those along the front are the obvious ones, but I cannot get excited about most of them. Here is the best of an indifferent bunch:-

La Présidence
HR(M-L)   *1 bvd. de Verdun   35.84.31.31   Open every day   CB AE DC EC*

It does what it sets out to do extremely well. If I were looking for a comfortable modern hotel, with spacious sea-viewed bedrooms, and didn't mind paying 320-515f, I could hardly find fault with La Présidence. In fact if you translate these sums into English equivalent, it begins to look like a bargain for what's on offer. Year-round efficiency, but predictably impersonal (88 rooms). Restaurant le Panoramic: allow 280f upwards.

Epsom
(H)M   *11 bvd. Verdun   35.84.10.10   Open year round   AE EC V*

My preference for a smallish (28 rooms), moderately priced hotel (220-270f). Newly refurbished, it is bright and cheerful, and has its share of sea views.

Plage
(H)M   *20 bvd. Verdun   35.84.18.28   Open year round   EC V*

Not my personal pick of the pops, but readers disagree with me:
'We find it pleasant, comfortable and reasonable in price considering its position. This is the third time we've stayed there.' 245–280f.

Hotel Aguado
(H)M   *30 bvd. Verdun   35.84.27.00   Open year round   EC, V*

The ultimate in plastic, but again it has a faithful following:
'Friendly and helpful welcome. A warm and happy night in clean comfortable rooms with all amenities, modern bathrooms, good deep baths, better than average lighting and at a negotiated price below that quoted'. – Mrs. L. Herman. 300–390f

The restaurant scene is somewhat better, but lacks a star:-

A La Marmite Dieppoise
(R)M   *8 r. St-Jean   35.84.24.26   Cl. Thurs. p.m. o.o.s.; Mon.; 20/6–1/7; 30/12–15/1   CB*

An old and reliable favourite. Set in a side street near the harbour, it is small, rustic, and busy. The marmite dieppoise from which the restaurant takes its name is definitive. Otherwise it's 80f for midweek lunch, or 190f upwards.

Armorique
(R)M   *17 Quai Henri IV   35.84.28.14   Cl. Sun. p.m.; Mon.; 15/6–30/6   CB*

Fish and nothing but the fish. You can buy it from the counter to take home, or eat it, the freshest of the catch, in the smartish (if crowded) restaurant on the first floor, with a good view from the window tables of the marine activity always going on in the harbour down below, or in the more basic café-style room downstairs.

Fish never comes cheap, but I consider l'Armorique offers excellent value for money. No eyebrows are raised if you order just a bowl of superb moules à la creme (30f), or a dozen stuffed oysters (48f). At the other end of the greediness scale, a 'royal' plate of fruits de mer costs a royal 250f, and would feed a family for a week (for lesser mortals, their plâteau comes at 95f).

Basic fish prices are fair – a large sole, for example, is 85f – but there are chef's specialities too – filet de barbue (brill) en écailles vertes, beurre d'échalotes costs 100f. So you gets what you pays for, and should be very well satisfied.

La Petite Auberge
(HR)S   *10 r. de la Rade   35.84.27.20   Cl. Wed.; 15/12–1/2*

Turn off the quay to find what the name says – a little auberge, tucked away from the tourists. Dead simple, dead cheap. 36.50f buys crudités/ pâté/mackerel; roast chicken/fish à la crème; frites and salad; cheese/ pud. 60.50f qualifies for mussels/langoustines; skate with burnt butter/ coq-au-vin, salad, cheese and pud. The French recognise a bargain when they see one, and it is often full.

Café des Tourelles
(R)S   *43 r. du Commandant-Fayolle   35.83.15.88*

A new recommendation, which should certainly please those with time rather than money to spare. Menus start at 45f, and the food is copious and good, as the locals well know.

'The service is slow to full stop, but the food is marvellous. The place was full of French having their Sunday lunch and there was a lovely relaxed atmosphere and we ate with no sense of time.' – Richard Coen.

Don't blame me if you miss the ferry.

La Mélie
(R)M   *2 Grande Rue du Pollet   35.84.21.19   Cl. Sun. p.m.; Mon.   CB, AE, DC*

I didn't enjoy my evening at La Mélie, but perhaps I went too soon after it opened, since readers have been happy here, and Michelin has re-awarded its rosette to M. Brachais, who used to be at Le Petit Pain (another restaurant I could never appreciate). So, slightly against the grain, I must report that menus are 150f or 200f with wine included, which I judge somewhat excessive for what is, after all, a simple and not very well decorated bistro. Good fish, I understand.

Map 7D   **DOMFRONT** 61700 Orne. 40 km SE of Vire; 98 km S of Caen

(T) *r. Dr Barrabé (in season) 33.38.53.97*   (M) *Sat.*

Although personally I find this stretch of Normandy rather dull, Domfront makes quite a useful stopping place, being an easy drive from Cherbourg well on the way south or west. An old cobbled pedestrianised street leads picturesquely up and away from the through-traffic blare to a square with what must surely qualify as the most hideous modern church in France (and that's some qualification). I think it must be a joke.

Unfortunately there are no hotels up here in the lofty calm and the only two options, the Poste and the France, are down on the busy main road. Neither of them has much charm, but here is a recent experience at the France:-

Hotel France
(H)S   *r. Mt. St. Michel   33.38.51.44   Cl. Mon. p.m.; Tues. o.o.s.; 6/1–14/2*

'The room was adequate for a one-night stay, but rather over-priced at 220f, as it was small with no wardrobe. It was also on the main road, so there was some traffic noise. However, dinner was one of the best meals we had in the whole holiday. 85f for moules à la crème, brochette de gigôt and profiteroles.' – Mrs. B. Paine.
Rooms 90–260f. Menus from 65f.

Map 7D   **DOMPIERRE** 61700 Domfront, Orne. 9 km NE of Domfront

Just a flowery crossroads on the D 21.

Restaurant du Bon Laboureur
(R)S   *33.30.44.90*

I couldn't resist including this extremely simple 'bar-tabac' restaurant in F.E.3 in order to point out that France can still be very cheap indeed if you know where to look and are not going to fret about lack of mod. cons. Madame Humbert-Lafontaine claims that her chambres have 'tout confort', but let's just say that it's all relative. It is rather for a food stop that I include Le Bon Laboureur and I was deighted to have this confirmation:

'We called on this restaurant, which was a few kilometres out of our way, simply on your recommendation, and had a really first-class lunch there. Madame Humbert has as assistant chef her son, a nice young lad, very keen and enthusiastic, who has just finished an apprenticeship at La Rochelle. Mother and son are very anxious to do well and make a success of their little restaurant. They certainly gave us a warm welcome.' – Pamela Waldy.

Madame Humbert used to be too occupied with 'banquets' at weekends to cope with overnight guests, but I hope that, with her son's help, her rooms will soon be as good as her food. Reports welcome.

Map 6B   **DRAGEY** 50530 Santilly, Manche. 14 km NW of Avranches by D 911 and D 143

> **Le Grain de Sel**
(R)S-M   *33.48.93.34   Cl. Sun. p.m.; Mon. o.o.s.; 1/1-28/2;1/10-10/10   CB*

One of the most exciting new discoveries for this book. Catherine and Thierry Bussière have turned the old granite house into a light and bright restaurant, modern and soigné. The cooking is remarkable for the prices involved (69f weekdays) and 138f for a menu du terroir which included rabbit marinaded in herbs, monkfish with a tomato coulis, cheese, and a superb hot apple tart. Arrowed for good value in an area not noted for the quality of its cuisine.

'We have dined here four times in a fortnight and have always had excellent imaginative food at very reasonable prices. For 88f we ate wonderful foie de volaille au porto and an escalope de veau with a mint and mustard sauce which beggars description. Mme. Bussière speaks astonishingly good English.' – David Dickinson.

Map 7B   **DUCEY** 50220 Manche. 11 km SE of Avranches

Ⓜ *Tues.*

Take the pleasant little D 78 rather than the main roads to find the village of Ducey.

> **Auberge de la Sélune**
(HR)M-S   *33.48.53.62   Cl. mid-Jan–mid-Feb.; Mon. o.o.s.   DC, EC, V*

This perfect little country inn has gone from strength to strength during the years since I first found it. The good news is that success has not changed its basic attractions; the bad news is that it is extremely difficult to get a booking. Discriminating tour operators like VFB (go to them if you want a package deal in small country hotels like the Sélune, all carefully vetted) have been sending satisfied customers here for years, and very few F.E. readers have not vowed to return there after the first visit.

Its charms include the welcome of the hard-working M. and Mme Girres, the exceptional standard of the food, prepared by Jean-Pierre, the simple comfortable countrified bedrooms, the pleasantly peaceful garden, with the hotel's namesake, the river Sélune, threading through and a pleasant flowery terrace. And the prices:- 200–220f for rooms, menus from 90f (red Michelin R).

'The meal was the best we had – delicious stuffed rabbit, crab pie, etc., all on an 80f menu, and perhaps the best thing of all – a kingfisher on the bush by the river!' – Mrs. James Ridell.

'This was the only hotel which required a deposit, but it was definitely the best of the trip – the setting and the rooms were lovely. We went for the gourmet dinner, which was fantastic. I still drool at the thought of the trout stuffed with trout soufflé. But breakfast was

disappointing – we had to make do with leftovers – all the croissants had gone by the time we came down.' – Virginia Barstow.

No dissension whatsoever that this is arrow-worthy, for position (on the route to Brittany), in a very pleasant setting, welcome, consistency, food and value.

There is now some opposition down the road. The old burnt-out mill has become the three-star Moulin de Ducey. Reports welcome.

Map 3G **DUCLAIR** 76480 Seine-Mar. 20 km NW of Rouen; 71 km SE of Le Havre

---

 Tues. a.m.

Spoiled by the heavy lorries that thunder through the little town or queue up to cross on the ferry to Brotonne, and with little attraction in the form of welcoming cafés or shops, but still a good place to observe the great cargo ships on their way between Rouen and the sea. The best view comes from:

Hotel Poste
(H)S *286 quai Liberation   35.37.50.04   Cl. Sun. p.m. Rest. cl. Mon.; 1/7–14/7; 1/2–15/2   AE, DC, V*

Bag a table by the window in the upstairs dining-room to get the benefit of the view of the quayside activity. They no longer serve the duckling rouennais, for which they have long been famous, in fourteen different styles, but it is still a popular choice.

The 70f menu is outstanding value (red Michelin R) and although the exterior of the hotel and the décor of the rooms is far from exciting, there have been few grumbles about the cost: 160–200f.

'Our room was on the top floor, with marvellous views of the river, with the ferry crossing every 15 mins and various cargo ships and barges. The cost was 130f for a simple room plus shower and a separate w.c. The restaurant has been lavishly decorated in pink and green, with extensive drapes and murals, very French. We had the middle price menu (98f), which was excellent, and the whole atmosphere was friendly and welcoming.' – Anne Beresford.

Le Parc
(R)M *av. du Cdt-Coty   35.37.50.31   Cl. Sun. p.m.; Mon.; mid-Dec–mid-Jan.; 1st week in Aug.   CB, AE, DC, EC*

Readers have maintained a profound indifference to my recommendation for Le Parc, but I shall persist. Its prime charm is in fine weather when you can eat in the garden, overlooking the river.

In order to find it you must double back from Duclair on the Route de Caudebec and take the turning along the riverbank signposted 'Route des Fruits'. The combination of fruit trees, as far as the eye can see to the right, and mighty river to the left is a heady one and slightly unreal.

It's all a bit too neat and miniature for France – the houses are for dolls the assorted livestock in the enclosures look as though they have been arranged by a child: one fat cow, two clean pigs, a Mummy-sheep with three baby lambs, four brown hens, one collie dog .... The scale is more Home Counties than Normandy, but very very pretty. Not very far along this route is Le Parc, an imposing turn-of-the-century mansion, slightly faded, with a large garden running down the river.

The food is determinedly traditional Norman, and menus start at 170f.

Map 2E   ÉTRETAT 76790 Seine-Mar. 28 km NE of Le Havre

(T) *(summer) pl. de la Mairie 35.27.05.21* (M) *Thurs. a.m.*

It's a pleasant easy drive along the coast out of Le Havre to the little seaside town of Étretat. Make for the beach, instantly familiar because of its much-photographed, much-painted, distinctive white rocks, and take a stroll along the prom, made colourful by the brightly painted fishing boats pulled up nearby.

In summer it's a lively little resort, full of happily squealing children, precarious windsurfers and dozens of souvenir shops and cafes; in winter it dies.

There are good walks on either side of the beach, to the left after a steep climb, past the golf course, to the Falaise d'Aval; to the right, up to the church, standing sentinel over the town.

Notre Dame is a justification for another agreeable walk, past typically French holiday villas, rose-covered, white-shuttered. It is a wonderfully simple Romanesque church, nine centuries away from the 20th-century 'amusements' on the prom.

Hotel Falaises
(H)S-M *bvd. R. Coty 35.27.02.77*

'A pleasant clean hotel'. – Frank Etherington.

This is the most comprehensive report that I have had from readers, although most of them have liked the little town. The bedrooms are comfortable, if on the small side, and cost 180–300f.

Some restaurant recommendation would obviously be welcome, since the Falaises does not have its own, but again I lack up-to-date information. The last two I tried, L'Escale in the pl. Mar-Foch and the Roches Blanches, in the rue Abbé Cochet, were both averagely-priced, averagely-good.

Map 5G   EVREUX 27000 Eure. 120 km SE of Le Havre

(T) *1 pl. Gén-de-Gaulle 32.24.04.43* (M) *Wed., Sat., Sun.*

For a Norman town, a situation near the provincial border has always meant a history of sack and pillage. Evreux from its earliest days has faced hordes of destructive enemies – Romans, Goths, Vandals, Normans, English, French, and finally Germans, whose 1940 attacks left the city burning for a week. After each devastation the townsfolk have picked themselves up, dusted themselves down and started all over again.

It's truly a miracle that any part of Notre Dame, Evreux's cathedral, has survived but there it is, rising up above the rivulets of the river Iton, still the focus of the town, an assembly of every phase of Gothic to Renaissance architecture, with astounding 15C glass,miraculously intact after being removed to safety during the war.

It's pleasant enough to stroll along the river walk and admire the cathedral from the outside, but there are other towns in the vicinity where I would rather stay, particularly as the hotel restaurant scene is somewhat limited.

Hotel de France
(HR)M   *29 r. St-Thomas   32.39.09.25   Cl. Sun. p.m.; Mon.   CB, AE, DC*

The best position, overlooking the river, and hard to miss. Some rooms have been redecorated in style, at 345f, better value than those at 115f. A well-qualified new chef has revolutionised the cooking here and the 160f menu is now something special. Others at 220 and 260f also recommended.

Le Gavroche
(R)S   *r. St-Thomas   32.33.78.78*

'Run by M. and Mme Prunier, who are a nice enthusiastic young couple; she speaks English; cheerful friendly accueil. It was jam-packed with locals. The Pruniers have a house in Ibiza and it shows – tapas and an Ibiza salad with the local seaweed spinach. The 75f menu included a bottle of red wine.' – Robin Totton.

Auberge de Parville
(R)M   *rte de Lisieux   27180 St. Sebastien de Morsent   32.39.36.63   Cl. Sun. p.m. and Mon.   EC, V*

On the main RN 13 exit, some 2 miles outside Evreux. A sophisticated upmarket restaurant, serving sophisticated upmarket food – langoustines with passion fruit, a terrine glacée et aux trois chocolats – on copious, good-value menus from 145f.

Map 5E   **FALAISE** 14700 Calvados. 34 km S of Caen

Ⓣ *32 r. G-Clemenceau*   Ⓜ *Sat., Wed. and Fri. a.m.*

It does seem hard that this little town, in such a dramatic setting in a ravine in the Ante Valley, with a uniquely romantic legend based upon it, should have had the misfortune to be in the path of the German soldiers as they tried to escape their 1944 destiny. It was completely devastated as a result and, although the yellow local stone which has been used to rebuild is an improvement on the concrete of many a post-war Norman town, it is a shadow of its former self.

However, the 12C keep of the castle was mercifully saved and continues to dominate the town and lends a good deal of character to it. It was from here that Robert, the younger son of Richard II, Duke of Normandy, is said to have watched the lovely seventeen-year-old Arlette, as she washed her clothes in the nearby river, and fallen in love with her. The proud Arlette declined secrecy and rode defiantly over the drawbridge to meet her lover, a liaison that resulted in William the Bastard (the Conqueror). His magnificent statue rears below the castle ruins.

A pleasant excursion from the town is northwards, via the N 158, to the Devil's Breach, a gorge hollowed out in the typical sandstone crests of the Falaise countryside. There is an interesting walk along the riverside path.

La Normandie
(HR)M *4 r. Amiral Courbet 31.90.18.26 EC, V*

In a side street and therefore not as traffic-ridden as most. It is modern (of course) without much character, but has been thoroughly approved of because of the friendly staff and good-value rooms – 140–200f. Menus from 60f.

'The castle is truly magnificent – a real castle, with spacious grass areas for people to enjoy and picnic in; the town is very French and nice to sit about in. Super camp site with open-air swimming pool would make it an attraction for families.

The Normandie is excellent. We had a beautiful room at the back, absolutely quiet, despite the busy main road just on the corner. The service was quiet, dignified and friendly and the food quite delicious and plentiful. This needs a better mention.' – Susan Leyden.

Happy to oblige.

Poste
(HR)M *38 r. G. Clemenceau 31.90.13.14 Cl. Sun. p.m.; Mon.; 15–26/10; 20/12–15/1 AE, EC, V*

Recommended for food, which wins local approval and a red Michelin R, but not for accommodation, which could be very noisy. Menus from 65f.

La Fine Fourchette
(R)M *52 r. G. Clemenceau 31.90.08.59 Cl. Tues. p.m.; Wed. p.m. o.o.s.; 1/2–22/2 EC, V*

Highly recommended as a good-value, distinguished restaurant, where I had the best meal of a long tour. From 60f.

Map 4F **FAUGUERNON** 14100 Lisieux, Calvados. 5 km NE of Lisieux on the D 263A

A hamlet in deepest Auge country.

La Vache
(C)M *31.61.13.31 Open all year*

A typical house of the region, set in an apple orchard. There is one guest room for three people, with private shower for 175f. M. et Mme Serge Sassier are hosts.

'The bed was blissful, warmed by sheepskins, and the whole place was very warm and comfortable. We had an excellent breakfast, with plenty of coffee and home-made jam. Mme Sassier also ran a market stall and sold butter and farm produce.' – Evelyn M. Walter.

Map 2F **FÉCAMP** 76400 Seine-Mar. 40 km N of Le Havre

(T) *pl. Bellet and quai Vicomte in summer* (M) *Sat.*

Readers have been quick to rush to the defence of Fécamp, which I found somewhat disappointing. Perhaps it was a wet day when I last visited.

'We find it a fascinating town, combining a fishing port, a seaside resort and an excellent market on Saturday.' – David Felton. He could be right.

The harbour is certainly the heart of the town – France's fourth fishing port – and most of the interest centres on the quays. By far the biggest tourist attraction, however, is the Bénédictine distillery a few blocks back. It was on the chalky cliffs sheltering the harbour that the 16C monk Vincelli originally found the herbs he used to make the famous liqueur; although the exact recipe is a secret, visitors are welcome to inspect the 27 plants and spices that are used to produce that distinctive flavour. A tour round the salle des plantes in the museum is certainly a feast for the nose as well as the eye. A guided tour takes one hour, daily, mornings and afternoons from early March to mid-November. *35.28.00.06.*

I am pleased to see that the new edition of the green Michelin has upgraded La Trinité, which it mysteriously used to disapprove of. I have always loved Richard I's church, a hotchpotch of architectural styles from the 12th to 18th centuries.

I failed to find any hotels in the town, but just 2 km S, at St. Leonard, on the D 940 is:

Auberge de la Rouge
(HR)M *35.28.07.59 Cl. Sun. p.m., Mon. and three weeks in Feb. CB, AE, DC*

This very popular old coaching inn, named after the flaming hair of the original owner, now has eight very agreeable rooms for hire. They open onto a little garden, via a loggia, and cost a reasonable 260–310f.

The cooking has become progressively more ambitious, but is still generous in quantity, and reasonable in price at 90f (weekdays) and 170f.

L'Escalier

(R)M   *101 quai Berigny   35.28.26.79   Cl. Sun. p.m. o.o.s.; Mon; 23/10–5/11   CB, DC, EC*

Consistently good value is this little restaurant overlooking the yacht harbour, dedicated to serving good honest fresh fish, simply cooked (what could be better?). If you like grilled halibut, or oysters from St. Vaast, or marinated herrings, or moules marinières, on 80f menus, this is the place for you.

Le Maritime

(R)M   *2 pl. N. Selles   35.28.21.71   EC, V*

The first-floor dining-room with panoramic view, if you get there early (or book), earns a red Michelin R for its 88f menu. Personally I prefer the Escalier, but I seem to be odd man out in Fécamp, so pay your money and take your choice.

➤ Le Grand Banc

(R)S   *63 quai Berigny   35.28.28.68   Cl. Thurs.*

I have a soft spot for this discovery, made by strolling further along the quay, away from the smarter restaurants, and taking a chance on an unpromising exterior, and was mightily chuffed when readers confirmed that my one enjoyable meal there had not been an isolated example.

However, it is not to be recommended for those who object to sitting in extremely close proximity to the rest of the (entirely French) clientele, at ten tables miraculously squeezed into a tiny step-up-from-the-street room.

The young owners, M. and Madame Marchand, are as unpretentious and delightful as the food they serve, which is way above usual cheap menu (65f) standards. There are several house specialities, like wild boar terrine, fillets of haddock with sorrel and excellent pastries, as well as the usual fishy selections. The wine or cider will not be out of keeping with the modesty of the bill. Arrowed for good value.

Map 7D   **LA FERTÉ MACÉ** 61600 Orne. 6 km N of Bagnoles de l'Orne

Ⓣ *13 r. Victoire* Ⓜ *Thurs.*

If Bagnoles is too smug and contrived, La Ferté Macé might be a nearby remedy. It's a pleasant little French town, with not a lot going on after nightfall.

Tire-Bouchon
(R)S   *13 r. Barre   33.37.38.21   Cl. Sun. p.m.; Wed.;   EC, V*

A lively little restaurant, decorated in art nouveau style, with a good-value 60f menu.

Map 4D   **FLEURY-SUR-ORNE** 14123 lfs, Calvados. 4 km S of Caen by D 562

 Sat.

Virtually a suburb of Caen, yet so different. The river Orne flows by and provides a delightful excuse to escape the city in order to walk by its banks, working up an appetite for:

L'Île Enchantée
(R)M   *1 r. St-André   31.51.15.52   Cl. Sun. p.m.; Mon.; 31/7–31/7   CB, AE, DC, EC*

A 19C house, covered in vines, with a most attractive first-floor restaurant looking out over the river banks. The chef-patron, M. Blaise, has an impressive culinary pedigree but wisely concentrates on local ingredients for the foundations of his menus, of which the 110f version is a bargain. So is the 130f. Stuffed pigs' trotters may not be the ideal summer food, but the Caennais are happy to come out here year-round—and not just for a salad. Rouen duck cooked in cider and oysters from Isigny are further regional treasures presented with style, and everything is as fresh as can be.

Map 6E   **FONTENAI-SUR-ORNE** 61200 Argentan, Orne. 4 km SW of Argentan

---

Argentan suffered badly in the 1944 tragedies and there is not a good deal in its modern reincarnation to detain the visitor for long. If a stay in this area is indicated, I would certainly drive out of the town to:

Le Faisan Doré
(H)S   *33.67.18.11   Cl. Sun. p.m.   EC, V*

The kind of little French country hotel, in this case run by the same family for 30 years, that is fast disappearing. Catch it while you can. It is comfortable (19 bedrooms, all well furnished at 140–280f) and the food is good quality and value. Menus from 70f.

Map 6F **GACÉ** 61230 Orne. 27 km E of Argentan; 27 km W of Aigle

(T) *Mairie 33.35.50.24* (M) *Sat. p.m.*

Not a very exciting little town – just a few streets radiating from the
main square, with its Saturday afternoon market.

Le Morphée
(H)M *r. Lisieux 33.35.51.01 Cl. Jan. and Feb. EC, DC, V*

A 19C delightfully eccentric French town house, tall and paper thin,
chequered brick, imposing entrance, fronted by murky pond set in
ragged lawn.
　　The bedrooms are charming, quiet and elegant, all with bathrooms –
excellent value at 240–290f. The fantasy continues with their romantic
names – Rêverie, Crépuscule, Aurore.

Le Morphée

Map 5H   **GIVERNY** 27620 Garny, Eure. 63 km SE of Rouen

House of Claude Monet
Open from early April to late October, with long lunch closing; cl. Mon.; Easter Whit Monday. The garden is open throughout the day during the same period.
32.51.28.21

A must for any tourist in the region, or anywhere nearby for that matter. The rub is that 'any tourist', American, Japanese, French or Brit, knows that, and the place gets swamped at busy times. Try and contrive a walk round the garden at least in a quiet period, when you can appreciate (and photograph of course) the evocative green bridge over the water-lily pond. Monet's planting of chrysanths, dahlias, Michaelmas daisies, provides a blaze of autumn colour in the garden around the house.

The house itself is surprisingly simple, with painted furniture in the sunshine-yellow dining-room, and the blue-tiled kitchen has gingham curtains and rows of gleaming copper pans.

The 50-odd famous, huge panels of water-lilies, inspired by the lake here, were painted in Monet's old age in the newer of the two studios here. He is buried in the family plot ten minutes' walk away, overlooking a Norman vista of poplar trees and apple orchards.

The only pity is that there is no obvious hotel nearby to suggest, to complement the delightful outing.

Map 5F   **LA GOULAFRIÈRE** 27390 Montreuil-l'Argille, Eure. 10 km S of Orbec on the D 134

A hamlet in the middle of a maze of D roads, in deepest Norman countryside.

Au Sire de Goulafre
(R)S   *32.44.51.58   Cl. Tues. p.m.; Wed.*

I am mortified that I have lost the signature of a splendid reader from Sunderland who has sent me several recommendations, all of which have proved winners. The following is one such, and I hope she will forgive me if I quote her experiences in full to make up for the lack of credit.

'I took the D 819 out of Orbec and a short distance after a big wiggle in the road spotted a sign on the right saying "Au Sire de Goulafre". (NB where the lane forks by the isolated house on the right, take the left unmarked fork.) From the outside it looks a bit like an English country pub. Inside entirely French. It's tiny (six tables), tinier bar, and more tables on the terrace.

Amazing range for such an isolated wee place. I took the cheapest menu and selected the starred menus: the smoked ham was beautifully presented and quite perfect, the poulet au cidre was accompanied by a big dish of pommes de terre rissolées, crisp and golden and cooked in goose or duck fat. Yum! Since the poulet was cooked in cidre bouché, made by the little farmer up the road, I chose the same to drink. It was the best I have ever tasted. Fresh field flowers on every table, not a scrap of plastic in sight and accueil as genuine as the cooking. Locals in work-gear, thirsty from working in the fields were as welcome as a dining guest.

No English is spoken and they're chuffed if a visitor speaks French. The local accent is a bit hefty, however. I really cannot speak too highly of this little place. It's a gem and I'm going back. As often as possible. And I shall buy a dozen bottles of the little farmer's cidre bouché.'

Jean-Pierre, the patron, tells me that he arranges une soirée 'Couscous' every Friday evening and a 'Fruits de Mer' on the first Saturday of the month. 'At the first sign of sun,' he says, 'you can be assured of service on the terrace.' I think my un-named correspondent is right – a gem.

Map 5D   **GOUPILLIÈRES, HALTE DE GRIMBOSQ** 14210 Évrecy, Calvados. 8.5 km N of Thury-Harcourt; 20 km S of Caen

One reader actually witnessed a train on the single track that crosses the D 171 here at the Halte. I don't think the noise from passing traffic, road or rail, would be too serious a problem in this case, though. The village of Goupillières is a kilometre away and the fishermen who populate the banks of the shallow river Orne here at the Pont de Brie are not given to jarring rowdiness. All is very peaceful, very serene and the wooded hills of the Forêt de Grimbosq, rising from the river towards the main D 562, provide the perfect backcloth to the delightful rural scene.

Auberge du Pont de Brie
(HR)S-M   *31.79.37.84   Cl. Wed. o.o.s.*

On the edge of the lovely Suisse Normande, the auberge has proved very popular with readers seeking rural comfort and tranquility. For 25 years it has been run by the same family, the Dris, and now the daughter of the house, Danielle Démont, is in charge of the cooking.

Her claim is that she produces simple family cooking, but her specialities include home-made foie gras, paupiettes of salmon, and a ragoût of scallops, which is not like any home-cooking I can muster. The menus start at 70f, but in order to get a choice it is necessary to pay considerably more. The rooms are modern, good-sized and comfortable. Some have bathrooms, and the price range is from 100–220f, according to the amenities on offer.

'The room at the top of the house was excellent. A bed-sitting room, with bed settee, separate toilet and shower, then up a modern wooden staircase to a double bedroom, with telephone and TV. The cost for the two rooms was 210f.' – Mrs. Audrey Barritt.

There have been recent quibbles about the prices of both food and wine accelerating, and so the arrow must go, but the recommendation for modest peaceful accommodation still stays. With Thury-Harcourt down the road, you can always eat out.

Map 1A   **GOURY** 50440 Auderville, Manche. 26 km W of Cherbourg

---

Goury lighthouse, at the extreme NW tip of the Cotentin peninsula, is a welcome landmark for sailors returning to safe harbour from extremely perilous seas. Here is a picturesque little port, good walks and spectacular views of wild rocks and wilder seas. There is a sleepy little customs office which only opens for a couple of hours here and there, a souvenir shop, and an excellent fish restaurant, way above what one would expect in such an isolated spot.

Auberge de Goury
(R)M   *Cl. Mon. p.m.; Sat. lunch*

The fish here comes straight from the local boats and is as fresh as can be. The menus are excellent value, with no choice but good quality throughout; the 65f is good, but the 90f menu de terroir is even better, with perfect crab mayonnaise and roast lamb. Who could ask for more? Well worth the detour, regardless of the other joys of the scenery. Arrowed for value and site.

Having lunched delightfully, continue the elevated mood by driving south on the D 401 for the best views of all, over the Baie d'Ecalgrain. At one hairpin bend the notices say 'Caution!'. As well they might, but in this case it's not for the bends but for vipers!

Map 5F   **GRANDCHAIN** 27410 Beaumesnil, Eure. 5 km SE of Bernay

---

Off the D 14 between Bernay and Beaumesnil.

Au Joyeux Normand
(HR)S   *32.44.47.16   Cl. Thurs. p.m.*

New young owners have taken over this simple little Logis de France, with phoney half-timbering, and coloured glass windows, and an entrance bar. They are friendly, helpful (they let me use their telephone and wouldn't take any payment) and trying hard.
M. Vigneron does the cooking in an open kitchen and can still offer incredible value – for example, where else could you hope to find leek flan, pork chop and cheese plus bottle of wine for 45f? If you can manage 86f, you get six oysters, salmon, cheese and pud.
The rooms are basic but clean, with shower and loo in the corridor. 80f a double and 125f for four people.

Map 6A   **GRANVILLE** 50400 Manche. 26 km SW of Avranches; 104 km S
of Cherbourg; 107 km SW of Caen

(T) *4 cours Jonville 33.50.02.67* (M) *Sat.*

Any excuse would do for me to visit Granville. It seems to me to be the
Norman seaside resort with everything – beaches, vistas, good
restaurants, a recommendable little hotel, interesting port, and enough
going on year-round to make an o.o.s. weekend feasible. It's fine for a
family holiday, or a stop on the road to Brittany. After the boring sand
dunes of the south-west coast of the Cotentin peninsula, it is a relief to
come across this busy commercial port, with a lively town divided into
two distinct sections.

The Lower Town encompasses shops, hotels, restaurants, in
complete contrast to the Upper Town, which has a timeless, fly-in-
amber atmosphere. There is a small museum up there, with nostalgic
photographs of Granville's recent past as an elegant bathing resort;
but through the narrow drawbridge, within the ramparts, the whole of
the Upper Town is a living museum of a much earlier age.

The quiet, steep streets are lined with graceful grey houses, 18C

Granvill

hôtels and flowery window-boxes. With few signs of commercialisation, it all makes a delightful excursion, from the central square where there is a tabac selling postcards, a bar, an épicerie, to the encircling ramparts with gorgeous views of the harbour, the Brittany coast as far as Mont St-Michel, and the Îles de Chausey (there is a viewing table at the Place d'Isthme to help sort you out).

Walk back through the stage-setting streets for refreshment at an exceptionally good crêperie:

L'Ercharguette
(R)S   r. St-Jean   Cl. Thurs. o.o.s.

Not only crêpes, but grills and excellent brochettes cooked over the log fire makes this pretty, rustic little bar a good choice for a simple meal. The only recommendation in the Haute Ville; in order to eat copiously it will be necessary to descend to the town.

▸ Le Phare
(R)M   r. du Port   33.50.12.94   Cl. Tues. p.m.; Wed. o.o.s.; 15/9–30/9; 20/12–30/1   AE, DC, EC, V

It's worth the journey to Granville just to eat at Le Phare, having wisely reserved a window-seat at the first-floor window, from which to observe the panorama of little ferry boats bound for Jersey, the fishing fleet, private yachts and shabby cargo ships.

It was a happy chance discovery many years ago, and dozens of readers have since written to agree about its virtues. Even Michelin, who always ignored the talents of Philippe Vercella (put off I suspect by the scruffy exterior), have relented and now list Le Phare. Whether that is a good thing I have still to discover. I suspect not – it was hard enough before to find a table, with all the locals well wised up about the value on offer. The prices have not yet become inflated – from 65f – but it may be the beginning of the end, so don't miss out on this one.

It is of course predominantly a fish restaurant – try the hot seafood mousse, served with lobster sauce, or a mammoth plateau de f. de m. and try and ignore the two minus points – the garish decor and the unsmiling and very slow service. An undoubted arrow.

'Superb in every way.' – Lt. Col and Mrs. Kopanski.

'You warned that the staff were po-faced but the food is worth the discomforts. There has certainly been no discernible lessening of quality over the past year. Menus from 62 to 240f, the latter including lobster. My Rabbi only allows me to eat shellfish if it is cheap.' – Steve Grainger.

Le Michelet
(H)M   5 r. J. Michelet   33.50.06.55   AE, EC, V

A delightful little very French hotel, on the hill above the town, just a few minutes' walk from the centre. It has tremendous character, and is quiet and spacious. The lack of restaurant is no hardship in Granville.

Good rooms, some with sea views, some with balconies, are from 90–190f.

'We had room 3 on the first floor, so the view was not perfect – no sea – but the owners were ready to laugh and the prices were very good. All the room prices, incidentally, were for a room with two beds, loo and bath or shower. What I wonder are the English hoteliers doing wrong?' – Steve Grainger.

Arrowed because I like it.

Chez Pierrot
(R)S   *r. Cl. Desmaisons*

A little restaurant, very central, very popular with locals, offering good honest value.

'Very crowded, very French. Prices are most reasonable, beginning at 45f; helpings are plentiful – something the management pride themselves on – and the seafood excellent. The patronne had time to welcome each customer.'

La Poste
(R)S   *r. de l'Abreuvoir*

As its name would suggest, near the Post Office, a little family-run restaurant, very popular with the discerning locals. The fruits de mer have been particularly recommended. Menus from 65f.

'The atmosphere is superb. Lots of noise and bustle, cheap and filling food, wine at ridiculously cheap prices – ideal for a three-hour dinner session.' – David Campbell and Vicki McLean.

Map 5C   **LA GRAVERIE** 14350 le Bény-Bocage, Calvados. 5 km N of Vire

Deep in the heart of the very green bocage country near the gorge of the Vire. Turn off the N 174 east on to the D 311 and then the D 109 to find:

La Chapelle Madelaine
(C)S   *31.68.20.43   Open all year*

A nice old stone house near the village of La Graverie, run by charming André and Yvette Lerebours. They charge 125f for a double room, with private bathroom.

'Highly recommended b. and b. Our friends who live locally use it regularly for their overflow.' – Judy Wright.

Map 5B   **HAMBYE** 50650 Manche. 23 km SE of Coutances; 26 km SW of
          St. Lo

Ⓜ *Tues.*

It all seems too good to be true. To find Hambye you take one of the
prettiest roads in Normandy, following the river Sienne from the
village on the D 13 towards Sourdeval-les-Bois and the Abbey of
Hambye. Add to the idyllic countryside one of my luckiest finds of all
time and you can't believe your luck.

The ruined Abbey, approached through a gateway thick with iris,
glowing with golden lichen, is illuminated by flaming torches on
weekend summer evenings, and the piped Gregorian chant floats up to
the Auberge nearby. The setting, in the valley, backed by a white
escarpment, river sparkling, fishermen posing, is pure picture-book.
Make sure the camera is well loaded.

Auberge de l'Abbaye
(H)S(R)M   *33.61.42.19   Cl. Mon.*

The file on this paragon is the thickest of any in F.E.3. Michelin
continues to ignore it, which is good news for getting a reservation

AUBERGE DE L'ABBAYE   HAMBYE

(not easy even so), but of course its popularity with F.E. readers means that you are likely to meet some fellow-countrymen there. Never fear – a more discriminating, intelligent, enthusiastic lot I have yet to encounter.

It's a nondescript building, with a terrace overlooking the little green valley hard by the Abbey gates. The rooms are simple, comfortable, and cheap. So what's all the fuss about? Well it's partly the welcome; Madame Allain has never ceased to make every guest feel special. Stories of illnesses and special diets cheerfully coped with, fractious children tolerated, crises dealt with, late arrivals and inconvenient departures accepted, fill the files. Within minutes of arrival I guarantee that the unwinding, coaxed by her cossetting, will begin, aided probably by a nice cup of tea.

The other exceptional bonus is her husband's cooking, which is way way beyond what one might expect in a simple country inn. Every dish, however simple, has the stamp of a loving cook. The china and table settings are elegant, the service is swift and efficient and the cheeseboard is exactly right. The wine list ranges from patron's home-made cider to premier cru clarets. Occasionally there have been murmurs of disapproval at the price of wines and the fact that the menus – now from 78 to 195f are out of proportion with the cost of the rooms, but I must dismiss these carpings. The Allains are proud of their restaurant and want to give their clients only the best.

If only there were more like them. A double arrow.

'Superb – all that you say. Cheap menu still a snip. Rooms lovely. Service A1.'

'Perfect interconnecting rooms (nos 7 and 8) for us and the children. Total cost 190f. Food excellent. Madame very understanding and helpful, whole place marvellous. If you find more like that, please do a limited edition of F.E. so that only you and I know.'

The loss of the Restaurant de l'Abbaye, whose popularity rivalled that of the Auberge, is a sad one. Readers write to say they can hardly believe that this ideal bargain stop is no more. We shall have to await developments. All reports very welcome.

Map 3E   **HARFLEUR** 76700 Seine-Mar. 3 km E of Le Havre

(M) *Thurs. a.m.*

The port of Harfleur, at the mouth of the Lézarde, once the most important in the north of France, now shelters a couple of barges and a few weekend dinghies. Harfleur has been almost engulfed by the industrial zone all round it and yet retains its identity as a small French town. Some of its oldest streets, around the lovely 15C church, have been pedestrianised to make very pleasant and peaceful strolling and shopping. The potential is there to make more, much more, of this surprising oasis; with a little more civic attention to its picturesque antiquity, it could again hold its own against its powerful neighbour, Le Havre.

One very good reason for exploration is:

L'Auberge du Prieuré
(R)M   *52 r. de la République   35.45.02.20   Cl. Sat. lunch; Sun. p.m.; Mon.*

Chantal Legendre and Michel Legros claim to offer 'quelque chose qu'on ne trouve pas au Havre.' You certainly cannot find a former 17C pharmacy serving superb food, with a courtyard in which barbecues cooked on a huge open fire may be enjoyed in fine weather.

The menus are inventive and original – a marinade of three different fish, in three different sauces, rack of lamb with fresh herbs – and the wine list is more than interesting. The 140f menu is the one to go for.

I'm not sure that I will get a huge post-bag from this new discovery, in order to qualify for the arrow that I believe is deserved. It is certainly not on the main tourist track (and all the better for it) and the timid might be nervous of tracking it down in the suburbs. (In fact it is next door to the fine Harfleur abbey.) Even Michelin has not yet found it. I imagine that only the gastronomes who are dissatisfied with lesser lights in the district will give it a whirl. I hope they will tell me about their experience.

Map 3E   **LE HAVRE** 76600 Seine-Mar. 86 km W of Rouen

(T) *Hôtel de Ville. Hotels can be booked from here (35.21.22.88), but not more than five days in advance* (M) *Every a.m.; Wed., Thurs., Sat. all day*

Le Havre has the doubtful distinction of being the most bombed port in France, and so her present aspect is almost entirely post-war. Old locals say that Le Havre lost its heart in 1944 and never replaced it. Architect Auguste Perret tried. He devised two cores- the Place de l'Hôtel de Ville and the Place Gambetta – and a grid system of roads leading to them, including the Avenue Foch, with which he intended to outdo the Champs-Elysées. These streets he lined with identikit concrete blocks of apartments, which give the town its distinctive grey and uniform character. It helps when the sun shines and the waters of the bassin sparkle, and in summer the Place de l'Hôtel de Ville is colourful enough with vivid flowerbeds. I cannot believe that Perret would have approved of a recent addition of wooden trellissed archways in the Place, but to my mind they are a softening influence.

The most boring part of the town is the triangle between the r. Royale, ave. Foch and the bvd. François 1er (François ordered the original Havre to be built in 1517, to replace the old silted-up port of Harfleur). Sadly this is often the only part that tourists see. The scale of the town puts them off walking too far from the port. They may get as far down the r. Royale as the pl. Gambetta, where the concrete igloos of the cultural centre effectively block off the only interesting view of the town, towards the bassin and swooping white bridge.

The real Le Havre begins behind the Town Hall, swerving round the r. Réné Coty into the bvd. Réné Coty, with the department stores and small shops which the Havrais rather than the tourists use. I cannot claim that this noisy main street is Normandy's finest, but at least there is animation here, even in winter, when the reconstructed Havre dies.

One modern building that is a great success is the **Musée de Beaux Arts** (10–2, 2–6 exc. Tues. and fêtes). Built entirely of glass and metal, with ingenious lighting, it looks out to sea on the point before the road swings back to Ste-Adresse. You proceed up and down ramps in this model of intelligent display to view the collection of Dufy (a native of Havre), Impressionists and Post-Impressionists, and of Boudin, born in Honfleur but attracted to Havre. Downstairs is a colourful exhibition of marine excitements – beautifully modelled boats, from fishing to steamer, and more paintings. A good bet for a wet day.

The rest of the pl. Gambetta is pleasant enough, with the smartest shops grouped around it, a bit of green, and a bar or two. And the arcades of the r. Royale are practical in the rain.

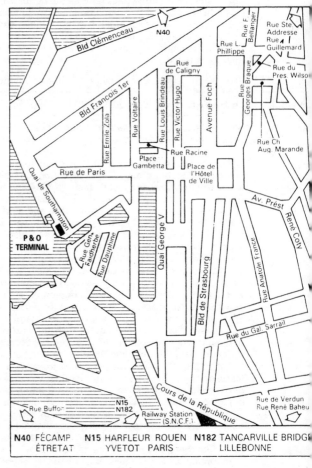

Quai de Southampton 76600 - Le Havre Tel: (35) 21 36 50

On to the pl. de l'Hôtel de Ville – vast again, but with some attempt at a bit of bedding-out. Do you know any other French town where the central square does not have a single lively café? There are, however, plenty of benches on which to study the brochures and maps supplied by the Tourist Bureau in the square.

SHOPPING

To the right and behind the Town Hall, some of the old town survives and vivacity begins. Along the r. Réné Coty are the little heterogeneous shops, some chic, mostly very un-chic, whose juxtaposition makes a quarter like this most interesting. Here is where the Havrais shop, but again, how odd – no cafés, no restaurants.

Monoprix, the French Woolies, is here, and a top department store, **Le Printemps**. **Les Nouvelles Galeries**, back in the pl. Gambetta, is another large store, with an excellent household department in a separate building.

I started to list best food shops, but the town is so scattered that the choice really depends on where the car is parked. However, assuming you are walking from the ferry, down what in the 18th century was a very elegant street, the r. Royale, you may be tempted to buy some oysters at 28f a dozen at the **Poissonerie Verel**, or perfume from the wide selection at **Perfumerie Univers**, which also sells interesting costume jewellery, less expensive than it looks. Good cheap vegs and seasonal fruits at **Fruits Primeurs**, the nearest tabac for p.c. stamps, and at **Antares**, those wonderful extravagant Leonidas Belgian chocs – the perfect take-home present.

Turn left into the pl. Gambetta for a very useful charcuterie – the **Rôtisserie Gaston**, which is open on Sundays and every other day except Wednesday from 11 a.m. to 10.30 p.m. Invaluable for last-minute purchases, and sells wine.

Over the other side of the Place is **Levèvre**, the biggest and best-known charcuterie in the town. Always queues here for made-up dishes, saucissons, pâtés, wines. Its own cellars are round the corner for quantity purchases.

Best shopping bet, if you're limited for time or if the weather's bad, is the **Halles Centrales** – Find them a street or two behind the pl. Gambetta, by walking along the r. Voltaire. The best cheese shop – **Cheinisse** is here, with a commendable assortment of cheeses, local and regional, served with pleasant advice on when to eat them. Wines too.

Cheap wine is best bought here at **Nicolas**, who always have packs of special offers available. It's all very convenient to push a trolley round the Halles, with easy parking right outside. Fruit and veg, fish and bread all on sale, and a supermarket for basics. Cheerful bar here is the **St Amour**, with tables outside for summer snacking.

Two hypermarkets serve the town. **Mammouth** is at Montivilliers, signposted from the Tancarville road, open until 9 p.m. Monday to Friday, 10 p.m. on Saturdays; and **Auchan**, which I prefer, in the Haute Ville. Take the Cours de la République (past the station) through the tunnel and follow the signs to the Centre Commerciale. Open Monday to Saturday until 10 p.m., it's a vast complex, with an entire village of boutiques outside the main food area, selling goods as diverse as tisanes and burglar alarms.

Not far from here is the **Forest of Montgeon**, 700 acres of trees, a boating pond, a camp site, all well laid out and ideal for picnics and family outings.

HOTELS

The uniformity of the blocks makes many of the hotels look alike from the outside, and I have difficulty in remembering which is which, so dull a bunch are they. However, the following have been re-endorsed by readers as fulfilling their function of providing a clean, inexpensive night's sleep not too far from the ferry.

Hotel Bordeaux
(H)M   *147 r. L-Brindeau   35.22.69.44   CB, AE, DC, EC*

The new owner has not changed the situation here – impersonal efficiency, comfortable well-equipped smallish rooms and all mod. cons. in a central position. 290–480f.

Hotel Foch
(H)M   *4 r. Caligny   35.42.50.69   AE, EC, V*

'Comfortable beds and good showers as always; we have known it a long time. What a pity our car was broken into during the night and suitcases stolen!' – Robert Clow. Rooms 165–260f.

There's the rub. Very few hotels have garages, which is why I propose, unusually, a chain representative:-

Mercure
(HR)M   *Chaussée d'Angouleme   35.21.23.45   AE, DC, EC, V*

You pay 450–550f for the peace of mind of safe parking and impersonal efficiency of a well-run chain. Some rooms overlook the water. Food is adequate.

Séjour Fleuri
(H)S   *71 r. E. Zola   35.41.33.81   V*

Rooms are 85–140f.
'Excellent value and friendly accueil.' – Patrick Nealon.

Celtic
(H)S   *106 r. Voltaire   35.42.39.77   EC, AE, V*

'We have stayed in this hotel regularly since 1981. It has always been a pleasure to do so. It is clean, very well kept and one is always assured of a warm welcome from M. and Mme Goussot. The breakfast is particularly appreciated. It is the only two-star hotel we know which includes orange juice on the breakfast tray. There is never any difficulty over arriving late.' – Dr. M. J. Tilby. Rooms 152–198f.

Le Richelieu
(H) *132 r. Paris   35.42.38.71   EC, V*

Rooms: 82–220f.
'M. and Mme Barbara were extremely helpful and hospitable. They were very cooperative about our possible late arrival time – something that we found to be a problem with other places we tried. We had a comfortable double room with shower and WC for 170f. The hotel was spotlessly clean and very good value.' – Dr. Suzie Fiske.

The restaurant scene in Le Havre is definitely looking up. And about time too. The big problem is finding somewhere not specifically geared to tourists that is open on Sunday and Monday evenings – just when British weekenders have most need of them. I have suggested one or two old favourites near the ferry, and some new ideas, which will probably require a town map (tourist office will supply.)

La Chaumette
(R)M *17 r. Racine   35.43.66.80   Cl. Sat. lunch; Sun. o.o.s.; 24/12–2/1   CB, AE, DC*

This incongruously thatched little restaurant in the Place Gambetta, whose fake beams provide a welcome relief from all the aggressive modernity outside, continues to improve. Its chef is Madame Frechet, who incorporates some Breton dishes from her home territory in the predominantly Norman repertoire.
Both include fish, and here it is of the freshest, and cooked with a light feminine touch. Interesting ideas include lobster cooked with a touch of horse-radish, bitter-sweet veal kidneys with sweetcorn, and superb scallops. Go for the 149f menu.

La Petite Auberge
(R)M-S *32 r. Ste. Adresse   35.46.27.32   Cl. Sun. p.m.; Mon.; 4/2–13/2; 6/8–28/8   CB, EC*

An old favourite, now with a new patron. The weekday 100f menu is remarkable. No fireworks, just the kind of traditional old-fashioned French food you come to France for. If you feel like a splurge, the other menus at 115f and 170f are equally recommended. Well worth making the short journey (from the Place de l'Hôtel de Ville, r. Braque, r. d'Etretat, which becomes the r. Ste. Adresse) for the rewards at the end, but make sure you have a reservation first.

La Bonne Hôtesse
(R)S *98 r. Pres. Wilson   3521.31.73   Cl. Sun. p.m.; Mon   AE, EC, V*

Continues to please and offers good value on the menus from 60–100f.
'By 12.15 on a Saturday it was almost full. No hope at all of getting a table later unless you book, as I thankfully did. The 90f menu is a whopper! To go à la carte is not expensive either. For a solo traveller there is the opportunity to have a 25 cl carafe of wine instead of the 50 cl. There is a Corbières at 30f and a good selection around 50–60f.

Really good food, away from the usual tourist route. We were the only English there, thank goodness.' – Keith Whettam.

Le St-Louis
(R)S-M *1 r. St-Louis 35.22.56.00 Cl. Sun. p.m.; Mon.*

I got absolutely no feed-back on this one last time, but I shall persist in recommending it, because it is something different, and light-hearted. Eric Millet has capitalised on the long narrow proportions of his little restaurant to reproduce fin-de-siècle train decor. You sit in little compartments, with luggage racks above. Fish and vegetables are particularly well cooked, but I also enjoyed some succulent sweetbreads and the range of home-made desserts. Good value at 75f. Look for it (not too difficult) in the St. François quartier.

And now for some new discoveries, all of which need more reports please:-

Lescalle
(R)M *39 pl. de l'Hôtel de Ville 35.43.07.93 Open every day (bravo!) CB, AE*

Hooray that at last the central Place once again has a meeting place (terrace in summer) and a bit of life injected. You can even dance there at weekends though the decor might put you off your beat a bit. What even more valuable is that Lescalle fulfils that long-felt need for somewhere to sit before or after dinner and sip a glass of wine. The impossibility of buying just one glass of drinkable plonk in France has long incensed me, but fret no longer. The food is not at all bad – monkfish cooked in cider, magret with blackcurrants, good chocolate cake – and the service is proficient. 87f menus good value.

Le Montagné
(R)M *50–52 quai M-Fere 35.42.77.44 Cl. Wed.; 17/2–24/2; Aug.*

If I had to bet on the first Michelin rosette for Le Havre, it would be on Bruno Barboux, newly installed (1989) on the Isle St. François (near the Bassin de Commerce). He is a chef of great distinction, having served his apprenticeship at many great Parisian restaurants – Ritz, Café de la Paix, etc., as the diplomas round his walls testify. His all-pink decor is comfortable, soothing and classy – just what the Michelin inspectors like. His food too is sophisticated enough for their tastes – a bouillon laced with white wine, topped with chopped artichoke, monkfish cooked in red wine, caramelised apples in orange butter. Again, the advice is to go soon, while you can take advantage of the remarkable 130f menu (carte from 270f). And he's open at weekends.

Local recommendations not recently tested by me are:
Athanor (R)M, 120 r. Guillemard, 35.42.50.27, 100–240f.
Gritnot, 43 r. Racine, 35.43.62.07, à la carte only. Open late, tables outside.
Palissandre, 33 r. de Bretagne, 35.21.69.00 (for fish).

Le Lyonnais, r. J. de-la-Fontaine. This one, run by a Roux protégé, looks like a winner, and I should particularly like to have more details. Good bars are Le Spi and Le Southampton on the quai Southampton. The former plans to open a small restaurant shortly.
See also Ste. Addresse and Harfleur.

Map 3B   LA HAYE DU PUITS 50250 Manche. 46 km S of Cherbourg

(T) *r. E-Poirier (cl. p.m. o.o.s.) 33.46.01.42* (M) *Wed.*

A useful stopping place for a bit of shopping (good market) on the route south.

Le Haytillon
(HR)S   *33.46.10.33   Cl. Mon.*

A reader commends the simple good value on offer in this Logis de France in the market square. Meals served in the rustic-style dining-room with good log fire start at 70f and the eleven rooms cost from 95–185f.

Map 2F   HÉRICOURT-EN-CAUX 76560 Doudeville, Seine-Mar. 10 km N of Yvetot on the D 131

A sleepy little village on the crossing of two minor roads, where the river Durdent flows tranquilly through unspoiled countryside.

Auberge de la Durdent
(HR)S   *35.96.42.44   Cl. times not disclosed*

An idyllic site. The river not only flows through the garden but through the dining-room! Under glass that is. It's an old, timbered, typically Norman building, balconied, hung with flowers, in the middle of some of the most attractive countryside in this otherwise lack-lustre Caux region. It also makes a useful overnight stop en route to or from the northern Channel ports.

The Auberge has had a chequered history French Entrée-wise. It was very much 'in' originally, with a confident arrow. Then it deteriorated, the victim of its own popularity the management changed twice, and the complaints file swelled. I warned off in the last edition of F.E.3, but asked for up-dates, and it looks as though the news is good:-

'We approached it with some trepidation, as we had read your doubts about it in the 1987 edition. Having had a coffee in the bar, we spoke to the owners who told us that they had replaced the owners who had replaced Mme Lebarq (who had not made a success of the hotel and were only there a short time). The new people have spent a

Auberge de la Durdent

ton on the hotel bedrooms – all the beds are new and very comfortable and they have plans to upgrade the breakfast room/bar.' – Janet Balmforth.

How long will it be, I wonder, before the potentially perfect Auberge de la Durdent can be arrowed again?

Map 3E   **HONFLEUR** 14600 Calvados. 57 km SW of Le Havre, 60 km E of Caen

(T) *Vieux Bassin*   (M) *Sat a.m.*

Still my No. 1 choice for a short-break destination. One or two readers don't share my affection for the place, finding it too tourist-ridden, but it would be surprising if anywhere with half the charm of Honfleur, combined with easy access to Paris and Le Havre, did not have its share of tourists. Count me among them any time.

Years of familiarity have not yet spoiled the impact of that gem of a harbour full of boats, water reflecting images of the lanky old houses surrounding it; cafés and restaurants humming, no matter what the season, picturesque and ancient Lieutenant's house guarding the entrance, fishing boats, unloading catches, gulls screeching overhead. I can't think of a more pleasant exercise than to join the strollers round the cobbled quays, watching the artists at work, peering down on the boats below, watching it all happen from one of the cafés on the harbour's edge.

In some ways Honfleur reminds me of St-Tropez – that other artists' haunt – but for me it has far more genuine charm and less superficial gloss. The outer harbour is a real working port and in the Vieux Bassin the pleasure boats come in many shapes and sizes, from ocean-racer to humble dinghy.

However hard to tear oneself away from the harbour, don't omit to climb up to Honfleur's other heart, the pl. Ste-Catherine; here is the site of the market, some colourful bars and restaurants spilling out onto the cobbles in summer, and a most unusual church, which gave the square its name. L'Église Ste-Catherine is built entirely of wood, boat-hulls forming the roof of the nave. It was the local shipbuilders who constructed it from the material they knew best, to give thanks that the English had at last departed after the Hundred Years War. It's not the oldest church in the town – that honour goes to St-Étienne on the quayside, built during the time when the English actually occupied Honfleur, from 1419 to 1450.

Little snippets of historical interest keep cropping up in this fascinating town. Throughout the eight centuries of its existence it seems to have bred a particularly forceful band of men. Intrepid sons of Honfleur, mariners, explorers, men of science, were forever taking to sea in search of new experiences. One discovered Brazil, one opened up the mouth of the St. Lawrence, Newfoundland, and one, Samuel de Champlain, filled his ship with pioneering Normans to sail to Canada and start a colony there.

In the 17th century, Colbert ordered the demolition of most of the town's old fortifications, built to keep out the English, and constructed the Vieux Bassin. He built three salt warehouses (greniers de sel) to store the salt necessary for preserving the fishermen's catch; two of these still remain behind the Mairie. There has been some clever restoration of this area recently and it is now a very pleasant place to stroll, between the stone and timbered houses, checking the menus of the numerous bistros that have opened there.

The 19th century saw the beginning of a new rôle for Honfleur – that of an artistic focus. Painters like Boudin and Jongkind, musicians like Erik Satie, writers like Baudelaire, were born or lived here. The town art gallery is named after Boudin; it is in the r. Albert Ier, an interesting building, half-modern, half-chapel, though I can't claim that the examples of Boudin's work there do him justice. He was the centre of the group of young artists fascinated by the effects of the crisp Northern light on the estuary waters, who attempted to capture their impressions on canvas, and later become known as the Impressionists and Post-Impressionists. Their meeting place was an inn owned by Mère Toutain, now metamorphosised into a fashionable hotel, the Ferme St. Siméon. Monet, Sisley, Cezanne, Pissarro, all knew it well; Courbet portrayed it on canvas in 'Le Jardin de la Mère Toutain'. The museum is primarily devoted to the Honfleur school of painting, in and around the Seine estuary. It has recently been much improved, so any reader who tried it some years ago and retired hurt, like me, should persevere. The great Boudin is well represented, plus Courbet, Monet, Jongkind, Dufy and Villon. On the first floor there is a display of Norman costumes and furniture.

For a pleasant drive from the town centre take the steep and winding D 513 coast road along the picturesque Côte de Grace, to find the 17C chapel of Notre Dame de Grace, the Mariners' Chapel. The walls and nave inside are crammed with thanksgivings for lives saved at sea. Whit Monday is dedicated to a special pilgrimage here for all men of the sea.

It has long been a problem that hoteliers, after a while in the town, begin to capitalise on its popularity and offer poor service at high prices. It has been difficult to back up my recommendation to go to Honfleur for a short break with a specially good hotel. Now I am happy that there are two superb answers.

➤ Hostellerie Le Belvédère

(H)S(R)M   *36 r. Emile-Rénouf   31.89.08.13   Rest cl. Mon. lunch o.o.s.; 15/11– 25/11; 10/1–20/1   EC, V*

An old favourite that actually manages to get better every time I visit. Michelin lists it as a restaurant with rooms, which perhaps is a bit hard on the rooms (simple, but perfectly adequate and good value in this town at 165–210f), and it is certainly true that the cooking here is outstanding. It is usually full, with a high proportion of English (yes, you have to be prepared to take breakfast with your fellow-countrymen, but what discerning countrymen they must be to have found Le Belvédère); the standard continues to improve all the time.

Menus start at 90f and are both copious and imaginative; I found general agreement among the locals that this is the best restaurant in the town – I would certainly concur. One big advantage to my mind is that Le Belvédère is quiet: an unfortunately rare asset in Honfleur. This outweighs the fact that it is a ten-minute walk from the centre, in a not very attractive quartier. Having arrived and climbed up the first flight of stairs to reception, however, a pleasant surprise appears in the shape of a long and leafy garden, dotted with welcoming white tables and chairs. In fine weather, it is most agreeable to sit here peacefully, rather than in a stuffy bedroom in the town hotels. Breakfast is cheerfully served here too, or else in a particularly pretty breakfast room, newly decorated with pink-tulipped wallpaper and white cane furniture.

M. Hauberdière is a most attentive host and always available to help his guests enjoy their stay. He has plans for ten more rooms in 1990–91, making 16 all together, and another dining-room, extending down the garden.

Where would Madame prefer to eat? Or perhaps in her bedroom? Wherever, whatever, pas de problème. Coffee comes in a jug, but if more is needed, or more bread, or another croissant or more orange juice, that's no problem either. How refreshing, how delightful. Arrowed on every count.

Le Castel Albertine

(H)M-L   *19 cours Albert-Manuel   31.98.85.56   Open year round   AE, DC, EC, V*

A 19C manor-house set back from the main approach, with the bonus, unusual in Honfleur, of an extensive leafy garden, with a little lake, bridge, and rowing boat. As for rooms, you get what you pay for – from 520f for my favourite No. 3, all green and cream, with tall windows opening onto the garden – to a comparatively small double-bedded room overlooking the road (but with little traffic noise at night) for 300f. In between is a variety of combinations of double/twin/bath/ shower, but all are freshly and delightfully redecorated. State your preference when you book. Good breakfasts with fresh o.j., and particularly friendly and helpful owners.

The combination of comfortable elegant rooms, the welcome and the certainty of a good night's rest within walking distance of the town earns the arrow.

Motel Monet

(H)M   *Charrière du Puits, 14600 Equemauville   31.89.00.90   Cl. Jan.*

A new discovery, which I think will be very popular with F.E. readers, because it is both practical and inexpensive (by Honfleur standards). The name motel might be off-putting, with associations of impersonality, but have no fear. The patron is welcoming and helpful and the only similarity between this and our idea of a motel is the ease of parking and access: it is particularly recommended for the disabled. The rooms are modern, clean and functional, at 250f. It is a little way from the town, on one of the routes to the Côte de Grace, but still within walking distance.

'We found it conveniently placed (8 minutes into town on foot), there was no problem with parking, it was small, very clean, quiet and the rooms were spacious. It was a little pricey at 230f, but we did have a bath and w.c. and the prices in Honfleur are inflated anyway.' – John and Georgie Roberts.

L'Ecrin

(H)M   *19 r. E. Boudin   31.89.32.39   Open year round   E, DC, EC, V*

An impressive 18C hotel, set back in its courtyard from a quiet street, near the town centre. No expense has been spared over its restoration, to impress and astonish with the lavishness of the furnishings – four-posters, drapes, swags, gilt mirrors, crimson plush and mod. cons. – film-star bathrooms, colour TVs. The ritziest of these rooms costs 850f. On the top floor are rather simple rooms, still extremely comfortable, at 280f. Breakfast is particularly good. Definitely a hotel with character!

'Mix-up over booking dates was sorted out without fuss and gave us a taste of two rooms. Both were very comfortable and the substitute room on the first night was particularly full of character, with sloping ceilings and dormer windows. The position too, is excellent: half way between the town centre and the Côte de Grace. Breakfast starts the day beautifully, as it is taken in an airy conservatory overlooking the garden (30f).' Vicki Palacio and Richard Elliott.

La Ferme St. Simeon
(HR)L   *rte. A. Marais*   *31.89.23.61*   *EC, V*

Nowadays I include the Ferme more as a tourist attraction – a drink on the terrace will be expensive but worth it – than as a serious suggestion for a self-paying holiday. Rooms now cost from 690 to 3600f and a meal with wine upwards of 500f. But everyone should try and pay a visit here some time, if only to call in and ask for a brochure, because of the Post-Impressionist associations.

La Ferme Saint Siméon

It was here in Mère Toutain's slate-grey farmhouse that they used to meet, and drink the home-made cider and argue about how to depict the light on the water of the estuary below (no oil refineries then). Too poor to pay for a bed down in the town, they were only to happy to accept Mère Toutain's hospitality in return for a sketch of two, that would buy the whole building nowadays.

The place gets grander by the minute. Now there are annexes and a new bar and extended dining-room and the original half-dozen rooms have grown to 40-odd, all very pretty and highly luxurious. A swimming pool and fitness centre was being planned when I visited. Make no mistake, I would happily accept the largely American clientèle, the un-Frenchness of the atmosphere, the huge prices. Just as long as I wasn't paying.

Château de Prêtreville
(H)M   *Gonneville-sur-Honfleur   31.89.37.06*

A 19C 'château' run by the helpful and friendly Rémi and Mina Bodet. Mina used to teach in Wales, so you can rely on easy conversation. Their accommodation is a series of 'studios' which they let by the day, week or month, sleeping from two to four people. Each one is well-equipped, spacious, with good bathroom, kitchenette and dining area. Some are furnished with antiques; others are entirely modern. Guests have the use of elegant salon, extensive grounds, swimming pool and, for an extra charge, sauna, clubhouse, tennis court.

Preparing one's own breakfast and picnic lunch, pouring out one's own drinks etc. can knock a lot off a normal bill, and driving 3 km into Honfleur for dinner sometimes would be no hardship. This would undoubtedly make an excellent family base and, with the Bodet children around, some entente cordiale might well be engendered.

The prices are highly complicated, depending on length of stay and season. Obviously they are geared against a one-night stay. A rough idea would be around 400f for two people for one night, 650f for a weekend, but a phone enquiry is essential.

'We were delighted with it. The weather was very hot, so the pool was a godsend. M. and Mme Bodet were charming and we would definitely go again. In fact we liked it so much we stayed there four nights instead of the originally intended two.' – Barbara Watson.

Arrowed for unusual but practical accommodation and friendly hosts.

For those who seek modern hotels, functional, central, there are now two choices in Honfleur. The Mercure chain is probably the best of its kind and the newly built (1989) representative in Honfleur is not at all a bad buy at 330–360f for a double well-fitted room. It is situated in the town centre, with a main road between it and the fishing boat tie-up. Apart from my preliminary check on the bedrooms there have been no first-hand reports yet. La Tour on the quay Tour nearby is similar, smaller and has been going long enough for several approving letters, including one from a disabled reader who found the staff helpful and friendly. Rooms are 250–280f.

➤ Au P'tit Mareyeur

(R)M   *4 r. Haute   31.98.84.23   Cl. Fri. lunch; Thurs.; 1/1–15/3   EC, V*

I discovered this pretty little navy-blue and white restaurant in one of the most attractive streets in Honfleur just in time for the stop-press of the fourth edition of F.E.3. Now, I am delighted to be able to enlarge on my initial good impressions.

Acceptance has been rapid. Even the conservative Michelin has gone so far as to award a red R for the 119f menu, and readers all agree that it is probably the most agreeable restaurant in town nowadays. Certainly you must book if you wish to eat there – it is tiny. Fish, obviously, is its prime concern, but local produce from field as well as sea is exploited by the friendly owners, Chantal and Christian. Prices have rocketed, I have to admit, but I agree with Michelin that the set meal at 119f, including oysters and other prime ingredients, is still exceptional value in this overpriced town.

The anticipated arrow is awarded with great pleasure.

➤ L'Assiette Gourmande

(R)M   *8 pl. Ste. Catherine   31.89.24.88   Cl. Tues. lunch; Wed.   CB, AE, DC, EC*

News-flash: M. Gerard Bonnefoy has abandoned his Auberge Normande at Carentan, a long-time arrowed restaurant, in favour of a prime site in Honfleur. He can hardly fail. The old Tilbury restaurant, whose premises he has taken over, managed to fill up mostly by virtue of its position in the Place Ste. Catherine. Gerard Bonnefoy can do better than that. He has completely gutted the interior and its new image might be described as 'modern-Norman'. His cooking, worthy of a Michelin star, is easily the most sophisticated and skilful in Honfleur, where he will continue to use regional ingredients and recipes. Menus currently start at 140f. Go soon. Arrowed, even without further reports, on the strength of past achievements.

➤ Le Bistrot Du Port

(R)M-S   *quai de la Quarantaine*

My affection for Le Bistrot stems in part from its willingness to accommodate all tastes at all times. It's the place we turn to if one of us wants a plate of moules, another a full menu, another a ham sandwich and another a steak. Each of these is dished up with no eyebrows raised. It looks somewhat garishly over-folksy on the quayside alongside other more expensive restaurants, but inside is another story. It's a very old timbered building, with cross-beams and mind-your-heads dividing the upstairs restaurant. Downstairs there are a few tables and a welcome log fire, and of course there is the terrace for summer scoffing.

Prices are remarkably good value. The cheapest menu, at 85f, offered us moules à la crème, rabbit in a mustard sauce, cheese, and a creditable range of desserts. Their 90f plâteau de fruits de mer keeps

Parisian weekenders happily dissecting for hours. And there's carafe wine to keep the bill reasonable. The owners, even in remarkably hectic peak periods, remain helpful and efficient.

Arrowed for consistent good value.

Le Vieux Clocher
(R)M-S *9 r. de l'Homme de Bois   31.89.12.06   Cl. Mon. p.m.; Tues.; 5/1–25/1; 15/11–30/11   CB, AE*

An old favourite, after a bad patch, revived. It's a charming little restaurant in the delightful r. de l'Homme de Bois, approached by a steep cobbled side road off the Place Ste. Catherine, or from the harbour. The menu (88f) is encouragingly simple (rare in this town) but not dull – monkfish in saffron sauce, oysters with wild mushrooms, grilled plaice.

A possible arrow, so more reports please.

L'Ancrage
(R)M *12 r. Montpensier   1.89.00.70   Cl. Tues. p.m. o.o.s.; Wed.; 2/1–4/2   CB, EC*

An old-established brasserie-type restaurant, long favourite with the French, rather than the English. It is solidly reliable, with its straightforward cooking of fruits de mer, moules, grilled fish, and is always full. Overlooks the harbour opposite the Lieutenance, with a summer terrace. Midweek menus are 92f, otherwise it's 140f.

'A superb restaurant, full of Frenchmen – not an Englishman to be seen. We were treated with courtesy and curiosity. Huge platefuls of moules, veal in cream and mustard sauce at a reasonable price, including dessert, cheeses, wine and coffee. The fruits de mer, at 220f for two, looked amazing value.' – Pauline Bennett.

L'Écluse
(R)M-S *2 quai de la Quarantaine   31.89.18.09   Cl. Mon.*

Another pretty, beamed, small restaurant, this time on the quayside, which looked after us very well on a bitterly cold December day, when most of the other restaurants had shutters up (no matter what they claim as their opening days). We found its 78f menu good and the 130f version even better. It is rightly popular and always crowded, so book or arrive early. Terrace tables in the summer ease the congestion.

Chez Laurette
(R)S *29 quai Ste. Catherine   31.89.05.34   Cl. Thurs.*

There are several bars and crêperies round the quay and as long as you stick to simple dishes you can't really go far wrong, but Laurette is the one that gets most plaudits for food and smiles. The place to make for if you feel like a plateful of moules and not much else. Open in winter too.

'Chez Laurette is every bit as good as you found it. Their Beaujoulais Primeur was superb.' – Ken Hampson.

La Tortue
(R)S-M   *36 r. de l'Homme de Bois*   *31.89.04.93*   *Cl. Wed.*

Pretty little beamed restaurant, with prices to match its location – in a back street rather than by the quay. 90f bought a terrine of salmon (or 9 oysters), a brochette of lotte, cheese, salad and apple tourte (covered pie) with crème fraiche or Calvados. I had both.

La Lieutenance
(R)M   *12 pl. Ste. Catherine*   *31.89.07.52*   *Cl. Tues.*

One of the several restaurants with tables spilling on to the colourful Place Ste. Catherine. The food is not elaborate – good fish and grills – but of good quality, well presented, on menus at 88f and 126f. Certainly the locals recommend it and, served in such an attractive setting, who could ask for more?

Le Marelot
(R)S-M   *Equemauville, r. de la République*   *31.89.37.68*   *Cl. Sun. p.m.; Mon. o.o.s.; 10/6–21/6; 15/11–30/11*

A restaurant for the locals, away from the tourist beat, on the main approach road to the town. Reliable traditional cooking on menus from 60f. Good value all round, and a change from chi-chi.

Particularly in winter, when the sun does not lure visitors to outside tables, it is very agreeable to find a good salon de thé, at which to rest the feet from cobbled stones and warm up a bit. Not to mention sampling a French pastry or three. Honfleur has recently acquired an ice cream parlour on the quay, and of course there are numerous bars, but it is strangely short on tea places. All the better news then is La Petite Chine at 14 r. du Dauphin, where not only can you sit and sip 50 different tea varieties (fancy lotus flower? or violet?), but get a superb view over the harbour at the same time.

Map 3C   **ISIGNY-SUR-MER** 14230 Calvados. 11 km E of Carentan; 61 km SE of Cherbourg

---

 Wed.

Not really *sur-mer*, but near the mouth of the Vire, which means oysters and all manner of other shellfish. There is a little quay, with green and red fishing boats tied up, and sheds full of baskets of assorted crustaceans. Not only the heart of the dairy industry but *pré salé* country, the salt marshes where the tastiest sheep come from.

La Flambée
(R)S

Right on the quay and un-missable. Go through the crowded smoky bar to an unexpectedly attractive dining-room, with raised log fire, beams, saddle leathers. The house speciality is brochettes – kidneys, scallops, sausages, all mixed with peppers, onions and mushrooms and charred to order over the fire, for about 50f. Delicious and just right for a quick cheap meal.

'Monsieur was very jolly. Food and atmosphere excellent.' – M. A. Warrender.

Map 6H   IVRY-LA-BATAILLE 27540 Eure. 17 km S of Pacy-sur-Eure

 Wed., Sat.

Heading north from Dreux, perhaps after a visit to the Loire, with too much main-road driving, I often opt to take the scenic route, following the little D 143 along the meandering course of the Eure. It is all very green, very relaxing, passing through flower-strewn villages, with glimpses of water and good picnicking possibilities.

Le Moulin d'Ivry
(R)M-L   *10 r. Henri-IV   32.36.40.51   Cl. Sun. p.m.; Mon.   AE, EC, V*

A change of management meant the loss of a Michelin star for this ridiculously picturesque restaurant on the very banks of the river, but little has changed, and its charms are no less. A young chef, Gilles Beaudriller, has been engaged by the new proprietors, M. et Mme Michel, to liven up the old traditional menu with some new ideas, but it is still based on regional products and old-fashioned recipes like duck cooked in cider and fresh foie gras.

A special occasion treat, with menus from 130f during the week and from 180f at weekends.

Au Grand St. Martin
(HR)M   *9 r. d'Ezy   32.36.41.39   Cl. Jan.; 20/8–31/8   CB*

This little village restaurant now has ten rooms, recently refurbished, to retire to after enjoying the rural surroundings and a good dinner. Demi-pension is obligatory, at 325–475f per person. Menus start at 120f.

Map 1A   JOBURG (NEZ DE) 50440 Beaumont-Hague, Manche. 26 km W of Cherbourg

---

I insist that all visitors to the Cotentin peninsula explore its NW corner. They will of course exclaim 'It's just like Cornwall' – and it probably is, but more so, in that it's just like Cornwall used to be, singularly lacking in crowds, hotels, souvenir shops. The narrow lanes, banked with hollyhocks and honeysuckle, lead to sleepy villages where grey stone cottages support tumbling old-fashioned roses, whose names have long since been forgotten.

The Nez de Joburg is the Land's End of the peninsula, the highest cliffs (128 metres) in Europe, with spectacular views, in all directions, of mighty rocks and bays and coves and tumbling seas. The Channel Islands, viewed through the telescope, loom very near.

The odd coach does rumble thus far and there is a solitary restaurant/bar on the point, battered by the winds, bleakish. Expectations are tuned to tourist food at tourist prices, which makes the reality all the more delightful.

➤ Les Grottes
(R)M   *33.52.71.44   Cl. Mon. lunch; Tues.; 15/10–25/3   CB*

For many years now M. Fauvel has stuck to his recipe for providing simple fresh food, superbly cooked, at realistic prices. No fancy long menus – his are still based on what the region does best: lamb, seafood, and his famous crêpes and omelettes. 89f buys an omelette filled with smoked ham, roast gigôt with potatoes Normand (like dauphinois, but with *Norman* cream!), vegetables and a sweet crêpe.

The log fire cheers the bleakness away; there are candles and waitresses in Norman costume of an evening, and altogether this is a restaurant that would merit the détour even without the view. Arrowed for consistent honest cooking.

Au Moulin à Vent
(R)M   *33.52.75.20   Cl. Sun. p.m. Mon.; 23/12–9/2   CB, EC*

Run by a charming young couple, M. et Mme Briens, who have turned this nice old stone house next to an ancient windmill into a restaurant full of character.

M. Briens sensibly cooks local ingredients simply and well. The menu is short and changes according to the market; the food is unpretentious but beautifully presented, as advised by their guide and mentor, M. Fauvel at nearby Les Grottes. I heartily recommend the 75f menu featuring, for example, asparagus in cream, a mouclade of mussels, grilled red mullet, interesting fruit desserts.

A possible future arrow I believe.

Map 3G   **JUMIÈGES** 76480 Duclair, Seine-Mar. 28 km W of Rouen

---

'One of the greatest ruins in France' states the green Michelin about the Benedictine abbey that dominates the village of Jumièges. Founded in the seventh century, it was razed by the Vikings, then rebuilt and consecrated in 1067, with William, Duke of Normandy, in attendance.

After the Revolution the monks were dispersed and a public auction

Abbaye de Jumièges

was held to dispose of the building. A timber merchant made the successful bid and used his new acquisition as a stone quarry. It was rescued 130 years ago and now belongs to the state.

You get a lot of ruin for your money. The entire nave, though roofless, still soars 90 ft. high, and some of the chancel and transept remain. The twin towers either side of the main door will be familiar from posters and photographs; the reality is every bit as impressive. A most rewarding hour could be spent here wondering and wandering through the grounds; there are more treasures in the complex of the church, St. Pierre, the chapter house, cloisters and storeroom.

Open from mid-June to mid-Sept. all day; closed from 12–2.30 pm. the rest of the year.

Auberge des Ruines
(H)S (R)M   *35.37.24.05*

In the square just outside the abbey walls and recently taken over by new management, who have transformed the old and dusty restaurant into something altogether smarter and so popular that Sunday lunches are now out of the question without a booking. Good terrace for drinks

All ingredients are market-fresh and the food is straightforwardly cooked and plentiful. Menu 72f (not weekends), otherwise 135f, 185f and 235f. Four very simple bedrooms are reserved for restaurant clients (160f), but I have my doubts.

'We found the couple who run this hotel extremely welcoming and nice. We stayed one night and actually chose to come again a few days later. The dinner was very good – imaginative and delicious and there is a splendid log fire. The bedrooms are basic but adequate. We had a table and two chairs, a view of the ruined abbey and warm radiators. The room cost us 110f (there was a cheaper, noisier one at 90f) and dinner was 115f.' – N. Fixsen.

➤ Restaurant du Bac
(R)S-M   *35.91.84.16   Cl. Tues. p.m.; Wed.; Mon. p.m. o.o.s.; Aug.*

One of the established favourites; everyone is enchanted with the little black and white restaurant, beamed and cosy with log fires inside, bustlingly busy in fine weather, when the large garden overlooking the river overflows with families enjoying the view and the fare.

From here you can see the little red and white ferry fussing to and fro with its car loads, along with all the other absorbing river traffic; it's all very restful and other-worldly.

The service can get overstretched at busy times – I would avoid sunny Sunday lunches unless you are happy to spend most of the afternoon here, though I can think of worse fates.

But at other times satisfaction is guaranteed, with menus featuring M. Morisse's famous chunky terrines, Norman recipes, cheeseboards left for personal and repeated selection, huge fruit tarts.

Arrowed for the same reasons as before – setting, food and atmosphere. The 70f (not weekends) menu is the one to go for – four good and plentiful courses. The 120 and 140f versions add yet another course – allocate a whole afternoon (as do the French family parties) to do justice to these.

Brigitte Chatel
(C)M   *r. du Quesney*   35.37.24.98

The brother and sister-in-law of the popular M. Chatel, who is no longer in the b. & b. business, run this way-above-average chambre d'hôte not far away. They have three double rooms with private loo and two shared bathrooms, and charge 150f for two people b. and b.

'The house is a few minutes' drive from the village in a quiet country road. It is a beautifully renovated old Norman farmhouse, all beams and character. All delightful and scrupulously clean.' – Margaret and Brian Day.

Map 4E   **LEAUPARTIE** 14340 Cambremer, Calvados. 15 km S of Pont-Audemer; 87 km SW of Le Havre

---

The Auge region, either side of the autoroute from Pont l'Evêque to Caen, is full of fascination and well worth a diversion. Immediately deeply rural, as if no main road were within miles, it is a countryside of rich pastures and small farms. Many of the farmers' wives have taken to catering for visitors and there are numerous gîtes and chambres d'hôte to choose from. Here is a typical example, which has pleased readers over a number of years:-

Suzanne Guérin
(C)S   *Le Bois Hurey*   31.63.01.99   *Open year round*

To find the Guérins' pretty stone farmhouse, look for the bridge over the Dorette or ask in the village. Madame Guérin is a friendly, nothing-too-much trouble hostess and a stay in one of her two bedrooms – one double, one for four people sharing a bathroom – will be a happy experience. They cost 135f for two people, and a super farmhouse-style meal can be booked for the evening.

'Wonderful welcome, wonderful food. I had telephoned in advance fortunately, as it was a weekend and she had many visitors from Paris. She set a trestle table outside and twelve of us sat down to a most excellent meal. Course after course, as much as we wanted, with plenty of cider – more than plenty. We were the only English and it was a most memorable evening. Dinner lasted from 8.30 until we drifted away three hours later. Sunday night there were only seven of us, in the garden again. The main course was a delicious piece of beef, which she announced was from one of her own cows.' – Audrey Barritt.

An arrow for confirmed simple perfection. You can also rent a gîte from Mme Guérin, and a stay in this area would please both purse and palate.

Map 4F   **LIEUREY** 27560 Eure. 15 km S of Pont Audemer

Ⓜ *Thurs.*

A typical little market town, usefully situated in the middle of the Pont l'Evêque, Lisieux, Bernay, Pont-Audemer quadrangle. In the main street of its otherwise unremarkable main street is the kind of old-fashioned French staging post that is increasingly losing ground to the flash, the tawdry, the cheap 'n' nasty, or the quick buck.

Le Bras d'Or
(HR)S   *32.57.91.07   Cl. Mon. o.o.s.; 15/1–15/2   V*

M. Deschamps has won many prizes for his dedication to Norman-speciality cooking, and many regional dishes feature on his remarkable 78f menu. My mousseline of moules – tender baby mussels cooked in a cream and saffron chervil-flecked sauce gratinéed, the chef's terrine flavoured with port and left on the table for self-service and the cassoulet of chicken liver were all memorable. The less adventurous can rely on trout with almonds.

Map 5E   **LE LION D'OR** 14370 Argences, Calvados. 3 km S of Méry-Corbon; 23 km E of Caen

The oddly-named hamlet (there must be a story there) of Lion d'Or is on the main Caen-Lisieux road, the RN 13, in the commune of Méry-Corbon.

➤ **Le Relais du Lion d'Or**
(R)S-M

Much prettier in than out, with two small rooms, stone walls, flagged floors, cane chairs, an open fire, and a hazardous, granny-fatal, spiral staircase leading to the loos. Run by a charming husband and wife team –Philippe who cooks, and Catrine who, with the help of one young girl, efficiently takes all the orders and serves the food.

We stopped on the off-chance one wet and windy Sunday lunchtime, desperately disappointed at the 'Complet' sign on the door, and she somehow squeezed us in among all the lip-smacking happy French families. What's more, she then made us feel welcome. I added insult to injury by saying I wasn't very hungry, could I please have just two starters on the cheapest (90f) menu, and it was only later that I realised that her concern was for my lost opportunity to sample Philippe's cooking. Never fear, Catrine, I shall be back. And back.

The very fact that they continue to offer this cheap menu on a Sunday is a big plus in their favour – most restaurants simply delete their lowest-priced version on that well-patronised day. So – I had sea trout, marinaded with fennel, and home-made terrine campagnarde with winter salad, both unusually delicious and unskimped. (Alternatively, I could have had a feuilleté of moules with chervil.)

Husband chose from the 160f menu a terrine of pleurottes, presented prettily but without chi-chi-ness, and then a mousseline of pike with a wonderful shell-fish sauce. By this time, seeing what I was missing, I weakened and decided to have a main course too and I can only tell you that my steak with marchand du vin butter was tastier and more tender than one eaten earlier that trip costing twice the price of the whole menu.

I personally don't care for iles flottantes – those fluffy puffs of sweetened air – but they are a house speciality here and looked mighty impressive, brimming over the plates, topped with crunchy almonds, sitting in a rich caramel sauce. I settled instead for délice de chocolat with a caramelised orange sauce, and Husband had the definitive Tarte Tatin. It's a difficult dish to achieve perfect components – flaky buttery pastry, quarters of *eating* apples, deep and impregnated with caramel. Hundreds of versions I've fought my way through in Normandy, but this was the star.

A fruity Muscadet-sur-Lie was £5. Altogether fantastic value, and arrowed.

Map 4E   **LISIEUX** 14100 Calvados. 78 km SW of Le Havre

(T) *11 r. Alençon   31.62.08.41* (M) *Wed., Sat., Fri. (animals)*

Not really a place to stay. The traffic, the war-time destruction of most of the old town, the hordes of pilgrims decanted by the coachload throughout the year but particularly around the feast day of Ste. Thérèse, all make for hassle. With the lovely countryside of the Auge all round and no shortage of accommodation nearby, I would rate Lisieux worth the odd rainy hour and no more.

Spend that hour in the cathedral of St. Pierre, an example of very early Gothic architecture, begun in 1170 and finished two hundred years later. The kindest word for the basilica of Ste. Thérèse is 'impressive'. It is one of the largest churches built in this century. You can visit the Carmelite Chapel where the saint is enshrined and her home, Les Buissonets, where Thérèse Martin lived until she was 15 years old.

Lisieux is surrounded by a wealth of fascinating manor-houses and abbeys, details of which may be obtained from the tourist office. Some of them are open to the public, but even a drive round the outside is rewarding. Look for St. Germain-de-Livet to the south, moated, glowing with the pinks, blues and greens, of mosaic tiles. To the north-west, an attractive drive through country lanes to Pré-d'Auge would find the 16C Victor, another mosaic-tiled house in a particularly lovely setting, and not far away is the former abbey of Val-Richer; but making your own discoveries is half the fun.

I checked all the hotel possibilities and failed to find one that I would wish to return to. Either they were noisy, or tourist-orientated at the expense of any personality, or just plain poor value. The only reader recommendation I have is:

La Coupe d'Or
(HR)M *49 r. Pont-Mortain 31.31.16.84 Open every day CB, AE, DC, EC*

'We received a warm welcome from M. Lion. Both he and his wife speak excellent English. Our room on the first floor faced a busy road, but it was well sound-proofed, warm and comfortable, with TV and mini-bar. Cost 225f. The cheapest menu at 82f was all fish; there was a tourist menu at 85f, another at 120f, which we had, and a gastronimique at 175f. We chose a pâté de canard which was enjoyable and not too nouvelle. Then a 'plateau de grillades', cheese, and a fair choice of dessert, including chocolate fudge gateau and a mille-feuille (ours are infinitely better). A carafe of house rosé and coffee were included. Not perhaps a memorable meal, but very welcome on a cold winter evening when the rest of Lisieux was shuttered. I would not mind a return visit for the warmth of the patron and the hotel.' – Audrey Martingell. Rooms 140–295f. Menus from 140f incl. wine.

If I had to choose a Lisieux hotel I would opt for once for the entirely modern, on the outskirts of the town:

Gardens Hotel
(R)M *rte de Paris 31.61.17.17 Open every day CB, AE, DC*

At least the rooms are spacious, well-equipped and quiet, and there is a swimming pool and garden. It's all predictably impersonal with even breakfast run as a do-it-yourself buffet (good though). Rooms 270–310f, and there is a restaurant.

One reader, whose views on the Gardens Hotel coincided with mine – 'pleasantly staffed, efficiently-run international plastic hotel' – found that he had to eat out on Sunday night and discovered:

Auberge du Pêcheur
(R)M *2 bis. r. Verdun 31.31.16.85 AE, DC, EC, V*

'Very quiet, reasonably priced and most enjoyable meal.' – Michael Cooper-Cocks.

Menus here start at 90f, and as it is open every day, it might well prove a salvation for other Sabbath travellers.

Restaurants now are another matter. Lisieux is the capital of the region and all those business men and farmers have to eat somewhere, but even here the best are just out of town:-

Le Parc
(R)M *21 bvd. Herbert Fournet 31.62.08.11 Cl. Tues. p.m.; Wed.; 20/1–20/2 CB, AE, DC*

An old organ-loft has been cleverly transformed into a sophisticated restaurant. From the well-spaced tables you can watch the chef, M. Reudet, in his kitchens, prepare dishes based on local ingredients –

turbot on a bed of edible seaweed, veal kidneys cooked in Pommeau, honey and nougat ice cream. The 130f menu is the best value, though there is a cheaper 92f version at lunchtime mid-week. Interesting and different.

La Ferme du Roy
(R)M   *122 bvd. H. Fournet   31.31.33.98   Cl. Sun. p.m.; Mon.; 18/12–24/1; 28/6–5/7   CB*

A pleasant old stone farmhouse a mile or two out of town on the Deauville road. Inside it's all oak beams and as Norman as they come. Patron M. Gouret does the cooking, aided by his son, and Madame Gouret welcomes warmly. They make a point of serving local produce like the andouilles made in Vire and local duck as one of their specialities: Cannette au cidre; the whole experience is a very pleasant one. Menus from 85f (weekdays) or 147f.

'Madame Gouret's accueil was unfussy but amicable, professional but nice. They've owned the place 12 years. I asked her recommendation on wine for my meal, and on looking up the price, found that it was one of the cheaper ones. But she really meant it. I took the 120f menu and had salmon marinaded in oil, lemon and peppers, with caviar and parsley garnish – a dream; then canette au cidre – incredibly tender with a yummy coulis of carrots and perfect celery, then cheese and desserts. My meal total was 230f and not a penny wasted. This place should be the main cultural attraction of Lisieux, with the Cathedral beaten hands-down.' – Robin Totton.

I think Robin enjoyed his meal. An arrow for the best food in town.

La France
(R)M-S   *5 r. au Char   31.62.03.37*

A limited choice (how wise) on well-judged menus. Eveline and Patrick Leroux are patrons – he cooks; she, an open friendly type and enthusiastic about her métier, welcomes and serves. The 80f menu is good value.

Map 5E   **LIVAROT** 14140 Calvados. 18 km S of Lisieux

 Thurs. a.m.

Home of one of Normandy's great cheeses, golden-rinded, strong-smelling, made here for over 600 years. A 'conservatoire' des traditions fromagères explains the different stages in its production. There are some nice old houses, all the more peaceful nowadays, since the town has mercifully been by-passed.

Le Vivier
(HR)S   *pl. G. Bisson   31.63.50.29   Cl. Sun p.m. o.o.s.; 25/9–9/10; 22/12–16/1*

There is little choice of eating-places around this area, but no matter –

the little Vivier feeds its customers well and cheaply, as it has done for many years. Ask any local and he will direct you there without hesitation. The simple well-cooked menus start at 68f and there are eleven equally simple rooms (though some now have bathrooms) from 100–260f.

Map 2H **LONDINIÈRES** 7660 Seine-Mar. 27 km SE of Dieppe

Ⓜ *Thurs. p.m.*

A pleasant drive from Dieppe, following the river Eaulne along the D 920.

Auberge du Pont
(HR)S *35.93.80.47 Cl. 25/1–28/2 EC, V*

The bridge which gives the auberge its name crosses a small stream running along the rear of the bedroom annexe of this small (13 rooms) modest hotel. Good value for an overnight stop at 105–175f, and menus from 52f.
  'A convenient overnight stop en route from Calais to Normandy. The bedrooms are modest but clean and comfortable and attractive. All very peaceful. The menus in the restaurant were not exciting but well-presented and good value. And the clock golf in the garden provided an ideal diversion for the children in the hours between arrival and dinner.' – Richard Beck.

Map 2F **LOUVETOT** 76490 Caudebec en Caux, Seine-Mar. 7.5 km N of Caudebec

A village on the D 33, in the heart of the farming Caux area.

Au Grand Méchant Loup
(HR)S *35.96.01.44 Cl. Fri. p.m.; Sat. lunch; Sun. p.m.; 16/8–31/8 EC, V*

Useful to know about this modest, very French hotel, in an area not over-blessed with accommodation. The 24 modern rooms cost from 185–225f and menus start at 65f with good carafe wine.
  'The food still good. The local hunting parties were using it the Sunday we were there, so that must be a recommendation.' – Mike Souter.

Map 4D **LOUVIGNY** 14111 Calvados. 4 km SW of Caen by D 212

A hamlet on the banks of the peaceful willow-fringed Orne, which could provide a merciful escape from the city on a hot summer's day. Take the Venoix exit from the ring road.

Auberge de l'Hermitage

(R)M   *11 La Haule   31.73.38.66   Cl. Sun. p.m.; Mon.; and three weeks end of August*

The Auberge is a creeper-covered old house with a pink-tinted dining-room. The patron, M. Grandsire, wisely presents a short menu, which is interesting without being eccentric. Fresh asparagus is cooked in layers of flaky pastry; farm chicken is allied with crayfish; fresh summer fruits are served in a pastry cornet. Menus from 150f.

Map 3H   LYONS-LA-FORÊT 27480 Eure. 36 km E of Rouen

 Thurs.

30 km to the east of Rouen lies the old hunting ground of the Dukes of Normandy, the forest of Lyons. To drive there makes a perfectly delightful excursion, with all kinds of possible diversions: to follow the valleys of the swift-flowing rivers, Andelle or Crévon, to visit the castle of *Vascoeuil*, the abbeys of *Fontaine-Guérard* or *Mortemer*, to walk amongst the massive beeches, some of them 140 ft high, and picnic in their shade. Or of course you could go, in time-honoured fashion, to pray for a husband at the Source Ste-Catherine.

In the centre of the forest, approached by the charming D 321, is the picturebook town of Lyons-la-Forêt. Centring on the old wooden covered market hall, the crooked Norman houses, black timbers, white plaster, red geraniums, are the focus of many an American and Japanese camera, and the fact that many of the shops are *antiquaires* is no coincidence.

It was once a delightful tranquil place, but is now so obviously tourist-orientated that I would not choose to stay here. The two main hotel/restaurants never lack for custom, and that's a sign to be wary of. However better to resign yourself to forking out for an enjoyable meal than economise on one you will regret (and if anyone knows a cheap good alternative in this town I should very much like to know.)

Le Grand Cerf

(HR)M   *pl. du Marché   32.49.60.44   Cl. Tues.; Wed.; 15/1–18/2   CB, AE, DC, EC*

Philippe Colignon's prices may be on the high side, but they reflect high standards. He searches Rungis for the best produce and makes his own bread every morning. His dining-room in the picturesque old inn in the centre of town is delightful and his 150f menu will offer classy cooking like scallops and clams in aspic, a plait of salmon and sole and good daily-baked gâteaux.

He has eight pretty bedrooms looking out on the ancient market hall, costing 250–300f.

Map 6E   **MACÉ** 61500 Sées, Orne. 4.5 km NW of Sées on the D 238

Clearly marked, via various narrow lanes, is:

l'Ile de Sées
(HR)M   *33.27.98.65   Cl. Sun. p.m.; Mon.; 15/1–15/2   EX, V*

Unexpectedly imposing gates lead to the little Logis. Built recently but nothing stark or aggressively modern about its creeper-clad appearance. Nice garden, tables, utter quiet. Inside is plush decor with comfy lounge and smart dining-room. Bedrooms too are very comfortable indeed. They all have bathrooms and cost a reasonable 210–230f. Menus from 80f.

Just one caveat. The new brochure boasts of a 'coin disco pour animer vos soirées.' I do not wish my soirées to be animated by a disco, and would be sure to get some assurance, when booking, that the animation would be out of ear-shot of the bedrooms.

'Unwise as we were to go to France over Whitsun weekend without booking, we were lucky to get the last room, small, at the back in the new part, but with excellent bath and separate w.c. and soap and good towels at 230f. Dinner was excellent – beautifully moist salmon and vegetable moulds light as a feather. Mme Orcier said they only use fresh vegetables – what a change. The lowest menu at 78f looked okay, but ours was well worth an extra 29f, very well cooked indeed. Busy dining-room, friendly staff. Another wing being added on. We will return to this one for sure.' – Diana Holmes.

Map 3H   **MAINNEVILLE** 27150 Étrepagny, Eure. 10 km NE of Étrepagny

Take the D 14 out of Gisors and head north on the D 17 towards the deep and verdant Forêt de Lyons to find this hamlet. Lovely walks in the Levrière valley.

Ferme Ste. Geneviève
(C)M   *32.55.51.26*

At the southern entrance to Mainneville, turn left 100 yards up the hill and the farm is set back on your left. The road is signed Le Timbre. It's a real working Normandy farm, spotlessly clean and spattered with geraniums. Nice Mme. Marc has four guest rooms, each with private loo, basin and shower for 170f, or 240f for three.

'It's gorgeous. You have a vast downstairs room with two vast loft rooms above. Old oak table and 8 ft. fireplace downstairs, bathroom and two double beds up. All this on the other side of the yard from the house and it is all yours. Mme Marc is much loved. Youngish, quiet, gentle, helpful, ungrasping. My impressions confirmed by a cycling family who stopped overnight. They arrived tired and Mme Marc took one look, went indoors and came back with fresh lemonade. They couldn't bear to leave and stayed several days. The rooms are heated

by central heating, fuelled by straw! Idyllic, less than three nights would be a waste.' – Robin Totton.

I haven't been to stay here yet – can't wait. A future arrow by the sound of things.

Map 3C   **MAISONS** 14400 Bayeux, Calvados. 3 km NW of Bayeux

---

Just a dot on the map, approached from the D 100 between Tour-en-Bessin and Port-en-Bessin.

Manoir du Carel
(C)L   *31.22.37.00*

Charming Monsieur and Madame Jacques Aumond are newcomers to the châteaux b. and b. game, and are trying particularly hard to please their guests. They are still in the process of converting their superb fortified medieval manor-house, part of which is still a working farm, into a luxurious home. The parts they have finished have been done with the greatest possible style and attention to detail, with no expense spared. I particularly like the huge glass door they have let into the sitting-room, allowing the natural light to illuminate the beautiful galleried room, with its grey and honey stone walls.

The bedrooms likewise have been restored and furnished with taste. Each has its own luxurious bathroom and costs from 250 to 450f. Dinner is 250f inclusive, and breakfast 40f.

Steeped in history and surrounded by the peaceful green Bessin countryside, this is a lovely and memorable place to stay. Arrowed accordingly.

Map 5B   **MARIGNY** 50570 Manche. 14 km NE of Coutances; 14 km SW of St. Lo

---

 Wed.

An unremarkable little market town, with an outwardly unremarkable little restaurant in the market square (busy on Wednesdays).

Restaurant de la Poste
(R)M   *pl. Westport   33.55.11.08   Cl. Sun. p.m.; Mon.; 15 days in September; 1/1–15/1   AE, DC, CB*

What a feeble lot F.E.3 readers are! For years now I've been nagging them to go to this remarkable little restaurant, offering all they are looking for, and after three arrows I have only one letter as feedback. Well, serve them right, they've lost the bargain the Poste offered when I first found it; Michelin and Gault-Millau have latched on, and I wouldn't be at all surprised if a rosette wasn't in the offing before very long.

And well deserved it would be. Joel Meslin has been dishing up superb food, based on the best that Rungis and the local producers can offer for a long time now and his consistency is obvious. Perhaps he has grown in confidence, but he still prefers to rely on the dishes of his region (both he and his wife are dedicated Normans), like wonderful John Dory cooked in cider, hot Isigny oysters, duckling in Pommeau, crêpes Normandes – and most of the vegetables come from the garden that he tends himself.

Take time to consider his wine list, which contains some treasures for every pocket. And go *soon*, while his menu costs only 135f (100f weekdays). You won't want to eat again that day, I'll warrant.

Here is what the one wise man had to say: *'Our meal so easily became a special occasion that we ate there a second time rather than try anywhere else. We stayed with the cheapest menu and between us tried everything from it. Nothing could be faulted. Next year we may savour the more expensive menus. Just the anticipation should be a joy.'* – J. R. Shipman.

Map 6C   **MARTILLY** 14500 Vire, Calvados. 2 km W of Vire on the Villedieu road

---

Le Relais Normand
(HR)S   *31.68.08.67   Cl. Sat. o.o.s.*

Several readers have been delighted with the welcome, the modest bill and regional cooking here. Madame Goure, wife of the patron-chef, speaks good English, so communication is no problem. M. Goure wisely sticks to local specialities like rabbit in cider, sausages prepared in Vire, and veal in cream and calvados. Rooms from 100f and menus from 55f.

'Dining room unfussy and typically French local – obviously regulars eating M. Goure's delicious fare. We looked at rooms – clean and adequate, if old-fashioned, one or two with bath. M. and Mme most welcoming. Lunch – pâté de pie aux champignons, tarte au beurre et aux amandes for 36.50f.' – Mrs. D. Court.

Map 1G   **MARTIN ÉGLISE** 76370 Neuville lès Dieppe, Seine-Mar. 7 km SE of Dieppe

---

If you take the D 1 out of Dieppe, the suburbs come to an abrupt halt only just before Martin Église; one minute its factories and lorries, then, all the more welcome for the surprise, rolling fields and cows.

Auberge Clos Normand

(HR)M   *Les Vertus*   *35.84.83.10   Cl. Sun. p.m.; Mon.; 5/1–13/1   CB*

A lovely old mellow building facing on to the village street, with large leafy garden running down to the river Eaulne. Bedrooms are in a converted stable block, creeper-covered, balconied, faded timbers.

The chef-patron M. Delaunay cooks on an open range at one end of the delightfully rustic, beamed and coppered dining-room, bright with red gingham cloths and lots of flowers.

So far so good, and some time ago this was my favourite hideaway in the region. Nowadays the reports are less enthusiastic. Hard to analyse, and I'm sure that one day it must come good again, so please keep   on writing. Meanwhile the meals, whose menus don't seem to have changed since I was first there – tarte aux moules, which I remember as being superb, duckling with apple, and apple tart – now cost a hefty 200f à la carte and demi-p. is obligatory if you stay, at 340f per person.

Auberge du Clos Normand.

Map 7F   LE MÊLE-SUR-SARTHE 61170 Orne. 20 km NE of Alençon

 Wed.

A not particularly interesting town, but there is now an artificial lake complete with beach and a variety of water sports, and the countryside is lovely.

Le Poste
(HR)S   *33.27.60.13   Cl. Sun. p.m.; Mon.; 1/10–15/10; 1/2–15/10;1/2–15/2   EC, V*

An unpretentious little hotel, useful for an overnight stop, with clean and wholesome rooms in an annexe, for 85–220f, and a local reputation for good honest cooking, on menus at 50–180f. A Michelin red R for the 50f menu makes this a popular destination, and you should book for Sunday lunch at least.

'The rooms were very quiet and overlooking a little public garden. We had a very good 72f menu and wine was available in carafe.' – Jenny Leeves.

Map 4E   MERVILLE-FRANCEVILLE-PLAGE 14810 Calvados. 6 km W of Cabourg

 Thurs. a.m.

Head west from Cabourg on the coast road D 514 to find this quiet little seaside resort, completely devastated in 1944. A museum has been contrived in one of the wartime shelters that used to house a 150 mm gun with a range of 20 km.

Chez Marion
(H)S(R)L   *10 pl. de la Plage   31.24.23.39   Cl. Mon. p.m.; Tues.; 3/1–31/1   CB, AE, DC, EC*

The H(S)R(L) says it all. This Logis de France is a restaurant with rooms, more dedicated to superb food than any other Logis I know. The rooms are merely somewhere to collapse after partaking unwisely, but understandably, of M. Marion's collapsity.

Personally I am happy to allocate the francs with this order of priority sometimes, but on the whole F.E. readers are not; the consensus has been shock at the size of the bill. There is a limited 97f menu, but the temptation to go for the lobster seems a good idea at the time. The wines are not exactly cheap either. Here is one reader's experience, which puts the situation far better than I could:-

'I immediately felt that this place was right and so it proved. We had a superb and vastly expensive fishy lunch à la carte. A huge lobster, shared by the younger generation was, according to weight, 594f! We all ate à la carte, which is not the most economical procedure, but

enables us to miss out the pudding. My poached langoustines with pasta and lobster sauce were stunningly good. I followed up with turbot, then coffee and a glass of 1968 Gruolt Calvados from M. Marion's 'Calvados Library', which included Calvados as old as 1922. I was almost sorry I gave up smoking last year when I read of his other 'Library' – of cigars.

I felt that this restaurant was so ideal that we went there again the following day and tried the 175f menu. My wife had a super plâteau de fruits de mer (not surprisingly without any lobster!) to start with and I had a nicely-turned-out plate of foie gras and truffles with a glass of Sauterne. This was followed by bass – amazing for 175f.

I think we endeared ourselves with many words of appreciation for food and wine. The young patron is quite a character in his brown suit and turned-up cuffs and the staff could not have been nicer. I should think the hotel is a good place to stay for a few nights – we were very impressed.' – Bobby Furber.

Map 3G   **MESNIL-SOUS-JUMIÈGES** 76480 Duclair, Seine-Mar. 5 km S of Jumièges; 74 km E of Le Havre

---

The main road cuts across the neck of the deep loop of the Seine and mercifully misses Jumièges. The détour, following the river all the way, via Mesnil to Duclair, is well worth the time and effort. It's a peaceful little stretch, free of commercial traffic, lined with simple houses whose owners sell the produce of their orchards in due season. Cherry-time is particularly colourful, with stalls piled high with glowing fruit; then come the apples and pears, and always on fine weekends there are families from Rouen and environs setting up their sophisticated picnic-tables and whiling away their weekends engaged in their favourite occupation.

La Pommeraie
(R)S   *35.37.94.87   Cl. Mon. and Tues.*

This little rustic restaurant, red and white inside and themed to the apple, had just changed hands when I wrote about it before, so I am delighted to be able to confirm that it is now even better. Locals think so too and the half a dozen tables in the cool stone interior and all those set under the apple trees outside are bound to be full at busy times. The 75f menu is very good value, so it's worth booking.

Map 1H   **MESNIL-VAL** 76910 Criel-sur-Mer, Seine-Mar. 4.5 km S of Le Tréport; 27 km N of Dieppe

---

In a virtual gastronomic and hospitality desert, it is a blessing to find a recommendable hotel in a peaceful hamlet like Mesnil-Val, complete with its own (tiny) beach. Here is the ideal mid-way break between northern Channel ports and Normandy, but good, indeed, in its own right.

The village, which only comes to life (and that's relative) in the summer, nestles in a break in the characteristic chalk cliffs, but is only a short distance from the more awake Le Tréport.

➤ **La Vieille Ferme**
(HR)M   *35.86.72.18   Cl. Sun. p.m. in March and from 4/11–16/12; 1/1–22/1   AE, DE, CE, V*

Extremely picturesque, all black and white timbers, stone walls, geraniums and lovely cooking smells wafting from the old farmhouse dining-room. Because of its position and good value, it is well known and popular, so the biggest disappointment that readers have expressed is not being able to get in. Persevere, plan ahead, and the rewards will be considerable.

'An old favourite of ours. The food gets better every time we go there, though the rooms are still pretty basic, but comfortable. Madame Maxine charges 285f per person demi-pension, which is a very good deal. The dinner is superb, with a great choice; starters include six oysters or crab, main course, sweet and cheese.' – G. M. Somper.

The accommodation, for the most part, is in two detached houses, in the grounds of the hotel. Rooms are 245–385f. The garden is terraced, well kept, and boasts a pleasant terrace for summer sipping, and a tennis court. Arrowed on many counts – peacefulness, intrinsic Frenchness, excellent food (menus 89f except Sats), welcoming management. A winner in fact.

'The prettiest hotel of all. A handsome building and our room across a courtyard 325f, with TV and a big bathroom. A notice on the door insisting on proper dress for dinner. This was our dearest meal – 425f for two and worth it. Continental breakfast, with jam in a bowl, total bill 815f. A good hotel, but not for disabled or infirm visitors – steps in the courtyard and 14 steep steps to our room.' – Valerie Hughes-Narborough.

Map 7A   **MOIDREY** 50170 Pontorson, Manche. 7 km S of Mont St. Michel; 2 km N of Pontorson

---

Turn off the Pontorson road onto the D 80 and then right, in attractive countryside, to find Moidrey.

Au Vent des Grèves
(R)M   *33.60.01.63   Open every day in summer; cl. Wed. o.o.s.*

The well-known proprietor of the famous La Mère Poulard, *the* restaurant on Mont St. Michel, has taken over this formerly modest restaurant, in an old farmhouse, and converted it into a delightful new alternative to the fleshpots down the road. He has kept the rusticity but embellished it with a new sense of style. The south-facing terrace is a particularly appealing prospect for summer eating.

The food is kept surprisingly simple, dedicated to local produce – crab and lobster from Chausey, sole meunière and pré-salé lamb, naturally grown vegetables and home-made desserts. Menus at present start at 85f, so catch this one before others do.

Map 3G   **MONT CAUVAIRE** 76690 Clères, Seine-Mar. 20 km NE of Rouen

---

Very green, very rural, very near Rouen. Mont Cauvaire is a hamlet between the D 151 and the D 155, on the D 3.

Château de Rombosc
(C)L *35.33.39.87*

Poor Francis and Catherine Rolland-Marescot had a bad deal when they took on the crumbling château from the previous owners, who had built up a disastrous reputation as b. and b. hosts. It takes a long time for the word to get around that things have changed, and the timing was bad for French Entrée – just too late for recommendation and correction of the old image.

I am happy now to be able to restore the balance somewhat. All reports are that restoration has worked well and that the new hosts are kindly, welcoming and efficient. They certainly speak good English and are doing everything they can to please their guests. Rombosc, dating from the 16C, but not particularly grand, needed tender loving care to bring out its many good features, and it is a great pleasure to see the transformation. A very comfortable double room, with bath, costs from 660–830f.

Map 5B   **MONTPINCHON** 50210 Cerisy la Salle, Manche. 12 km SE of Coutances

---

Take the D 7 out of Coutances, turn left onto the D 27 and follow signs to:

Château de la Salle
(HR)L *33.46.95.19*   *Cl. 5/11–10/3*   *CB, AE, DC*

An imposing, if somewhat severe, one-time prison, member of the Relais et Châteaux chain – its sole Cotentin representative.

Château de la salle

The setting is quite perfect. A walk through the beech woods behind the Château, misty with bluebells in April, down to the little stream in the valley, will make home cares seem more than a day away. Their prices, like everywhere else, have increased substantially since I first recommended the château as an ideal luxurious hideaway and, at 728f per person for obligatory demi-pension, expectations are high. Several readers have not been happy here, especially if they drew one of the smaller rooms, cramped, monastic-like, with midget bathroom carved out, sit-up-and-beg bath. You should go for the more expensive versions, dignified, tapestried, four-postered – or not go at all.

The food, on the other hand, is good value at this kind of level, as long as you abjure the carte. The 155f menu, prepared by Claude Esprabens, a youthful chef from the Basque country, includes sophisticated entrées like the best pigeon (cooked in honey) I've ever tasted, and delicate beurre blanc with the freshest of fish. The dining-room, furnished with antiques appropriate to the nobleman's house this one was, and the table settings, are appropriately elegant.

There is a 100f weekday menu. The 230f version is also good value, with more choice of courses, and M. Lemèsle's cave is superb.

The arrow goes, alas, for the moment, since there have not been enough enthusiastic reports to justify its retention.

Map 4E   **MONTREUIL-EN-AUGE** 14340 Cambremer, Calvados. 16 km
NW of Lisieux

In some of the most charming countryside in Normandy, the Auge
region, on the well-indicated Cider Route from which it takes its name.

La Route du Cidre
(CR)S   *31.63.00.63*

A typical Norman farmhouse, perched on a hillside, with big windows
making the most of the view. It is particularly popular on Sunday
lunch-time, when it is essential to book a seat in the rustic restaurant,
where copious traditional food is dished up on menus starting at 75f.
Reports please on the rooms.
  *'Well worth finding, but use a map. Good food, pleasant service and
cider at 22f a bottle.'* – Bob Smyth.

Map 7A   **MONT-ST-MICHEL** 50116 Manche. 22 km SW of Avranches

Ⓣ *Corps de Garde des Bourgeois 33.60.14.30*

'Le Merveille' they call it, which says it all. Like Venice, Mont St-Michel
exceeds well-briefed expectation every time. I have known it in winter,
grey with the sea and the sky, eerie and remote, in the spring when its
colours change like those of nature from sullenness to sparkle, in
autumn when it swims in early mists and catches fire from late sun,
and in the summer – when it is best left to other tourists and admired
from afar across the dazzle of fast-receding water. It never fails to
captivate the imagination. From a northern approach particularly it
dominates every landscape, glimpsed from little seaside resorts
around the bay, to Avranche's heights, to marshlands surrounding; the
magnetism is undeniable.
  The Archangel Michael, whom it honours, is said to have become
irritated with the neglect of Aubert, Bishop of Avranches, who failed to
build the customary hilltop shrine in his honour on Mont St-Tombe, as
the mount rising from the forest was then called. A few preliminary
dream visitations failed to spur Aubert into action, so Michael tapped
him so forcibly on the forehead that he dented his skull – there for all
disbelievers to see for themselves in St-Gervais in Avranches.
  Left in no doubt about his boss's wishes, Aubert built the first
oratory in 907, replaced by a Carolingian abbey on which successive
generations piled more and more elaborate edifices in Romanesque
and Gothic styles. Each one demanded formidable dedication of skill
and industry, with granite blocks having to be imported from the
Chausey Islands and Brittany and hauled up to the crest of the Mount.
  The many sections are too complex to describe here, but those of the
Merveille (14C) to the north of the Mount are certainly not to be
missed. Allow more time than you think necessary. Ideally a

Mont Saint-Michel.

circumference on foot (having first checked the tides!) is the way to get bearings and assess the scale. You may have to paddle a little.

The combination of this man-made miracle, set in the natural miracle of the racing water, which leaves only a causeway for the pilgrims across the water meadows – and at new and full moons surrounds the Mount completely - has always drawn admirers. Modern pilgrims come by car in the summer in their thousands and shove and jostle their way up the narrow lane to the summit between souvenir shops and crêperies. Restaurants there open only for a few short weeks and know they must extract the last shekel then. I strongly advise avoiding their rude avarice and that a picnic eaten amongst the sheep in the meadows is a better way to find space and calm to marvel at the Merveille.

I have always avoided staying in close proximity to the biggest tourist attraction in France, but it seems that my caution was misplaced:-

Relais du Roy
(HR)M   *33.60.14.25   Cl. 15/11–15/3   AE, DC, EC, V*

'We stayed at one of the several hotels situated on the main road leading to the Mont causeway, not to be confused with the hotel of the *same name on the Mont itself. An excellent hotel. Room with en-suite bathroom, w.c., and view of the estuary for 183f, extremely clean and comfortable. The hotel was opened in 1983 and is very well run and maintained. Food in the hotel restaurant was superb and was our second gastronomique feast of the week* (after the Cantepie – see Clécy) *and cost about the same –16 per person. Would thoroughly recommend an arrow for restaurant and hotel.'* – Wendy Forrest-Webb.

An arrow it shall have, Mrs. Forrest-Webb, as soon as I can get there to see for myself. Certainly sounds good news.

Les Terrasses Poulard
(HR)M   *r. Principale   33.60.14.09*

I realise that I mustn't duck the question of which of the dozens of eateries to choose, if a meal on the Mont is indicated.

I think that in spite of the through-put – more than 800 covers at peak periods – the Terrasses has most advantages. It has a marvellous view over the bay and the service from the waitresses, in local costume, is efficient and sometimes even smiling. The 60f menu is pretty basic, but it must be given credit for even trying to produce one at this price in this environment. There are others at 75, 120 and 140f, or you could just take an omelette, excellent fruits de mer and gigôt from the salt marshes below.

There is a new hotel under the same management not far away from the restaurant, which is said to have comfortable if smallish rooms from 300–750f, as yet uninspected.

Map 7F   MORTAGNE-AU-PERCHE 61400 Orne. 38 km NE of Alençon

Ⓣ *pl. Gén-de-Gaulle   33.25.19.21*   Ⓜ *Sat.*

'Sur-montagne' says the road sign. Well more of a hill really, but none the less an appealing setting for the little town spilling down from its crowning 'Place'. Behind the 18C Town Hall is a small public garden with a 'vue panoramique': a gentle panorama of venerable trees and the softly rolling countryside of the Perche.

The same forgivable exaggeration evidences itself in another road sign: 'Mortagne – le plus beau bourg de France'. That might be pushing it a bit, but it's certainly a charming little town, rich with old houses and the Church of St. Denis set in an area of echoing cobbled streets. The old market halls have been dashingly restored into a light and bright Tourist Information centre. Tourist info. is badly needed in this area, which local hoteliers grumble is poorly publicised. Certainly it seems little-known to the Brits, and that is a pity because it has much to offer. Not only is it a strategic staging-post on the way to the Loire, or Chartres, Brittany, Channel ports, but it has enough charm in its own right to merit a longer stay.

A pleasant excursion is to the La Trappe and Perche forests, divided by the river Avre, to the north-east of the town. Good picnicking here by one of the many lakes.

Another reason for a halt here is a delightful hotel and restaurant:-

➤ Hostellerie Genty Home
(HR)M *4 r. Notre Dame* *33.25.11.53* *Open every day* *EC, V*

This lucky F.E.3 find has proved as popular as I had hoped. The hard-working Mme De Gournay has endeared herself to readers by the warmth of her welcome and the good value she offers. Her compact establishment in an ancient stone house is squeezed into a side street parallel with the main square.

The Genty Home is a restaurant with rooms (four). They are extremely comfortably furnished, if on the small side, in the same style as the restaurant below, i.e. in the elaborate mock-Louis XV decor so beloved by French restaurateurs. Each has a shower, loo and basin and costs a modest 265f.

The dining-room is intimate and best by candle-light, when the chandeliers and boudoir-ish atmosphere look more appropriate than on a hot summer's day. That said, there is certainly no shortage of customers at lunch-time, especially on Mondays when all the other restaurants in the district shut up shop. Local business men are regular customers.

For 65f (another at 95f) the menu offers remarkable value, especially considering that it is served in a luxurious setting of sparkling glasses, dazzling napery and expensive china. One starter option is the hors d'oeuvres displayed in the window – over twenty different dishes to choose from. Main courses are getting more adventurous, with the use of oriental spices and recherché dishes like an osso bucco of fish! I advise sticking to the classics, and you can't go wrong. A good cheeseboard is included, and the sweet trolly is amply loaded. Service is pleasant and smiling. An arrow on all counts.

'The two days spent at the Genty Home were the most delightful of the whole holiday. We were charmed by the high bourgeoisie elegance of the decor and by Mlle Laetitia who welcomed us, served the meal and worked all hours. Good breakfast began each day well; superbly cooked and presented evening dinner completed it.' – Mary Shannock.

➤ Château des Carreaux
(H)M *Courgeoust* *33.25.02.00*

Listed as an annexe to the Genty Home, this elegant 18C château is five minutes' drive outside the town, set back from the RN 12.

Mme de Gournay has decorated the bedrooms in similar style, but here the elaboration seems more appropriate, since the rooms are spacious and gracious. There is a comfortable salon in which to sit, and green and leafy grounds in which to stroll. The proximity of the nationale does not intrude, and altogether the château is an extremely peaceful and comfortable alternative to the town Genty Home. Good value again at 295–365f for a double with bath, and arrowed accordingly.

Hotel du Tribunal
HRM   *4 pl. du Palais   33.25.04.77   EC, V*

A charming old stone building, both 13C and 18C, with an interior garden, set in a strikingly quiet square. I felt that recent 'improvements' to the decor have been unfortunate, and readers' reactions have been mixed. Rooms are 110–360f and menus start at 70f.

'We took one of the cheapest rooms in the renovated part above the dining-room and it was rather small and directly overlooked by an office. We moved to Room no. 1, which overlooked the courtyard and was excellent, with private bath, spacious, good bed and very comfortable – worth every bit of the extra. Food was exceptionally good. Basic menu included a help-yourself buffet hors d'oeuvre from which you could have made an entire meal, and a most delicious selection of desserts – candied fruit cream pud – yummy. Very good value indeed. Dining area in the bar rather gloomy, so we took breakfast elsewhere.' – Susan Leyden.

Map 6E   **MORTRÉE** 61500 Sées, Orne. 16 km S of Argentan on the D 198

In pleasantly hilly, intensely rural countryside, where the pace perceptibly slows down and a little diversion from a long drive seems a very good idea.

Le Chateau d'Ô
33.35.33.56

Everyone within striking distance of Mortrée should visit this chequered fairy-tale castle, rising from the waters of lake and wide, wide moat. It takes the strange name from the family of Jean d'Ô.

The inner courtyard is enclosed by three pavilions, one Gothic, one early Renaissance and one 18C, and a balustrade. You can tour the interior, but there's really not a lot to see. Better spend the time in the surrounding park, which is spacious and green – perfect for a picnic on a stone bench. Cl. Tues., visits from 2–5.30 p.m.

But if it's not that kind of weather, another excellent reason for a visit to Ô would be for its unusually good restaurant.

Restaurant de la Ferme d'Ô
(R)M   *33.35.35.27   Open year round, but telephone in advance if possible*

In the old stable wing a most appealing restaurant has been contrived, with cool stone-flagged floors, a log fire in winter and menus from 90f. Way above the usual tourist-attraction trash. Stop off for tea or coffee if it's not time for a tuck-in.

Just 4 km away is another beautiful chateau, **Médavy**. Far less grand than Ô, it was built of mellow stone in the 18C. Dominating the grounds are two impressive towers, one now a chapel, which are all that is left of a mediaeval fortress, all surrounded by a moat full of the fattest most complacent trout.

The chateau is still inhabited by the Médavy-Grancy family and is open to the public from 14/7 to 14/9, from 10–12 and 2–4.

Map 2B   **NÉGREVILLE** 50260 Bricquebec, Manche. 22 km SE of Cherbourg; 8 km W of Valognes

---

Turn off the D 13 at St. Joseph on the D 146 and follow the signs.

➤ **Le Mesnil Grand**
(HR)M   *33.95.09.54   Cl. Sun. p.m. and Mon.*

Don't even think of approaching Le Mesnil Grand from Valognes, as I did. I couldn't begin to explain the micro-lanes and villages I rushed through and back again, nor the number of times I stopped to ask, in order to find it tucked away in the kind of deepest countryside that is normal just off a Norman main road but inconceivable in England. All the more galling to find how easy it was to track it down from the other direction, a mere 15 minutes from the port.

By whichever route, it's worth the détour, just so long as utter peace and quiet and seclusion is what you're after.

It had been open only two months when I found it in June '89, with just three delightful bedrooms open for guests; 11 more are planned. It is run by a nice young couple, the Boekees. James is English and had been teaching in a hotel school; Pascale, French, has worked in leading hotels. Sickened with southern English prices, they bought a derelict farmhouse and gradually and painfully transformed it to the charmingly rustic, extremely comfortable hotel it is today.

The rooms are spacious, well-equipped, not at all plastic, with luxurious bathrooms. With breakfast for two, they cost a bargain 300f. Dinner in the elegant dining-room offers both traditional Normandy cooking and international dishes on menus at 95 and 120f.

I am confident this one will be a winner; arrowed accordingly.

Map 2H   **NEUFCHATEL-EN-BRAY** 76270 Seine-Mar. 36 km SE of Dieppe

Ⓣ *6 pl. Notre-Dame (June-Sept.)   35.93.22.96*   Ⓜ *Wed. and Sat. a.m.*

An unexciting town in the heart of the cream cheese country of the Bray. Neufchatel cheese has its own 'appellation d'origine', which insists that it can only be produced locally; the various farms produce it in different shapes and sizes. 10 km to the SW is the miraculous forest of Eawy (pronounced Eeahvee), the most beautiful and extensive

(16,500 acres) beech forest in Normandy, cut through by a straight divide, the Allée des Limousins. It covers a jagged crest, bordered by the Varenne and Béthune valleys, and makes a delightful excursion in this predominantly flat area.

There are two goodish restaurants, Les Airelles and the Grand Cerf, both with rooms, about which I have no information other than their prices – both in the S-M grade – but here is one satisfied customer:

Hotel du Lion d'Or
(HR)S   *17–19 pl. Notre Dame   35.94.77.94*

Rooms from 120f; menus from 65f.
'The hotel was good value and the staff were most helpful and particularly tolerant of our late arrival.' – Jonathan Matthews.
More reports needed.

Map 7F   **NOCÉ** 61340 Orne. 8 km E of Bellême on the D 203

 Tues.

Deep in the heart of the lush Perche countryside, near the forest of Bellême.

l'Auberge des Trois J
(R)M-L   *Grande Rue   33.73.41.03   Cl. Mon.; Tues. o.o.s.; Feb.; 1 week in Sept.   CB, AE*

What a bonus to find a restaurant of the quality of the Trois J in such deeply rural surroundings. Michelin thinks so too and has awarded a rosette, rare for the Orne département.

The Trois J are Father Joly and his two sons. The younger, Stephan, is a chef of outstanding talent. Catch him while he's young and you can afford his prices. The 110f midweek menu is outstanding value.

Their Auberge is an old Percheronne inn, beautifully restored to provide an elegant restaurant. Thierry, the older son, is a welcoming and efficient maitre d'., while Joly père looks after the admirable wine list.

Stephan's specialities show confidence for one so young – turbot with 'crêpes asiatiques', asparagus and langoustines stuffed into oursin shells, garnished with tiny deep-fried vegetables, plump poularde de Boissy (from a neighbouring farm) served as a ballotine stuffed with foie gras and truffles. Not exactly simple country fare. If all these novelties bewilder, plump for the menu dégustation at 200f, which for me included cucumber and salmon soup, hot oysters, lamb en croute and a 'corne d'abondance', which lived up to its name.

Map 3D   **NONANT** 14400 Bayeux, Calvados. 5 km SE of Bayeux

The hamlet of Nonant is in the triangle between the D 6 and N 13, in ridiculously rural countryside. I know it well, having recently been on the brink of investing in a stunning 18C house there (alas, the brink was as far as we got). The attractions were (and are) manifold. Just five minutes from Bayeux, no distance along the nationale to Caen, and yet in the kind of rusticity that is rare in England.

Mme Simand
La Poulinière   (C)M   *31.95.51.03*

'Madame Simand not only speaks immaculate English but delights in making you feel welcome. The main accommodation is based in a beautifully converted barn, where there are two apartments with shared bathroom/w.c. The barn sleeps a maximum of eight people and everything in it has been decorated with a great deal of thought and taste and is exceptionally clean. For b. and b. the charge was 130f single; 200f for a family of three. With the breakfast there was always a selection of beautiful home-made jams and marmalades.

Between Monday and Friday Mme Simand also prepares an excellent dinner, for 8, including apéritif, a bottle of wine and a four-course meal. We could find no fault with La Poulinière.' – P. Upton.

Map 3F   **NORVILLE** 76330 Notre Dame de Gravenchon, Seine-Mar. 45 km E of Le Havre

Just a name, high above the Seine on the D 428, 5 km SE of Lillebonne.

Auberge de Norville
(HR)S   *35.39.91.14*   Rest. cl. Fri., Sat. lunch; Jan.   V

A very useful stop, within easy striking distance of the port, in a peaceful setting, with surprising views of the river, and at modest un-touristy prices: 160–200f for a comfortable room, and menus from 70f. Its weekend closing times are a snag, but the Sunday opening is a rare bonus.

Readers have been well pleased with this recommendation, finding the interior a pleasant surprise; almost an arrow, but lacking recent recommendations.

'It has changed hands and is now run by M. et Mme Eliard. There are 10 bedrooms, 5 with shower on the south side, overlooking the Seine valley. The other five, on the road side, have no shower, with traffic noise in daytime but quiet at night. Rooms are small but adequate and the pleasant dining-room is well patronised. I enjoyed food and service, with ample choice. Norville is 40 minutes' drive from Le Havre.' – Lt. Col. G. C. D. Scott Lowe.

'A nice dining-room with the boats lit up as they travel down the

Seine in the middle distance. Large portions of pâté, salmon mousse, duck, veal, all tender and melting; followed by salad and a cheeseboard of mostly local cheeses, all well served and presented with subtle taste.' – Brian H. Cooke Smith.

Map 3G **NOTRE-DAME-DE-BONDEVILLE** 76150 Maromme, Seine-Mar. 7.5 km N of Rouen

---

Virtually a suburb of Rouen, but on the fringe of open country.

Les Elfes
(HR)S-M   35.74.36.21   303 r. des Longs Vallons   Cl. Tues. p.m.; Wed. p.m.; Sun. p.m.

A useful inexpensive stop if the thought of Rouen's traffic is intimidating. It's a modern Logis de France, spotlessly clean, hung about with pink geraniums.

It's always a good sign if the indication is that the establishment is a restaurant with rooms, rather than the other way round, because the Logis chain demand a minimum standard of cleanliness anyway, and you know you're going to get a good dinner thrown in. M. Deligne prides himself on his cooking, especially his seafood, and his menus from 80f are infinitely better than in most modest hotels. A giant vivier provides the cabaret while you're waiting for everything to be freshly cooked.

Map 5F **NOTRE-DAME-DE-COURSON** 14140 Livarot, Calvados. 10 km E of Livarot; 12 km W of Orbec on the D 4

Some of the most sensational scenery in the whole of Normandy is to be found in this little-known area, through which the river Touques twists its way south. I recommend following its course via the D 64. It is hilly, wooded countryside, with unexpected views in all directions of sleepy villages, church steeples, crumbling Norman barns – and little traffic. I strongly recommend a stop here, whether it be merely on the route south or for longer.

Hotel Château de Belleau
(HR)M   31.32.34.23

It should be longer if it's to be at Belleau, in order to appreciate the hotel's many virtues. I found it by accident, driving north and having discovered little of interest in the district – a gastronomic and hotel desert generally. I followed the sign and came across an eccentric, typically gallic, 19C, small, château, red brick, grey stone, slate roof, turreted, set in lovely grounds, backed by a lake.

It had only just opened, it was distinctly o.o.s. (and in this area that is no mean threat), but Mats Larsson, its friendly Swedish owner, was only too pleased to welcome me and show me his achievements.

They are considerable. These 19C châteaux dotted liberally about northern France can seem grim and daunting; here the furnishings have taken advantage of the light that floods in through the big windows, and the impression is cheerful rather than heavy. The decorating has been tastefully and luxuriously accomplished; the 10 rooms all have private bathrooms and there are comfortable lounges and a superbly panelled dining-room.

Food is important (not always the case in this type of hotel, which sometimes rely too much on the 'personal touch'.) The chef is a dab hand at transforming local ingredients into interesting dishes, and the Swedish penchant for all things fresh is evident.

A double room costs from 400–850f; the menu is 175f; breakfast is complimentary. For the standard on offer this is not expensive, and best of all the owners are trying (and succeeding) to please. An arrow and good wishes for success.

Map 1A   **OMONVILLE-LA-ROGUE** 50440 Beaumont Hague, Manche. 24 km W of Cherbourg on the coast road

---

This is an area of particularly pretty villages, reminiscent of Cornwall. Omonville is one such, with old stone houses in a narrow village street, and spilling over with flowers. It also has a little port, which I remember we were once only too pleased to discover, in a particularly unpleasant storm. Perhaps our relief at being able to step on terra firma, and then to have the good fortune to discover a little restaurant prepared to offer us succour, might have coloured my judgment then, regarding the Auberge du Port. As it has now changed hands and I approached it this time from the land, I can report more dispassionately:-

Auberge du Port
(R)S-M   *35.52.74.13   Cl. Mon.*

I suppose this is what it's still called – there's no name above the door and the car just says 'Bar-Restaurant'. Madame Colden has just taken over and no doubt will be sorting the matter out.

It's smarter than I remembered, with a vivier in the entrance. At lunch-time, mid-week, it was packed with business men, a surprise in their dark suits in this setting, hailing, I suppose, from the nuclear establishment nearby.

Strongly fishy, as you would expect, with some good à la carte suggestions and menus from 68f.

Map 5F **ORBEC** 14290 Calvados. 20 km SE of Lisieux

Ⓣ *r. Guillonière (May–Sept.) 31.32.87.15* Ⓜ *Wed.*

In one of the most attractive valleys of the Auge, Orbec is a lively little mediaeval town, full of character. The r. Grande is particularly colourful, with ancient wooden-gabled houses and glimpses of courtyards and gardens. In one of them Debussy was inspired to write 'Jardins sous la Pluie'.

This would make an excellent base from which to explore the Auge region, surrounded as it is by châteaux and manor-houses, some open to the public, some to be glimpsed down long avenues, mostly on minor roads, dominating tiny villages; some are well maintained, many are shabby and lead to surmise as to who can afford, or cannot afford, to live there. **Bellou**, **St Germain de Livet**, **Grandchamp**, the moated **Compesarte** and many others are all within an easy drive. The paper shop in the r. Grande has postcards of them all, and the friendly lady selling them advised us which ones to make for.

A pleasant little diversion is to the source of the Orbiquet; head south-east on the Vimoutiers road, then turn left onto the D 130 and D 130A to La Folletière-Abernon on the right bank of the river. Leave the car just before the bridge and follow the path to the spring, a perfect picnic situation.

Hotel de France
(HR)M *152 r. Grande 31.32.74.02 Cl. 15/12–15/1 CB*

Choose a room in the annexe for preference; these are light, bright and well fitted-out, at 320f. There are cheaper ones in the main hotel from 100f. The restaurant is convenient, if nothing else.

Au Caneton
(R)M-L *32 r. Grande 31.32.73.32 Cl. Mon. p.m.; Tues.; Feb. school holidays CB, AE, EC*

It was undoubtedly one of the most serious gastronomic tragedies to hit Calvados when the old Caneton, for forty years the favourite treat for locals and gourmets alike, closed down. Now it has risen again, under the patronage of Mme Tricot, who wisely has done little to change all the undoubted assets of the ancient, heavily beamed, tiny, and utterly charming restaurant.

Perhaps the menu is not quite so strongly orientated towards the restaurant's namesake as of yore, but duck certainly still features, along with lobster, pigeon, and other luxuries, simply cooked and well presented. Except on fête-days there is a 120f menu. Otherwise it is from 180f.

Map 4F   **OUILLY DU HOULEY** 14590 Moyaux, Calvados. 11 km NE of
Lisieux by N 13 and D 137

A hamlet (with a jokey unpronounceable name), delightfully lost in the green Norman countryside, which would make a rewarding excursion in every way.

Auberge de la Paquine
R(M)   *31.63.63.80   Cl. Tues.; Wed.; Feb.; 2/10–10/2   CB*

Unbeatable on a hot summer's day to eat in the flowery garden of this rustic auberge, at the edge of a little river. The simplicity does not extend to the food, except in price, when a mere 120f buys skilled interpretations by M. Champion of dishes like eels cooked with garlic and wrapped in cabbage leaves, fillet of beef with fresh herbs, peaches poached in wine with a sorbet based on St. Emilion.

Confirmations please for an arrow.

Map 4E   **OUISTREHAM-RIVA-BELLA** 14150 Calvados. 14 km N of Caen

---

Ⓣ *Jardins du Casino*   Ⓜ *Tues. at Ouistreham. 15 June – 31 August daily at Riva; 15 September – 14 June, Fri. at Riva.*

Since June 1944 the Côte de Nacre is probably better known for landings than mother-of-pearl. For those with memories of the drama as it unfolded, a visit to the Calvados beaches, Utah, Omaha, Gold, Juno and Sword, will be an illuminating pilgrimage; to post-war generations, here is history brought to life. To turn a corner in a sleepy Norman hamlet and find its square dominated by a souvenir tank makes the holidaymaker sit up and take notice.

The advent of the ferries has brought new life and prosperity to the erstwhile little fishing port, the Ouistreham part, at the mouth of the Caen canal. Its main square is lined with bars, cafés and restaurants, and hotels are busy building annexes to accommodate some of the new visitors. I find it still friendly and attractive, especially out of season, and look forward to a walk over the lock and along the canal path, or out towards the sea over the sand dunes. Along the front is a busy Friday market throughout the year – when local seafood stalls vie for attention with bargain-loaded clothes stands.

To the west it merges with Riva Bella, blessed with a wide sandy beach and popular with families at the bucket-and-spade stage. The seafront has little to recommend it, with a gaudy funfair in the summer months, but a few streets back it becomes the sedate Bvd. de la Mer, villa-lined residential, with all the shops concentrated on this one long street.

Few transient visitors bother to explore the 'bourg' of Ouistreham, a few km inland, which is a pity, because its 12C fortress church survived the devastation that removed so much of interest in the surrounding countryside, and it is well worth a visit to remark its ancient buttressed belfry and Gothic chancel.

The square outside is the scene of a Saturday market, which continues, as it has always done, to serve the locals not the tourists.

Normandie
(HR)M   31.97.57 71   ave. Michel-Cabieu   Cl. Sun. p.m.; Mon. o.o.s.; Jan.   AE, DC, EC, V

Christian Maudouit is looking very prosperous these days. He has seen his opportunity in Ouistreham's new-found celebrity to develop his little Norman-style hotel and restaurant into a three-forked Michelin establishment. (We all know what that means – the dining-room gets re-styled for a start.) Some readers have regretted his ambition, preferring the old style to the flossy menus and the increased prices – up to 290f.

The menu du terroir now costs 140f, but there is sometimes a menu Normand at 90f as an alternative. The quality is high and there are some interesting adaptations of local ingredients – a flan of Normandy mussels, free-range chicken cooked in cider and cream, local cheese served hot with a salad and Norman pears cooked in red wine.

The rooms have not changed. They are small but comfortable, with countrified white net curtains, and make a good overnight base at 220–280f.

Le Chalet
(H)S   74 ave. de la Mer, Riva Bella   31.97.13.06

The new owners, nice M. and Mme Fatta, have had to work very hard to cancel out an unfortunate inheritance left behind by the previous tenants, who allowed this once-favourite little hotel to deteriorate and disappointed many old and faithful customers. They are succeeding now, with a plan of restoration for all the bedrooms – good value at 150f for two, or 220f for a four-bedder – and a pleasant light and airy new breakfast room and bar downstairs. Ideal for an economical overnight stop or for a family holiday.

'I feel that you should reinstate the Chalet as a very useful, comfortable 2-star hotel, whose owners, a French couple, M. and Mme Fatta, were very attentive. He kept open until the early hours to receive late guests, who were all very satisfied with the place.' – A. E. Marsh.

M. Fatta has also bought a large house in Ouistreham (tel: 31.96.66.00), opposite the Normandie, which he uses as a pleasant annexe. Known as Le Chalut, it has ten rooms, similar to those at Le Chalet. One feels he is putting down firm roots in the community here and that an arrow for simple good value will not be far off.

L'Ambroisie
(H)M   59 r. E. Herbline   31.96.16.45   Open every day   CB

A lovely 18C stone house, set peacefully in a quiet area behind the town, recently restored by the owner of the Broche d'Argent hotel to provide ten comfortable and tasteful rooms. At 280–320f they represent, for me, the best proposition in town, but only one has a bath (the rest have luxury showers). No restaurant but a good breakfast for 30f.

Could be an arrow.

Map 5H   **PACY-SUR-EURE** 27120 Eure. 13 km SW of Vernon; 18 km E of Evreux

---

 Thurs

The river Eure is not very well known, overshadowed by its neighbour, the mighty Seine, but there are stretches of its banks that are well worth exploring, and the patches of rusticity here belie its proximity to the autoroute.

L'Etape
(HR)M   *32.36.12.77   Cl. 1/1–26/1   CB, EC*

You feel you're on a cruise as you dine in the salon, right on the water's edge. There is a pleasant green garden too. Mme Angot has nine rooms, at 97–191f, which are really accessories to the restaurant, but make excellent, inexpensive, overnight bases. During the week there is a bargain 87f menu; otherwise it's 142 and 201f, with straightforward dishes like rabbit stews and poached salmon.

   'Pleasant-looking and friendly old place, run by a nice family offering friendly service, and speaking English. The suite with one double and two single beds plus bathroom, and views up and down river, at 313f seems to be an excellent overnight bargain for a family. But you'd have to ring up and book from England. The food was copious and unpretentious.' – Robin Totton.

Map 3E   **PENNEDEPIE** 14600 Honfleur, Calvados. 1 km from Honfleur

---

Take a pleasant drive along the delightful Côte de Grace, west of Honfleur, to find:

Moulin St-Georges
(R)M   *31.89.12.00   Cl. 1/12–15/12; 15/1–10/2*

A faded old one-time mill at the side of the road, with a good local reputation for honest value. Particularly popular for Sunday lunch-time family blow-outs.

   'Once again we had an excellent meal, selected for the extensive table d'hôte menu. The service was both good and attentive.' – Claude Landes.

Menus from 65–149f make a pleasant change from Honfleur prices.

Map 2B   **LA PERNELLE** 50630 Quettehou, Manche. 32 km SE of Cherbourg; 10 km S of Barfleur

Inland the north-eastern Cotentin countryside swiftly reverts from stark coast to Norman lushness. The valley of the Saire is typically green and flower-studded, and the D 125 from Valcanville to La Pernelle is especially pretty.

Take a left turn from this road to the hamlet of La Pernelle, where a patchwork panorama unfolds far below the bluff, commanded by a dolls-house Mairie. A viewing table indicates Gatteville lighthouse to the left, Grandcamp cliffs to the right. On a clear day you can see for ever, or at least to the Percée Point, the islands of Tatihou and St. Marcouf and La Hougue.

Le Panoramique
(R)S   *33.54.13.79   Cl. Sun. p.m.; Mon.*

A very smart bar/crêperie; one is tempted to suggest that had it been situated in such a beauty spot in Britain, a certain amount of cashing-in would be inevitable. Not so here. Apart from simple snacks, it specialises in a generous plâteau de fruits de mer and lobster from local pots. Readers have found both the service and the food live up to the view.

Map 4E   **PIERREFITTE-EN-AUGE** 14130 Pont l'Evêque, Calvados. 5 km S of Pont l'Evêque

Turn west off the D 48 south of Pont l'Evêque on the D 280A, following the sign: 'La route des Douets'. Douets are the pays d'Auge streams, the Saulnier, the Houlbec, the Yvie, the Calonne, and the Chaussey, that emanate from the river Touques, and add still more character to the delightfully rural Auge country, unbelievably just a few km either side of the autoroute. Their characters are as variable as the hilly/wooded, open/cultivated, almost undiscovered countryside they traverse: at Clarbec the stream tumbles in a mini-cascade; at St. Hymer it fills the village lavoirs. A few hours spent following the trail will be well spent and long-remembered.

A visit to Pierrefitte, which must qualify as one of the prettiest villages in Normandy, is alone good reason enough for the detour from the hectic motorway so near and yet so far, but there is another justification:-

Les Deux Tonneaux
(R)S   *31.64.09.31   Cl. Mon.*

Hard to describe Les Deux Tonneaux. It describes itself as 'Café-Collation, Tabac-Epicerie', and goes on to insist 'Une Halte en famille qu'il faut faire.' I'd agree with that one. It's the kind of totally unspoiled, temps-jadis, over-the-top-picturesque village bar/bistro that it's now hard to find anywhere in the North of France, let alone so near the tourist beat. The two barrels from which the café gets its name dispense good farm cider, one sweet, one dry, for 12f a pichet, so you could just make this a liquid refreshment stop; but I strongly advise you to linger, either in the dark and cosy interior or on the 'terrasse panoramique', in order to try – and again I cannot better their description – 'les solides collations du pays'. All the ingredients come from local farms.

An omelette made from the eggs of 'poulets libérés' arrives the colour of Bird's custard and stuffed with cheese or ham. They determinedly stick to what they can do best – rillettes, salad, cheese, crêpes, tripes. Order ahead if you want a plainly-roasted farm chicken, plumply yellow, or try their home-smoked ham. Crêpes are reckoned to be the best in the region, so this is the perfect choice for a lunch-time escape, even if only to read the hilarious English menu.

An arrow for a truly individual discovery. There are a couple of chambres d'hôte in the village, about which I should particularly like some news.

Map 7B   **PONTAUBAULT** 50220 Ducey, Manche. 7 km S of Avranches on the N 175

---

13 Assiettes
(HR)S   *33.58.14.03   Cl. Wed. o.o.s.; 15/11–15/3*

1 km N of Pontaubault on the Nationale, this motel Logis de France on the main tourist route to Mont St. Michel is an obvious and well-known overnight halt. It seemed to me that they have a lot of practice in turning people away. If you do get in, you are likely to be satisfied, judging from readers' reactions.

The thirteen dishes of the hotel's name are the traditional ones served at old banquets in the region. The food today maintains the tradition of being copious and good, on menus from 50f, a price that has not changed much since the first edition of F.E.3. 35 chalets offer a peaceful night, from 115–200f.

Map 3F   **PONT AUDEMER** 27500 Eure. 52 km SE of Le Havre; 52 km W of Rouen

---

(T) *pl. Maubert   32.41.08.21* (M) *Mon., Fri.*

Viewed from the ring road, Pont Audemer is a disaster of dusty concrete, railway sidings, and traffic jams. You must penetrate into its ancient heart to appreciate the way it used to be.

Here rivulets from the river Risle thread their way beneath old bridges; beamy ancient houses overhang the water. There's really only one main street, the rue de la République, which closes to traffic on Mondays for the general market and on Friday for the marché maraîcher. It's probably the best in the whole area, and certainly the most colourful. The stallholders take particular pride in laying out their wares – pulses laid in mosaics of green flageolets, white haricots, orange lentils, all manner of dried fruits – fatter prunes, moister apricots, healthier figs than ever seen back home. And there are flowers everywhere – unsophisticated childish bundles of pink daisies and wallflowers, marigolds, narcissus, hyacinths, and tiny wild daffodils in season.

The church, St. Ouen, overlooks all this activity and is at hand for the headscarfed matrons to drop in for a quick word after their shopping baskets are full. Inside is some magnificent stained glass, some Renaissance, some Max Ingrand.

Well-served though the town may be by pâtisseries and charcutiers, there is unfortunately little choice of either hotel or restaurant. We all miss the admirably cheap little Hotel de Risle, and so far no obvious substitute has presented itself.

Auberge du Vieux Puits

(H)M(R)L   *6 r. Notre Dame du Pré   32.41.01.48   Cl. Mon. p.m.; Tues.; 2/7–10/7; 16/12–17/1   CB, EC*

This enchanting 17C inn, which takes its name from the old well

Auberge du Vieux Puits   187

described by Flaubert in *Madame Bovary* (when it was in the Hôtel du Cygne in Rouen), continues to charm its many faithful British clients. A real haven of calm from the ring road that incongruously passes its ancient door, it is ridiculously picturesque inside and out. The dining-room is furnished with sparkling copper, lots of flowers, log fires, the garden with welcome shade, flowers, and white tables and chairs for summer sipping.

Patron Jacques Folz sticks with his well-tried, well-approved favourites, recipes that have been stars on the menu since his father's time, – duck with bitter cherries, roast pigeon, and Trout Bovary, with champagne. He has little choice – his clients would rebel if they did not find them here. But nowadays the young chef, Denis Geoffroy, puts new life into their preparation, and if it is possible to improve on what many considered perfection, he has done so. Menus start at 155f (mid-week lunch); otherwise it's 250f or la carte. He now has six new bedrooms, all with bath, which are more spacious and comfortable than the previous eight which are only used in summer. None of them is big, but the price is right – 150–360f.

Generations of Englishmen have been more than satisfied with the Auberge and its arrow is for long-term service.

'Our stay here was most enjoyable and M. Folz guided us courteously through his delicious menu .... Excellent value, even if, inevitably, the other guests were all English.' – E. J. Ellis.

Map 6D   **PONT D'OUILLY** 14690 Calvados. 48 km S of Caen; 18 km W of Falaise

---

Ⓜ *Sun.*

In the heart of the craggy Suisse Normande, but unfortunately also in the path of the Falaise Gap devastation, so that almost the entire town was wiped out. The old market 'halles' survived and lend a certain character to the centre.

➤ **Auberge St. Christophe**
(HR)S   *at St. Christophe, 2 km N   Cl. Sun.; 21/1–17/2; 30/9–27/10   CB, AE, EC*

On the D 23, this little country inn has won universal praise from readers who looked for and found simple comfort, good food and realistic prices. The seven bedrooms are decorated in country style, bright and cheerful, and mostly looking away from the road and onto a pleasant rear garden. I liked the young owners, Gilles and Francoise Lecoeur, and thought his cooking was way above average in this price bracket.

'The bedrooms, like the whole of the Auberge, were extremely clean and very modern, but a little cramped; during the visit, the only occupants were British. The food we thought magnificent and Gilles Lecoeur is a first-class chef.' – Mr. and Mrs. J. Suffield.

'We cannot imagine anyone being disappointed in any way. The food was so good that we never found it worthwhile to venture from

the menu pensionnaire. The extensive local patronage proves how good an establishment the Lecoeurs have built up.' – Harold Towse.

An arrow for the value (rooms 230f, demi-pension at 250–350f obligatory in season, menus otherwise from 80f), good food and welcome.

Hotel du Commerce
(HR)S   *31.69.80.16   Cl. Sun. p.m.; Mon. o.o.s.*

A modern Logis in the main square, with an excellent local reputation. Menus from 60f; clean and wholesome rooms 100–250f.

'Our room at the back of the hotel had a beautiful view over the hills of the Suisse Normande, and the room itself was clean and adequate, with use of a hot shower nearby. We ate in the hotel and were extremely impressed – the best meal of our stay in France. We chose the 65f menu and had a superb four-course meal. House red wine was very palatable, especially at 25f a bottle. Local French families were eating here and I feel it warrants your continued praise, especially for such good value.' – Mrs. Lynden R. Cooper.

'We were well satisfied. The rooms are small but very comfortable, and there was a huge bath towel, though the shower cabinet took up a lot of the bedroom space. If anyone is a connoisseur of French hotel wallpaper, then this is the place to stay. The food was excellent and the second-price menu was ample, with a superb cheeseboard and reasonably priced wines. It's a very friendly place and would get an arrow in my book for its atmosphere and efficiency.' – David Dunham.

All that a simple French country inn should be, and arrowed accordingly, with the proviso that you should ask for a room at the rear (square can be noisy).

Yet another option in this thrice-blessed town:-

Hotel-Restaurant de la Place
(HR)S   *31.69.40.96   Cl. Wed. o.o.s.*

'Thanks to the Hotel de Commerce up the road being closed (le lundi), we discovered the above. Very good food and accueil. Small dining-room, check cloths, etc., obviously popular with French – unpretentious, friendly. A few tables and chairs outside, opposite the old market hall. Bedrooms, up two flights, have basin and bidet, those on first floor have bath or shower; all clean and adequate. Our excellent lunch for two, including cider and coffee, came to 71f.' – Mrs. D. Court.

Well worth investigating I should have thought.

Map 4E   **PONT L'EVÊQUE** 14130 Calvados. 48 km SE of Caen

Ⓣ *Mairie   31.64.12.77* Ⓜ *Mon.*

Not my favourite town, since the lorry-ridden main road is frenetic and dusty and the old timbered houses that once gave it some character are falling into ruins.

It is sad to see what was once the old 16C staging-post, the Aigle d'Or, crumbling behind its grimy facade. Chief claim to fame for the town must now be its cheese.

Auberge de la Touques

(R)M *pl. de l'Eglise* 31.64.01.69 *Cl. Mon. p.m.; Tues.; 4/12–18/11; 3/1–27/1* CB, AE, EC

A traditional Norman inn, facing the river Touques, serving traditional Norman food, like veal vallée d'Auge, tripes à la mode de Caen, andouillette cooked in cider. The patron, M. Froger, used to be a pâtissier, so you can rely on good desserts. Menus from 90f. Popular with locals for Sunday lunch, so make sure of a table by booking.

Map 7A   **PONTORSON** 50170 Manche. 22 km W of Avranches

Ⓣ *pl. Église (in season)* 33.60.20.65 Ⓜ *Wed.*

Right on the Brittany border and a popular overnight stopping-place. It's just one main street really, with some useful stocking-up shops, and a square centred on Notre Dame, a church said to have been founded in the 11C by William the Conqueror in gratitude to the Virgin for having saved his army from the Couësnon quicksands.

Montgomery

(HR)M *13 r. Couesnon* 33.60.00.09 *Cl. Tues. p.m. and Wed. o.o.s.; 23/10–24/11; Feb. school hols.* AE, DC, EC, V

The ancient home of the Counts of Montgomery. Lovely polished wood staircase, flowers, terrace, elegant dining-room make a lunch-time stop here a more-than-welcome break in a long journey. Most of the bedrooms overlook the garden and do not suffer from the main street traffic. The rooms have been modernised to a generally high standard of comfort; demi-pension is now obligatory, at 216–309f per person.

The food is said to be better than ever, and the patron M. Le Bellegard goes out of his way to please his clientele. Menus from 92f, and you should certainly book at busy times. A few more reports please for this potential arrow.

Le Bretagne

(HR)M *59 r. Couesnon* 33.60.10.55 *Cl. Tues. lunch; Mon.; 15/10–1/2* CB, AE, DC, EC

Not so obviously picturesque and historically interesting as its neighbour, but still pretty good news. The son of the house, aged 21, has recently revitalised the cooking, adding lightness and originality to the strictly conventional regional cooking. Menus start at 60f and the rooms (uninspected) are from 150–250f.

Map 3G **PONT ST-PIERRE** 27360 Eure. 21 km SE of Rouen

 Sat.

The scenery around Amfreville, with its great locks dividing the tidal from the fluvial Seine, is particularly attractive. Here is the **Côte des Deux Amants**, a lofty spur overlooking not only the Seine but the valleys of the Andelle and Eure. The two lovers in question were Caliste, daughter of the Baron of St-Pierre, and Raoul, a humble peasant. The baron decreed that in order to prove his determination to marry Caliste, Raoul must run to the top of the escarpment with Caliste in his arms, without pausing once for breath. The good news was that the handsome young man achieved his target, the bad that he dropped dead from exhaustion, and that Caliste had no alternative, in the best romantic tradition, but to die beside him.

Put all thoughts of tragedy aside, though, because this is a spot to contemplate all the joys of nature rather than its sadnesses. In the village of St-Pierre, a few km to the north, is:

La Bonne Marmite
(HR)M   *32.49.70.24   Cl. Sun. p.m. o.o.s.; Sat. lunch; 24/7–11/8; 20/2–10/3   AE, DC, EC, V*

Readers have approved of this old coaching inn in the centre of the town.

'We would definitely recommend a visit. Our room was comfortable and well furnished and the food was outstanding.' – A. J. Cooper.

'Our room cost 320f, and the cheapest menu was 165f, but it was a very enjoyable luxury on our last night in France.' – Kenneth Peters.

There are nine rooms altogether, from 295–385f; I had heard local rumours that the food wasn't as good as it used to be, but there is no dissension about the wine list, which is superb. Menus from 135–295f.

Map 3A **PORTBAIL** 50580 Manche. 45 km SW of Cherbourg; 10 km S of Carteret

---

 Tues.

An enchanting village, full of character, with wide chestnutted square, two ancient churches, a Gallo-Roman baptistery, and incomparable sandy beach.

Turn left before the old bridge for a glorious walk along the estuary, animated with wild life, and the perfect picnic destination, or cross the bridge, past little sailing boats galore, to find a private stretch of the sands.

Alas, the only hotel in the place, **Le Galiche** in the square, has been firmly given the thumbs-down by readers, even allowing for its cheapness, so there is, strangely, no recommendable accommodation in the town. (If you know different, please say.)

La Fringale is an atmospheric café-restaurant near the bridge, good for a drink outside or modest meal in its dim interior, but the nearest to a first-hand report is:

'Lively and clearly very popular with the locals, looked to be serving generous and delicious portions, judging by what we saw of the diners eating al fresco. Les Pecheurs gets a firm "thumbs down" from all of us.' – Commander Hugh Edleston R. N.

More reports welcome.

Map 3C   **PORT EN BESSIN** 14520 Calvados. 9km N of Bayeux

Ⓜ *Sun.*

The most attractive little fishing port on the Bessin coast, contrasting with the landing beaches on either side. Drive to it, via the D 60, through a lush green countryside, an altogether pleasant diversion from the more cultural attractions of Bayeux.

The fishing fleet pulls up along the quays of the deep inlet of the harbour, and it is most agreeable to stroll along the edge peering down into the holds of the colourful boats and checking on the catch. Continue further out to sea, to the end of the jetties, for a real head-clearer gulp of ozone, or climb up the cliff path to the old blockhouse for a good view of the harbour.

There are plenty of cafés for refreshment, some good fish restaurants, to justify the excursion, and a superb butcher, M. Criquet, selling the best charcuterie in the district.

La Foncée
(R)M   *12 r. Michel Lefournier   31.21.71.66*

An attractively intimate little restaurant in a back street near the port, specialising in locally caught fish, cooked by chef-patron Bernard Lechanoine. Menus from 85f.

La Chenevière
(HR)L   *1.5km S of Port en Bessin by the D6   31.21.47.96   Cl. 20/12–1/3   Rest. cl. Mon. o.o.s.*

Opened in 1988, La Chenevière will, I believe, come high on the list of luxury hotel favourites just as soon as news of its attractions spreads. Unlike other 4-star establishments situated in formerly glorious 18C châteaux, which have split up the lovely old rooms with cardboard partitions and generally have scant respect for the building's natural elegance, the owners of La Chenevière have not been greedy, but left the proportions of only fifteen bedrooms as they were originally, furnishing them with bright and cheerful fabrics, and covering the floors with polish and rugs rather than nylon wall-to-wall. The result is all airiness and light.

The food is sophisticated, but not pretentious – the 150f lunchtime menu, for example, consisted of oysters/smoked salmon terrine; duck/seafood cooked in a Noilly Prat sauce, and a choice of good desserts –

and the carte is admirably concise. Service both in the dining-room and in the hotel is efficient and caring.

Not cheap, alas, but I think good value for the high standards on offer. The rooms are 550–950f, and breakfast is a hefty 45f on top. You could make a preliminary recce by opting for an o.o.s. inclusive weekend for 1810f per person.

I look forward to some enthusiastic reports, before the award of an arrow.

Le Vauban
(R)S-M   *6 r. du Nord   31.21.74.83*

Tucked away behind the Hotel Marine, and more popular with the locals than with the tourists. The seafood of course is the thing to come here for, and a modest plateful of moules would make a good cheap lunch. Menus from 60f.

'We found it seven years ago, but the same couple still run it, with high standards and good fresh French fish cooking – plump fresh oysters etc. But ask for the sauce to be served separately!'

La Marie du Port
(R)S   *Quai Felix Faure   31.21.72.45   Cl. Sun. p.m.; Mon.*

A friendly little bar with restaurant on the first floor and tables on the pavement for summer dégustations. Seafood again, 'en directe du bâteau à votre table'. I believe them. Menus start at 58f. On the 86f version we ate oysters, lotte, cheese, salad and pudding, all good news.

Map 1A   **PORT RACINE** Manche, 50440 St-Germain-des-Vaux. 29 km W of Cherbourg

---

A tiny bay within a bay: 'Le plus petit port de France' proclaims the sign. High above it, with the best site of any hotel in the peninsula is:

L'Erguillère
(HR)M   *33.52.75.31   Cl. 15/11–15/3; Sun. p.m. and Mon.*

The view from the terrace is a wonder of sands and cliffs and green Norman countryside, with dramatic rocks out at sea when the tide recedes.

It has long been a favourite with the Germans and French as well as the Brits, and there are only ten rooms, so book well ahead. Nothing much seems to have changed in many years. The rooms are more pleasant and comfortable than large and luxurious, relying on the fabulous view for impact, but their prices have not increased horrifically since F.E.3. Then the most expensive was 247f. Now it is 272f. The restaurant is relatively expensive, with menus from 135–180f, but its local popularity for a Sunday lunch seafood treat augurs well.

Map 6D **PUTANGES-PONT-ECRÉPIN** 61210 Orne. 17 km SW of Falaise

Ⓜ *Thurs.*

Nice little twin towns of Putanges and Pont Ecrépin connected by a modern bridge (replacing the mediaeval one blown up in 1944) spanning the willow-fringed river Orne. The market on its banks has taken place there for over 400 years.

A few kilometres outside is the extensive Lac de Rabodanges, where you can bathe, picnic, take refreshment at a restaurant on the water's edge and mock the amateur windsurfers and water skiers.

➤ **Hotel Lion Verd**
(HR)S   *33.35.01.86   Cl. Fri. p.m. o.o.s.; 23/12–31/1   AE, EC, V*

A popular and well-documented Logis, so necessary to book well in advance. One reader has had problems over having his reservation honoured.

It's not surprising that Lion Verd is so well esteemed. It must be one of the most agreeable little hotels in the area, with gravelled terrace overlooking river, pleasant dining-room with above-average choice of menu – cheapest is 50f. Rooms are bright and cheerful, but regrettably refurbished not in country style but in fierce vinyls. A good-sized double with bathroom costs 250f; cheapest is 80f.

This is not the most recent report in my file of approving letters, but quote it because the writer is a respected restaurateur and might be expected to know a thing or two about the business:

'Once past the rather formidable presence of Madame, Le Lion Verd had many pleasant surprises. I could hardly believe that my wife and I could enjoy a room with bath, and our three children an adjoining room, all clean and well kept, for the princely sum of 202f. And that the prices of the menus should be equally modest. The service was too fast for the food to have been cooked to order but then what can you expect? It was very acceptable, and all menus contained the incomparable French frites and the delectable bread 'à volonté'. – Derek Grossman.

An arrow for good value in an attractive touring area.

Map 2A **QUERQUEVILLE** 50460 Manche. 9 km W of Cherbourg

Few passengers from the ferry discover Querqueville, a turning off the main road onto the D 45. I am always keen to find alternatives to staying in the ferry ports themselves, within easy reach but without the noise and expense, and so was pleased to have this recommendation, as yet unchecked.

Le Quervière
(HR)S   *17 r. Réné-Fouquet   33.03.35.84*

> *'We have stayed here several times and M. and Mme Laisney always make us most welcome. A comfortable double room costs 160f.'*
> Not a lot to go on, I know, so further reports would be particularly welcome.

Map 2B   **QUETTEHOU** 50630 Manche. 28 km E of Cherbourg; 10 km W of Barfleur

---

(T) *pl. Mairie   33.43.63.21* (M) *Tues.*

> Take the D 26 south off the D 901 towards St. Vaast, or follow the little D 120 along the valley of the Saire. Either way will lead through green, intensely rural countryside. Do visit the picturebook village of Le Vast, with the river flowing through, and call in at the well-known boulangerie there, where Madame Thonine serves her famous brioche. A local resident told me that he really prefers the other boulangerie in the village, but is too scared of Madame Thonine to take his custom elsewhere. Those without problematic local associations might like to see if he is right.
> The village of Quettehou has a wide central market-place and is the everyday shopping venue for the many gîtes in the district. Several regular visitors have recommended:

La Flambée
(R)S

> Good-value family food, well cooked and served with a smile. Menus from 55f.

La Chaumière
(HR)S   *33.54.14.94   Cl. Wed. o.o.s.i. 25/10–5/11*

> Opposite, larger, better known. Menus from 55–160f.
> *'The hotel side has been developed recently by the addition of six double bedrooms, all with full bathroom. While the rooms are scrupulously clean and very comfortable, it is the restaurant which is the main attraction. M. Orange is an imaginative and gifted chef, who leaves the management side to his wife and daughter. We stuck to the cheapest menu, which gave such a choice that, had we stayed for a week, we could have had three different dishes each night. 6 local oysters, clams in garlic butter, pâtés and mousses, then coq au vin, gigôt d'agneau (both particularly well cooked). There were five fish choices fresh from the port – sole, John Dory, skate, monkfish or salmon – the skate was excellent. We stayed at La Chaumière for four*

nights, and ate sumptuously. Our total bill for three, including enjoyable demands upon the bar, was 291f.' – M. George Lloyd.

Map 5B **QUETTREVILLE-SUR-SIENNE** 50660 Manche. 10 km S of Coutances

---

 Sat

On the N 971, a hamlet

Auberge de la Tournée
(HR)M   *33.47.62.91   Cl. Mon. o.o.s.; Sun.; 25/9–9/10; 26/2–17/3   EC, V*

No feedback whatsoever about this nice old-fashioned Logis, which is surprising because it is peacefully situated just outside a big town and convenient for the Brittany route. Very popular for local celebrations. The chef-patron Gilbert Deslands has become somewhat of a local celebrity by winning regional competitions for his specialities, such as snails in puff pastry, local salmon and home-made blackcurrant gâteau. His wine list is reasonable and his menus start at 80f. I have still not inspected the ten rooms, but they cost from 130–160f and all reports would be most welcome.

Map 1G **QUIBERVILLE** 76860 Ouville-la-Rivière, Seine-Mar. 16 km W of Dieppe

---

An unlovely stretch of coast, crowded in summer, with souvenir stalls dominant, but we enjoyed watching the fish being sold from fishing boats dragged up to the roadside, still alive and kicking in the housewives' baskets. With Dieppe's hotel shortcomings, this would certainly make a practical and stress-free alternative.

l'Huitrière
(HR)S-M   *35.83.02.96   Cl. Sun. p.m.; Fri. o.o.s.; 15/12–20/1   EC, V*

A spruce modern Logis, with surprisingly smart dining-room. It lost its Michelin red R, but still has 65f menus, featuring, naturally enough, lots of local fish. The bedrooms cost 150–260f, mostly with balconies overlooking the sea. The general impression is of a well-run and immaculate hotel.

'We confirm your opinion of the restaurant and the 90f menu. The double room had a sea view from the balcony, toilet, shower and, unfortunately, a TV, for 170f. Clean, simple and very convenient for Dieppe. The chef, M. Lapointe, was particularly friendly, as were three local fishermen in the bar.'

Map 2B   **QUINÉVILLE** 50310 Montebourg, Manche. 22 km E of
Valognes; 40 km SE of Cherbourg

From St. Vaast down to Carentan, including the landing beaches, the
coastline is flat, dreary and mostly badly-developed, with low-grade
caffs and no accommodation. Quinéville itself is no exception,
featuring sand dunes, a parking lot, a few deserted beach huts and a
habitually shuttered café.

King James II wept here in 1692, when he saw his last hope of
regaining the English throne literally go up in smoke: his allies in their
French ships were intercepted off Barfleur by an Anglo-Dutch force and
annihilated, in the four-day battle of La Hougue. He is said to have
stayed at:

Le Château de Quinéville
(HR)M   *33.21.42.67   Cl. 1/1–20/3; rest. cl. lunch 1/10–31/12   CB*

Even when I first found the château and described it as in need of both
a coat of paint and a hard-working gardener, F.E.3 readers loved it.
Today they would love it even more. The imposing 18C building now
stands in manicured lawns, with roses softening the grey stone walls,
the lake is well-groomed and there are plans to arrange boat trips on
the little river.

Chateau de Quinéville

The two nice ladies who run the establishment, Mlle Regnault and Mme Lemaire, make their guests welcome and comfortable in well-furnished rooms with lovely views over the green and peaceful countryside, at a well-spent 300–330f. Meals are served in the elegant dining-room, drinks on the terrace overlooking the lake. The garden supplies fresh vegetables and herbs for the table. Demi pension is obligatory in season, at 460–490f per person. Menus from 180f including wine.

Arrowed for comfort, style and position.

Map 2G   **RAINFREVILLE** 76730 Seine-Mar. 20 km SW of Dieppe

---

Turn off the D 925 west of Dieppe at Ouville-la-Rivière onto the D 152, pretty minor road leading to the middle of nowhere. At Rainfreville look for the D 270 on the left; the farmhouse is on the corner.

➤ **Le Clos Cacheu**
(C)L   *35.06.10.99*

The young proprietors, English Angela Stewart and French Gilbert Bankual, invested in this typical 18C Norman farmhouse a couple of years ago, with the lovely idea of guiding English prospective purchasers through the tangles of house-buying in France, while staying as p.g.s. in Clos Cacheu. Thanks to a Wish You Were Here programme, the p.g. operation developed to such an extent that the property side has faded away. They offer such a good deal to their guests that you have to be quick off the mark to book one of their four comfortable bedrooms, all with private bath.

Gilbert is a wonderful cook, with competition successes behind him, so the evening meal is all part of this highly recommended deal. For 420f for two people you get dinner, b. and b., the former taken with the owners and other guests.

There are all kinds of enterprises going on here – courses in music and cooking in the summer and involvement in many local activities. Gilbert and Angela are exceptionally enterprising and hard-working hosts and I guarantee a stay in their superbly renovated farmhouse will be a winner.

An arrow of course.

Map 6E   **RÂNES** 61150 Écouché, Orne. 20 km SW of Argentan

Ⓣ *in the Mairie* Ⓜ *Sat.*

A useful staging-post on the route south.

Hotel St. Pierre
(HR)S   *6 r. de la Libération   33.39.75.14   Rest. cl. Fri. p.m. o.o.s.   AE, DC, EC, V*

A modern Logis de France, stone façade, geraniums in window-boxes,

red iron tables outside, friendly patrons. 160–270f. Menus from 65f.
*'M. and Mme Delaunay are doing a good job; we were entirely
satisfied with both room and restaurant.'* – Keith J. Haldane.

Map 2B   **RÉVILLE** 50760 Barfleur, Manche. 32 km E of Cherbourg; 3 km
N of St. Vaast

Au Moine de Saire
(HR)S   *33.54.46.06*   *Cl. 12/11–31/12. Rest. cl. Sun. p.m.; Fri. o.o.s.*   *EC, V, P*

On the corner of the D 1, the Barfleur road, the centre of the village.
    I wrote in F.E.3 that only the French knew about the Saire Monk,
while the Brits all flocked to St. Vaast, but judging by the letters of
approval since then, this is no longer the case. Many readers have
been well pleased with the value here, often comparing it favourably
with its better-known neighbour.
    The twelve country-style bedrooms cost from 130f to 220f with bath,
and you can opt for twin beds if you wish. Meals in the charming
dining-room start at 60f.

Mme Réné Fouace
(C)S   *3 r. Guillame Fouace*   *33.54.48.75*   *Open year round by reservation*

Madame Fouace's farmhouse is a substantial creeper-covered building,
backed with barns and outbuildings, on the road to the Pointe. Her
bedrooms are comfortable and cheap – 130f for two including
breakfast.
    Bearing in mind the proximity of the good beaches, the village,
Cherbourg, and all the fascinations of this part of the Cotentin, I call
this a good deal.

Map 4F   **LA RIVIÈRE-THIBOUVILLE** 27550 Nassandres, Eure. 14 km NE
of Bernay

The river Charentonne, a tributary of the Risle, winds swiftly through
its damp-grassed valley, its teeming fish providing diligent French
anglers with ample reward for their perseverance. Local hostelries are
not slow to profit from this abundance and fresh fish features strongly
on their menus. For non-anglers, the area provides plenty of
opportunity for enjoyment in exploring the several Risle tributaries, in
country green with beech and studded with Norman castles and
churches.
    Unfortunately, La Rivière-Thibouville, looking so promising on the

map, straddling the streams, proves disappointing in reality. Sugar-beet mills dominate the little town, but it would make a good centre from which to spin off in exploration.

Soleil d'Or
(HR)M-S   *32.45.00.08   Cl. Wed. o.o.s.; Feb.   EC, V*

Having been put off by a less-than-warm reception, I perhaps dismissed the hotel somewhat cursorily in F.E.3., and was reproached accordingly:

'The sugar-beet factory cannot be seen from the hotel and certainly doesn't mar the other attractive properties and roads. We were in the newer part and it was not noisy at all; very few vehicles were on the road and the only noises came from animals and birds in the surrounding woods. The garden was well maintained and completed a very pleasant setting. The menu was excellent, offering at least four choices in each of four courses.' – Mrs. Yvonne Richards.

'Most luxurious bathroom of the tour, no problem with traffic noise, and pleasant views only over lawn and river ... but no feeling of real humanity, both under-manageress in reception and waitress were equally po-faced, as were the manager and the chef. They didn't even smile when the chef's poodle bit me. The 85f menu was pretentious and generally disappointing.' – Robin Totton.

I leave my readers to make their own minds up. Rooms are 160–280f and meals start at 83f.

Map 3H   **ROSAY-SUR-LIEURE** 27790 Lyons-la-Forêt, Eure. 6 km SW of Lyons-la-Forêt by the D 321

Deep in the forest.

Château de Rosay
(H)M   *CB*

An elegant Louis XIII château of rose-pink brick, offering many a rural blessing – total calm, apart from the rooks nesting in the ancient trees, the sound of water over the weir, and, if you're unlucky, a noisy wedding party. The rooms are spacious (250f) and the suites are even more so (400f). At these prices you must expect a slightly amateur approach and no slick service. There is no restaurant except for groups, which is a pity, but there are plenty of local eating possibilities

---

Map 3G   **ROUEN** 76000 Seine-Mar. 87 km E of Le Havre

Ⓣ *25 pl. Cathédrale*   Ⓜ *Tues., Wed., Fri., Sat.*

Rouen can be all things to all men. It is a year-round delight and an

Le Gros Horloge

ideal choice for a winter break. I would rate it No. 1, in fact, because of the diversity of treats there – the three wonderful churches, the Musée des Beaux Arts, the Joan of Arc associations, the shops, the excursions and the restaurants. It's good too in the shoulder seasons of spring and autumn, when the sunshine lures the Rouennais out into their pedestrianised streets, to stroll, to sit on the ubiquitous benches, to patronise the many cafés. Only in high summer, in common with most other French cities, does it die a little and many of the restaurants close.

It's always a good idea to start off at the Tourist Office for maps and guidance, but here it is worth a visit for its fascinating old building alone, just opposite the cathedral. In fact it's a city where it doesn't really matter in which direction you stroll; you cannot fail to catch glimpses of the ancient Rouen – narrow alleys where the top storeys of timbered houses almost meet, opening into sunlit squares, planted with trees and flowers, and everywhere cafés just when you need them most for sedentary appraisal. Its plan is compact, so that all the most interesting parts can be visited comfortably on foot.

Don't, of course, fail to walk from the Vieux Marché down the r. du Gros Horloge, where the familiar colourful clock is reinstated over the narrow passageway. I started to list some of the more interesting food shops here and in the rest of the city, but found so many excellent specimens, I gave up. But I must single out *Périers* in the r. du Gros Horloge for special mention. Delightfully old-fashioned, with wonderful pastries to be elegantly wrapped as presents or to be eaten there in the salon du thé. Behind this is a more attractive restaurant with central aquarium, and walls decorated with bakers' ancient utensils, and beneath this is a visitable 13C crypt. A good location not only for a cuppa and indulgences but for a light lunch (open till 7.30, closed Sun.).

The magnificent cathedral terminates the vista along the r. du Gros Horloge. Sit quietly in the square to take in some of the details. As Monet realised, it is a building of many moods. Fascinated by its complexity, he painted twenty versions, different times of day filtering different light on the façade and offering him twenty alternative visions; one is in the Musée des Beaux Arts.

The cathedral might serve as a catalogue of architectural styles, developed over nearly eight centuries. Each age has added what it considered its finest possible contribution to the original 11C building. Of the two main towers flanking the 16C west door, the Tour St. Romain on the left is a relic of the 12C church, early Gothic on a Romanesque base; the right-hand Butter Tower is pure Flamboyant Gothic. It got its name in the 17th century, when those who wished to indulge in butter in Lent were prepared to buy forgiveness by a contribution to the church. The openwork spire is the tallest in France.

At least two other churches are essential viewing, on even a short visit to Rouen: the charming church of St. Maclou, built in the 15C– 16C, all Flamboyant Gothic, and the Abbey Church of St. Ouen, 14C– 15C, where summer concerts are held in the beautiful chancel, making full use of one of the best organs in France.

Walk behind St. Maclou and between it and St. Ouen to discover the

Cathedrale Notre Dame

oldest part of Rouen. Skilful restoration is a continuous process here and a stroll along narrow lanes like the r. Diélette, full of antique shops will be orchestrated with cheerful hammering.

Your tour of discovery is bound to lead you past the *Palais de Justice*, formerly the site of the Normandy Parliament. Severely damaged in 1944, shell holes much in evidence, the restoration of this elegant building is still going on. The Renaissance *Hotel de Bourgthéroulde*, just off the Vieux Marché, has famous bas-reliefs of the Field of Cloth of Gold, *Joan of Arc's Tower* is the keep of the castle (1204) where she faced torture. *The Musée des Beaux Arts* (closed Tues. and Wed. a.m., entry 4f) is one of the most important art galleries in France, particularly strong on post-Revolution artists, like Géricault and David, and on Impressionists and Post-Impressionists.

Winter or summer, try and find time for a visit to the Rouen Corniche. Take a picnic lunch with you, perhaps, to Ste. Catherine Hill, where an astounding panorama of the whole of the city and the loops of the Seine lies spread out below. To do this, drive along the north quays and turn left just past the last bridge. The 'Rouen Corniche' is clearly marked from here. Follow its twists and turns for about 4 km and stop at a sharp bend where a viewing table helps identification of landmarks. All the city's many spires and towers rise up to the right, the industrial blocks to the left, and the bridges span the great shining river, dotted with ships and small craft. Eerie in the morning mists, spectacularly beautiful in the sunshine, exciting in the evening with the lights below beginning to sputter, not to be missed.

Rouen is hard-up for recommendable hotels, few of which have restaurants. It more than compensates, in my view, however, by housing a magnificent range of eating places, from Michelin-starred (three this year) to bistro. My file of readers' discoveries would engender a whole book in itself; as they seem to change hands fairly frequently, I shall not even attempt to list all the possibilities, but just make a few suggestions of my own favourites. You can't go wrong if you inspect the menus carefully and choose one well-patronised by the French.

➤ **Colin's Hotel**
(H)M   *15 r. de la Pie   35.71.00.88   AE, DC, EC, V*

The best Rouennais news for many a day is that at last the city can boast a comfortable, medium-priced, privately-owned hotel, in the heart of the old quarter. You can find it in the SW corner of the Place du Vieux Marché, conveniently placed for popping into Warin's next door for even more comfort and cheer.

The exterior is uncompromisingly modern – a sheet-glass profile on the rue de la Pie and another behind a quiet and ancient courtyard in the rue du Vieux Palais. All is surprisingly quiet and calm. Inside, the starkness gives way to soft pastels and deep armchairs in the reception area.

The 48 bedrooms likewise have expensive chintz drapes and

bedcovers to offset their simplicity. Mod. cons. but no fuss. For 440f (600 for a more spacious version) in this position, with parking facilities, I reckon this is outstanding value and an arrow follows.

Hôtel de la Cathédrale
(H)M   *12 r. St. Romain   35.71.57.95*

An ancient building, close to the cathedral and St. Maclou, with an unexpected and soothing flowery courtyard. The 23 rooms are all different and moderately comfortable at moderate prices – 200–250f. Diabolical parking, and problems even to unload the car, but the place does have character.

'Towels spare and very rough, but otherwise all was lovely. Kind helpful people and butter in pots. We were able to park outside long enough to unload.' – Miss Joan Taylor.

Hotel Québec
(H)S   *18 r. Québec   35.70.09.38   Cl. 23/12–3/1   AE, EC, V*

'The hotel is small, modern, central and extremely well-run by a charming Parisian couple who are firm Anglophiles. A big advantage is that the hotel has its own excellent small car park.' – Frank Wakeman-Long.

Rooms are 135–245f, so it all sounds extremely good news. More reports please.

Hotel Lisieux
(H)S   *4 r. Savonnerie   35.71.87.73   AE, EC, V*

Another modern small hotel, between cathedral and the quai Pierre Corneille, in a rather boring area, completely rebuilt. The rooms are characterless, but if an overnight stay is all that is required, this could be the answer. 100–250f.

'Couldn't have been nicer people. Slightly grotty plastic breakfast room. Comfortable purple bedroom with shower. Parking outside and very handy for all the sights.' – Mrs. J. L. Rankin.

Viking
(H)S   *21 quai Havre   35.70.34.95   EC, V*

'We liked this hotel very much and would return there again. We had a twin-bedded front room and found the double glazing very effective. On the fourth floor we heard hardly any traffic noise. With pleasant bathroom the cost was 240f, plus 20f for breakfast. We also paid 30f for locked underground parking. We found most other hotels had parking problems.' – Vic Oliver.

Other readers have confirmed that the Viking satisfied the overnight traveller's wants. Rooms 200–295f.

Carmes
(H)M   *33 pl. Carmes   35.71.92.31   AE, EC, V*

This one is a bit more colourful. A nice old house in a central square, without too much traffic. The 15 rooms are all different and furnished with real furniture. 260–375f.

Nowadays you can eat your way right round the Place Vieux Marché in any style and price range you choose. From very grand (*Couronne and Warin*) to wine bar (*Bouchon*), to foie gras (*Pierre Champion*), to fish (*Gentil* and *La Mer*), to light lunches and pastries (*La Moule au Gateau*), supplemented by a wide choice of bars open all hours, inside and out. It's also a Foodie's paradise, with superb charcutiers, chocolatiers and pâtissiers, not to mention all the stallholders in the central market. I cannot help ruefully comparing all this delightful animation and choice with Le Havre, whose central square lacks even one good bar.

A range of some of the most interesting restaurants, in various price brackets, now belong to one obviously enlightened owner, Darvin Cauvin, who has given each one tremendous character and individual style. In different moods and circumstances, this group alone, of four restaurants and a bar, the Mirabelle, could satisfy anyone's gastronomic requirements, from big splash to budget. All are open every day throughout the year. All deserve arrows:-

➤ La Couronne
(R)L   *31 pl. du Vieux-Marché   35.71.40.90   All credit cards*

'The oldest restaurant in France' has become the flagship of the Cauvin fleet. Once the best restaurant as well as the oldest in Rouen, its fortunes sagged for a while, but currently it is commendably not resting on its considerable world-wide laurels and is always encouraging new young chefs and brightening up its ancient décor. This is a serious restaurant for serious eaters, at serious prices, but for an investment of 195f (menu) you can eat increasingly well, where the great and the good have eaten for many generations before you.

➤ L'Orangerie
(R)M   *2 r. Th.-Corneille   35.88.43*

Tucked away in a quiet courtyard just off the Place, on the site of the 18C Hôtel de Ville, is this utterly charming restaurant, making the most of the old vaults, arches, pillars, and newly-cleaned yellow bricks. It has a strikingly light and airy feel, decorated with statues, balustrades and many tubs of greenery. On fine days there are white iron chairs set outside on the cobbles, white parasols, white cloths.

The specialities are fresh fish and the trolley of desserts; take the 90f menu and try their brandade of cod and mignon of beef.

▸ **Les Marâichers Bistrot d'Adrien**
(R)M-S   *37 pl. du Vieux Marché   35.71.57.73   AE, CB, DC*

My favourite of all the many Vieux Marché possibilites. The terrace of course is the place to sit if weather permits – all provincial French life is here – but in winter too the ambiance pleases. The 'retro' decor of a 1900s Parisian bistro is warm, friendly and amusing, the service good-humoured and efficient, right up to midnight, the food high in quality, low in price.

For 85f (not weekends), I ate nine oysters, a substantial feuilleté of salmon trout and spinach, hot goat's cheese salad and profiteroles. If you are an îles flottantes freak, try them here – they come puffed up to overflow the plate and are latticed with caramel.

▸ **Charles**
(R)S   *6 r. du Gén. Giraud   35.70.73.39   All cards*

The latest addition to the Cauvin fleet, the budget-priced representative. The retro theme again in a small brasserie setting. A splendid place for the young in heart to assemble in a cheerful atmosphere, from 11.30 a.m. till late, late, late.

Excellent value eating. 75f buys wild boar terrine, skate with black butter, chocolate gâteau and wine (except weekends). For à la carte allow a mere 100f.

The one asset that the Cauvins lack at the moment is a Michelin star. Rouen has three restaurants that have reached this dizzy height:-

Gill

At the time of going to press, this double-starred prodigy, Gilles Tournadre, probably top chef in the whole area, had abandoned his glossy restaurant in the rue St.-Nicolas and moved to the Quai de la Bourse. Time will tell.

▸ **Bertrand Warin**
(R)L   *7–9 r. de la Pie   35.89.26.69   Cl. Sun. p.m.; Mon.; 1/1–15/1; last two weeks of August*

Probably the prettiest restaurant in Rouen. Glass doors open onto a green courtyard and the dining-room is far from being gloomy in spite of its old beams and low ceilings. The food is simply superb. Bertrand Warin is in the very top rank of Norman cooks and more than merits his single star. He likes presenting dishes that look simple but involve perfect precision and imagination, like his langoustines with leeks – fish cooked to the point where a minute less and they would have been raw, a minute more and they would have become banal, lamb roast in thyme, with all its innards presented too, and all equally desirable.

Prices have shot up since I last raved about him. Lunch at 180f (midweek only) is the best bargain; otherwise it's a hefty but worthwhile 295f.

Arrowed for outstanding food and charming atmosphere.

→ Beffroy
(R)L   15 r. Beffroy   35.71.55.27   Cl. Feb.; school hols.; 1/8–22/8   AE, V

An old favourite in an extremely ancient building, tucked away in a
quiet backwater near the Beaux-Arts. Small, intimate, elegant, with a
talented lady cook, Mme Dorothée l'Herault. She sticks to traditional
food more than do the other top-notchers, on a menu at 200f, but all is
superbly presented. If you want to play safe, with dishes like turbot in a
saffron sauce, roast pigeon, paupiettes of smoked salmon, this is the
place. Michelin gives her one star.

L'Auberge du Vieux Carré
(R)M   34 r. Ganterie   35.71.67.70 Sun. p.m.; Mon.; 1/7–17/7

A charmingly elegant old restaurant, discovered in one of those
fascinating side streets, full of quirky little shops, off the main rue
Jeanne d'Arc. It is particularly recommended on a fine summer
evening, when you can sit in the quiet courtyard, lit by old-fashioned
standard lamps and relish the carefully preserved antiquity of the
surrounding old beams and tiles.

Inside, in an intimate dignified ambiance, are Louis XV armchairs
and old oil paintings – familiar décor for this classy but not-too-
expensive genre of restaurant.

M. Jacques Pinel's cooking is classic, but delicate – fillet of beef with
red wine sauce, and wonderful desserts like an 'impérial' of black and
white chocolate. Good value in this class at 90f, 140f including wine
(but not weekends), or 190f.

Les P'tits Parapluies
(R)M   46 r. du Bourg l'Abbé   35.88.55.26 Cl. Mon. lunch; Sun.; Feb. school hols;
10/8–18/8   CB, AE

Another very pretty little restaurant, this time in an old umbrella shop
behind the Hôtel de Ville. Décor an attractive mix of old-Rouen and
1920s. Popular with the young and chic. Chef Marc Andrieu specialises
in Norman produce and local seafood, and has gained unanimous
praise from F.E.3 readers. Midweek lunch is 140f. Other menus at 200
and 240f.

'We lunched at Les P'tits Parapluies. And would have cycled at least
15 miles against the wind and in the rain to do so. Looking back, this
was our most memorable meal. Every single thing about it was
perfection.' – Jeremy Cockayne.

La Marine
(R)S-M   42 quai Cavalier de la Salle   35.73.10.01   Cl. Sun. p.m. and Sat.; 1/8–20/8;
24/12–1/1   AE, DC, V

Unpretentious small restaurant specialising in fish, on the left bank.
Not a lot of character, but with good menus from 53f.

Pascal Saunier
(R)M-L *12 r. du Belvédère   Cl. Sun. p.m.; Mon.   CB, AE*

This is the place to make for on a fine summer's evening. It has a superb view from its lofty perch on the Belvédère, overlooking a wide loop of the river far below. The restaurant (with only 20 covers) has a pleasant garden for drinks and is decorated in soothing pastels. Pascal Saunier proposes two menus, one at 160f with wine included, which I consider a bargain for his extremely high standard of cooking, and another at 200f. Go for fish dishes and leave room for dessert.

La Poule au Pot
(R)S *13 r. Père Adam   35.71.09.53*

Thumbs up for one of the cheapest restaurants in this tourist-dominated area near the cathedral, which does not take advantage of its easy custom by serving disgusting food. Nothing special gastronomically, but good value. Three rooms have different character and different prices, so check before settling.

Gentil
(R)M *2 pl. du Vieux Marché   35.71.59.09   Open every day until 1 a.m.*

This old Rouennais institution has two claims to fame – it sells more oysters than anywhere else in Normandy and has (or so it claims) the longest fish menu in France.

Certainly you can take your pick from almost any known piscine variety and demand it cooked in any way you wish. Huge portions, good value, but sometimes variable cooking. Menus from 70f (not weekends).

Le Bouchon de Rouen
(R)S-M *20 pl. du Vieux Marché   35.89.39.69   Cl. Sat. p.m.; Sun.   CB, AE*

That gallic rarity, a wine bar, but in this case going one better in serving particularly fresh and interesting food to complement the wine – It's an excellent idea for a light lunch, to leave room for a gourmet dinner experience, or a wise precaution against post-prandial doziness on the auto-route.

You can settle for just a plate or fillettes or cheese, but the fresh salmon here is especially good, as is the 'gâteau' of mushrooms. Take the advice of patron Alain Simon in choosing an appropriate glass of wine. Allow anything from 50–200f.

Pierre Champion
(R)S *24 r. Rollon   35.07.36.08   Cl. Sun.; Mon.   CB*

New to Rouen (since 1988) is this concept of a 'boutique-restaurant'. Here you buy an enormous range of foie gras, but before you choose, sit down at one of the bistro-style tables and sample the possibilities. You can taste foie gras of duck or goose, cooked in Muscat wine to a famous recipe, or rillettes, cassoulets, magrets de canard, cheese. There are menus from 70f, which do not include desserts.

La Mer
(R)M   *14 pl. du Vieux Marché   35.89.95.96*

Not as expensive as it looks, and a wonderful fishy treat. The 78f menu offers, for example, soupe de poisson, sea trout and chocolate marquise. How can they do it for the price?

At Bonsécours, a suburb of Rouen, 3 km E by the N 14:

Auberge de la Butte
(R)M-L   *69 rte de Paris   35.80.43.11   Cl. Thurs. p.m. Wed.; Sun.; Aug.; 24/12–3/1   CB, AE, DC*

In the most unlikely setting, encircled by hypermarkets, Bricoramas, and parking lots, is a gem of a restaurant. The Auberge was a staging post when the road to Paris from Rouen cut through the countryside of Bonsécours. It has miraculously preserved its identity, along with its beams and odd corners, old furniture and paintings of a long-gone Rouen.
It is more than a restaurant, it is Pierre Hervé's home, and it shows in the warmth and personal welcome. He is a cook of the old school and you will eat traditional dishes cooked with a wealth of experience, outlasting culinary fads. Menu at 200f.

A few ideas for more modest occasions:-

Les Beaux Arts
(R)S   *34 r. Darriette   35.70.17.15*

Classic dishes well presented in a little restaurant in a street full of antique shops. Allow 100–120f.

Les Halles du Vieux Marché
(R)S   *pl. du Vieux Marché   35.71.03.58*

Cosy intimate atmosphere in old panelled, knick-knackery décor. Unpretentious and friendly. Allow 130–150f.

La Queen Mary
(R)S   *r. du Cercle   35.71.52.09*

An art deco style brasserie with good grills and fish. Open till 11.30. Allow 150f.

Map 3F   **ROUTOT** 27350 Eure. 18 km E of Pont Audemer

 Wed.

Turn off the autoroute at Bourg Achard and take the D 144 to find this pleasant undiscovered little town, with a huge market square.

l'Écurie
(R)M   *Cl. Sun. p.m.; Mon.; 16/1–10/2   EC, V*

Strange that there have been no reports on this useful stop, just a short diversion off the autoroute. As there has been a change of management since last I wrote about it, I decided to check again and found Danielle Thierry charmingly accueillante and her husband Jacques a very proficient cook. They are both trying hard to make it a success and they deserve to.

It's a well-groomed little restaurant in the square, rustically comfortable. Menus now start at 80f, and for this I ate mousse au foie and salad, sea trout, cheese and sorbets; only with the wine list would I quarrel – half a bottle of Cheverny cost 40f. It was all presented as carefully as for the expensive menu, with titbits offered here and there – nuts and raisins with the cheese, chocolate truffles with the coffee, smiles withal.

Map 3H   **RY** 76116 Seine-Mar. 20 km E of Rouen

 Sat. a.m.

Turn off the N 31 onto the D 13 to find this attractively green and rural area.

Ry is a favourite excursion destination for the Rouennais and it's not hard to see why. There is a notable and wonderful carved wooden 16C porch by the little church and the forest of Lyons surrounds the peaceful little town. The good people of Ry have designated it as the place where Emma Bovary went to live, and where she died. Fans of either Flaubert or *Flaubert's Parrot* would find the museum a must. It is a reconstruction of Homais' shop, plus mechanical dolls enacting scenes from the novel. I'm not sure whether Flaubert would have roared with rage or laughter.

Auberge de la Crévonnière
(H)S(R)M   *35.23.60.52*

How cynical to feel that anywhere as romantic, as ancient, as peaceful as La Crévonnière – with river Crévon cascading through its gardens, willows sheltering white tables, dovecots, roses, blackened beams – is highly likely to cash in. But here is the honourable exception to the rule that maximum natural attraction spells minimum proprietorial effort. Here the patron, M. Laine, goes out of his way to ensure that his many guests enjoy their visit.

I can't say that the food is a great gastronomic experience. I *can* say it is well cooked and presented and that an hour or two spent in one of the four delightful small dining-rooms should bring great pleasure. Specialities are entrecôte marchand du vin, filet de veau à la cauchoise and Tournedos Perigourdine, on menus from 92f. Packed at weekends, understandably.

There are four very pleasant countrified rooms (160f) with no more raucous sound than the splashing of the waterfalls to disturb a good night's rest.

Map 3G **ST. ADRIEN** 76240 Seine-Mar. 8 km E of Rouen

A hamlet on the outskirts of Rouen, by the N 15, direction Vernon-Paris, or by exit 21, direction Vernon, from autoroute A 13.

Le Manoir de St. Adrien
(HR)M *6 Chemin de la Source* 35.23.32.00

This 1914-constructed manor-house, all eccentric towers, gables, black and white timbers, is set in the midst of a large 'parc', overlooking the valley of the Seine. It's an ideal situation for those travellers who prefer the peace and greenness of this rural area to the fret of the city so close by.

It was restored in 1987 by the owner Madame Masset, who is most anxious to increase her British clientele. She has 18 extremely comfortable bedrooms from 310–400f, each with bathroom, and a restaurant serving traditional cuisine from 135f.

Map 3F **ST. ANDRÉ D'HÉBERTOT** 14130 Pont l'Evêque, Calvados. 7 km NE of Pont l'Evêque by N 175 and D 17 south

---

No-one would believe that by turning just a km off the nationale it would be possible to find such intensely rural, utterly unspoiled countryside as that of St. André d'Hébertot. I find it hard to decide which of the dozens of delightful hamlets and villages of the Auge region is the most picturesque, but this must surely be in the running. As you climb a steep hill you come across, to your right, a stunning château, whose lichened walls line the village street, hard by an ancient country church. Opposite is the old priory, set in green lawns, surrounded by gracious trees, and all so quiet you can hear yourself think.

➤ **Auberge du Prieuré**
(HR)M *31.64.03.03*

The interior is as good as the first impressions suggest. Natural oak

Auberge DU PRIEURÉ

beams support the roof; the floor is flagged black and white; a fire burns in the great fireplace; the walls are stone; the flowers from the garden. There are seven lovely bedrooms, decorated in appropriate country style, all with bathrooms; windows look out on the garden, in which breakfast is taken in summer. They cost from 310f. Menus are sophisticated and change with the seasons: 130f.

Arrowed for comfort and position.

Map 4B   **ST. AUBIN DU PERRON** 50490 St-Sauveur-Lendelin, Manche. 15 km NE of Coutances

St. Aubin is a well-kept secret, lying east off the Périers road. the château is even more obscure, since it isn't in St. Aubin at all but 3 km nearer Périers on the D 52.

➤ **Château du Perron**
(C)L   *33.46.63.69   Open all year*

This is the winter home of Mme Gauthier of the Hotel des Bains at St. Jean-le-Thomas. She has five guest rooms, three with bathrooms and one shower between the other two, for 150–200f for two, or 250f for three.

The 19C château is very French, very beautiful, slightly faded but certainly not seedy, and the grounds and lake are gorgeous. After exactly one hour's drive from Cherbourg, the peace and restfulness of the place are immediately soothing.

The rooms are all spacious but very different, so try and discuss priorities when booking. The two most stunning are on the first floor, with long windows overlooking the lake, one of them with swagged corona over a double bed, but these are the two without bathrooms. Those on the second floor are also assorted, some with bath, some with shower, with the nicest rooms on the front, the best views to the rear. All extremely comfortable and arrow-worthy.

The only meal served is breakfast in the dining-room, included in the price; there is an elegant salon to relax in and those fabulous grounds and allées to explore and picnic in. Plenty of restaurants to investigate for evening meals.

Arrowed for luxury at an affordable price.

Map 3H   **ST. DENIS-LE-FERMENT** 27140 Gisors, Eure. 8 km NW of Gisors

---

Take the D 14 and then head north on the D 17 to find this middle-of-nowhere village.

L'Atelier
(R)M   *Rue Principale   32.55.24.00*

Josiane and Marc Chevalier combine a studio for his paintings with their little restaurant in the main street. The one menu, at 100f, includes as much wine as you can take, red, white or rosé. They serve you with a jug of your choice and you refill from the barrel! The food is simple honest country fare, and you go as much for the atmosphere (and the wine) as for the grub. In summer, outdoor eating is ideal.

'All sorts eating there, but all French and half of them local peasants. Inside is smarter than expected, with pink linen table-cloths and immaculate settings. The meal left me feeling distinctly benign and Marc Chevalier's Calvados (offered to all customers) added to it. My criticism is that they offered nowhere to sleep it off. Customers all ended their meals smiling at each other and the world. Why? It wasn't the haute cuisine – it was just very enjoyable.' – Robin Totton.

Map 3A   **ST. GEORGES-DE-LA-RIVIÈRE** 50270 Barneville-Carteret, Manche. 40 km from Cherbourg; 2 km W of Barneville-Carteret

Between Carteret and Portbail there is a stretch of fine beaches, backed by dunes, with enough space for everyone, even in high season. Sand-sailing is a sport practised here that might intrigue the done-everything brigade.

Manoir de Caillemont
(C)L   *33.53.81.16*

A misleading address, since the Manoir is on the opposite side of the main road, the D 93, from the little sleepy village of St. Georges. Signposts clearly point the way down the lane.

It is a lovely late 18C building, with two suites for guests' use. Both have sitting-rooms; the 400f version has television and double bed, wood panelling and fireplace in the sitting-room; the 350f room has twin beds, a smaller sitting-room and again a fireplace. (Breakfast is included in the price.) Very nice indeed, especially as the use of a heated swimming-pool is included in the deal, the owners are particularly friendly and helpful, and the whole area is so delightful. No evening meal, but good restaurants are nearby.

An undoubted arrow, which I am confident F.E. readers will enjoy.

Map 4F   **ST. GEORGES-DU-VIÈVRE** 27450 Eure. 14 km S of Pont Audemer

 Wed.

Take the little D 29 out of Pont Audemer, signposted Campigny, for an intensely green and rural ride to St. Georges.

Hotel de France
(HR)S   *32.42.81.13*   *Cl. Tues.*   CB, AE, V

A little Logis de France, with just four rooms at 160–200f, and good cooking on menus from 65f by patron M. Vochelet.

'For 190f we had a room with double bed, basin, w.c. and shower; on the 76f and 128f menus we had excellent food, with very friendly family service. We would recommend it very highly.' – Patrick Reynolds.

Map 6C **ST. GERMAIN-DE-TALLEVENDE** 14500 Vire, Calvados. 5 km S of Vire on the D 577

Auberge St-Germain
(HR)S   *pl. Église*   *31.68.24.13*   *Cl. Sun. p.m.; Mon.; 21/8–14/9*   AE, EC, V

A restaurant with three bedrooms, locally renowned for its good cooking. Excellent value menus from 55f, good carafe wine and simple rooms at 90–120f.

'Initially, when staying in a gîte, we only ate there, but liked it so much that we eventually stayed three nights en pension. The food was superb. The bedrooms and bathrooms were rather limited, so probably not suitable for your guide unless they have been recently expanded. However the owners, M. and Mme Jonan, are charming.' – Heather Filmer.

Map 2B **ST. GERMAIN-DE-TOURNEBUT** 50700 Valognes, Manche. 5 km NE of Valognes; 25 km from Cherbourg

A hamlet in the maze of little lanes south of the D 902. No hardship if you do get lost trying to find it, since the pleasure of discovering such totally rural unspoiled country, seemingly unchanged for centuries, outweighs any frustration. A total change of pace and all a mere 18 miles from the port.

➤ **Au Bon Accueil**
(R)S   *33.41.13.12*   *Cl. Wed.*

A most popular find for F.E.3 readers, even after a change of ownership. It's a little bar/restaurant still known locally after the original owner, Louis Sanson. M. et Mme Sanson have now retired to live more quietly in the village, leaving their chef to run the business, apparently the successful mixture as before.

'We have visited four or five times and always everything has been excellent (even if they do not pay too much attention to desserts). The lamb and the fish – well, where could you find better – and those langoustines .... But there is always that certain something extra – the company, sometimes the full French family or grandparents downwards, and one memorable visit included several bottles of champagne with Henri and Guy – so we had fine renditions of Parlez Moi d'Amour and Auprès de ma Blonde.' – Bill Chapman.

'The new young owners are carrying on the former traditions admirably. The weekday 40f menu with no choices (sample: oeuf en cocotte, pork in cider, cheese and dessert) was a bargain. A trip to look at the Château, which offers gîtes, is worth the detour.' – Bob Smyth.

There is no choice usually on the menu, which will now be around 50f. An arrow for distinguished simplicity and good value.

Map 7B ST. HILAIRE-DU-HARCOUET 50600 Manche. 28 km S of Villedieu-les-Poêles

Ⓣ pl. Église (July–August) 33.49.15.27; Mairie (o.o.s.) 33.49.10.06 Ⓜ Wed.

One of those sadly characterless towns, thanks to the events of 1944, completely reconstituted in uniform grey. I would prefer to drive on to somewhere more uplifting, but it appears to be a favourite overnight stop for many readers, obviously because of its situation on a popular route south.

There are four hotels in the town, of which the one that gets most votes is:

Relais de la Poste

(HR)S r. Mortain 33.49.10.31 Cl. Mon. and Sun. p.m. o.o.s. EC, V

Functional hotel, with rooms from 90–180f and above-average cooking on menus from 60f. This personal experience sums it up well:

'Nothing to look at from the outside, on one of the main roads leading from the town centre. However inside it was clean and comfortable and the rooms were adequate, both with showers and one with w.c. Our meal on the 130f menu was excellent, but the coquilles provençales were out of this world. I only have to close my eyes now to recall them. I can happily recommend this restaurant.' – David Garnett.

Map 7B ST. JAMES 50240 Manche. 19 km S of Avranches

Ⓜ Mon.

The little market town of St. James is not on the main tourist route into Brittany and therefore caters mainly for its inhabitants rather than for migrants. And all the better for that. We only found it by accident, having broken down in the middle of nowhere, and being towed to the nearest garage, in St. James. The bad news was that the car could not be repaired until a spare part arrived from Rennes; the good news was that we found the Normandie, a very present help in trouble.

Normandie

(HR)S pl. Bagot 33.48.31.45 Cl. Fri. p.m. o.o.s. EC, V

A typical small-town French hotel/restaurant, with modern/rustic décor and stone exterior. In its brochure, it lists among its attributes 'Sa Simplicité, Son Bon Accueil' and I wouldn't disagree. The rooms at 140–250f are simple good value, comfortable and clean. It is the food that is so exceptional. We were not in the mood to be cheerful until we saw the quality and quantity of the 60f menu – cold salmon, contrefilet steak, salad, cheese and dessert. The plat du jour was a huge smoked pork cutlet, garnished with local vegetables, at 38f. The welcome and the simplicity were both much in evidence and much appreciated. Next time it will be a deliberate détour to eat here.

Mme Françoise Tiffaine
(C)S   *La Gautrais*   33.48.31.86

Take the D 12 from St. James, direction Antrain, to find the farm, 1.5 km from the town.

'The owners are dairy farmers, who speak very good English and offer a very high standard of accommodation, and a really wonderful evening meal. This includes: first course with home-produced cider; main course of meal and vegetables with as much wine as you want; apple pudding, cheese, coffee and calvados – made by the farmer and the best I have tasted. All the food is home-produced. They are a most friendly and willing couple, who make every effort to offer that personal touch. Other families who were staying were also very pleased.' – Peggy Watts.

I have since received a charming letter from Catherine Tiffaine, convincing me that a stay under her hospitable roof would be an excellent idea. The rooms open on to a green valley, through which flows a river; each has its own bathroom and costs 85f for one person, 110f for two, 147f for three and 170f for a family of four. She does not tell me how much her evening meal now costs, but I would guess around 55f. A likely arrow I feel.

Map 1A   **ST. JEAN-LE-THOMAS** 50530 Sartilly, Manche. 17 km S of Granville

---

 Sat.

A pleasantly sleepy village, with one main street leading eventually to the vast sandy beach, where the tide recedes for miles and the cockle gatherers gather. Mont St. Michel swims on the horizon.

Hotel Les Bains
(HR)S   33.48.84.20   *Cl. Wed. o.o.s.; 15/11–20/3*   AE, DC, EC, V

An old favourite with the British (and therefore booking essential). Its short season, red R in Michelin, small heated swimming-pool, and good value all ensure a full house. The patronne, Mme Gautier, well aware of the extra rooms she could fill, is now on the way to owning half the village. Apart from the main Les Bains, she governs not only the annexe across the road but two other nice stone houses nearby and another by the sea, all of which serve breakfast, with main meals taken in the hotel. It is therefore important to discuss what kind of accommodation you will be getting when making a booking. Bedrooms in the main hotel are on the small side, but cost only 110–229f, and the food is both copious and good.

'This was truly excellent in all respects. Beautiful room with bath en suite for 158f. Wonderful meal for 55f. Breakfast above average, for 22f.' – F. Guillonet.

See St. Aubin du Perron, where Mme Gautier has another property.

Map 5E   **ST. LOUP-DE-FRIBOIS** 14340 Cambremer, Calvados. 1 km S of
Crevecoeur-en-Auge

Le Prieuré
(C)M   *M. et Mme Rosset*   *31.63.02.09*

Turn off the D 16 heading for St. Pierre-sur-Dives, to find this picture-book old farmhouse, wisely restored to give the best of the old – beams, eaves, flowers – and the new – comfortable, well-equipped bedrooms, with the bonus of friendly efficient hosts.

M. and Mme Rosset sell the cider, Calvados and Pommeau they produce on their farm in the little sitting-room of their home. The atmosphere is simple, but more sophisticated than in most chambres d'hôte. Three rooms, 120–200f.

Recommended for charm and comfort.

Map 4E   **ST. MARTIN-AUX-CHARTRAINS** 14130 Pont l'Evêque,
Calvados. 52 km SW of Cherbourg; 6 km S of Deauville

On a very busy stretch of the N 177 at a crossroads with the D 58.

Auberge de la Truite
(R)M   *31.65.21.64*   *Cl. Sun.; Mon.; Feb.*   CB, AE, DC

A very well-known, well-respected pillar of local gastronomy. There is certainly nothing like la Truite in nearby Deauville, where fashion is paramount and solid bourgeois cuisine would not do at all.

Jean-Michel Lebon looks like a chef should look – massively well-fed and importantly moustachioed. He enjoys cooking as much as he does eating; with a strongly classic base his dishes show that he is not above experimenting – a ravioli made from lentils with his saddle of lamb; oysters are mixed with salmon and served in a light pastry crust. This is serious eating in a room sparkling with polished brass, polished glasses, polished cutlery. Don't nip in for a hamburger straight from the beach.

The 98f weekday menu is a bargain – snatch it if you can, otherwise it's 160 or 280f. Always full on Sundays.

A reader has explored further; just across the road in fact, and recommends the **Auberge du Douet de la Taille.**

'*A simple country bar-Restaurant, but full of lively French, eating simple but excellent food. We had lunch with a very good omelette, then sorbet; Madame and assistant were run off their feet but seemed to enjoy it. Highly recommended.*' – Dr. D. C. Lillie.

Map 7D   **ST. MICHEL-DES-ANDAINES** 61600 La Ferté Macé, Orne. 2 km N of Bagnoles de l'Orne

On the edge of the Fôret des Andaines.

La Bruyère
(HR)S   *33.37.22.26 Cl. Fri. p.m.; Mon. lunch o.o.s.; 15/12–1/1 CB, V, EC*

A useful-to-know little Logis de France, with 20 immaculate rooms from 120–260f and menus from 60f. It is furnished in mock rustic style and the older building housing the restaurant is comfortable, grey stone with flowery window-boxes. The hotel is modern.

Map 3F   **ST. OUEN-DES-CHAMPS** 27680 Quillebeuf sur Seine, Eure. 5 km N of Pont Audemer

There is a strange other-world region of Normandy that no-one ever seems to write about. And yet it is bounded to the south by an autoroute and to the north by the Tancarville bridge, and completely surrounded by major roads. It is a misty forgotten land of low-lying fields, swimming in mist, lakes and ponds and peasant farmhouses, straight from a Corot landscape. It is called the Marais Vernier.

There are no hotels in this tourist-neglected region, so I was particularly pleased to have the following report:-

La Vallée
(C)M   *32.42.17.25*

'The Marais Vernier is a magical chunk of the idyllic Norman rural past. The Blondins are genuine, kind, rustic Norman farmers – or were till an accident laid him up permanently. It is ideally close to Tancarville, though seemingly 1,000 miles and 100 years away, but you'll regret leaving yourself only one night there.

Beware, it is not at St. Ouen-des-Champs, which is on the other side of the uncrossable autoroute. As soon as you turn off the D 90 down the hill, i.e. first right, the landscape will become breathtakingly beautiful. (Don't try any clever short cuts. Get to it from the N 182 and D 90 – you could get lost very easily any other way.)

The rooms are on a staircase completely cut off from the Blondins' part of the house and are very comfortable. Not to be missed.' – Robin Totton.

The Blondins have three rooms in their Norman-style house, one with private bathroom and two with shared shower and loo. They charge 135f for two, including a good breakfast.

Map 7E **ST. PATERNE** 72610 Orne. 3 km SE of Alençon on the D 311, Chartres road

A rather dreary suburb of Alençon.

Le Château de St. Paterne
(C)L *33.27.54.71 Cl. Nov.–Feb.*

Is it cheating to include a property half in Normandy, half in the département of the Sarthe? I don't really care, for St. Paterne is so well worth bending the rules a bit. Especially so since the worthy Château de Maleffre is no longer functioning. (M. Gaetan de Nanteuil's many friends and clients will be sad to hear that his ill-health has forced him to abandon this, one of F.E.'s favourite entries.)

St. Paterne has in common with Maleffre the fact that it stands in its own grounds – 120 acres – within a short distance of the town centre, and that it is run by a very enthusiastic and dedicated owner. But there

St Paterne.

the resemblance ends, since this is an altogether grander concept. It is a glorious 15C château; its present patron, Charles-Henry, is said to be the youngest châtelain in France. Now 25, he has two years' experience behind him of the huge responsibility of running such a property, previously left abandoned to crumbling oblivion for thirty years.

Readers of F.E.8 will know of my admiration for Les Briottières in the Loire, which François de Valbray inherited from his mother and now runs as a b. and b. par excellence. He it was who encouraged his younger brother, Charles-Henry, to take on a similar venture at St. Paterne. The family capacity for infinite pains and determination to succeed is immediately obvious.

Charles-Henry, having wooed and won his bank manager's substantial help, had to face the appalling state of the château's disrepair, and bring it back to life, painting many of the walls in warm yellows to compensate a little for the lack of sunshine from Provence, where he was brought up. He has demonstrated considerable taste and flair in his choice of drapes and wall covering, giving each of the five rooms so far restored a totally individual character, as he uncovered treasures like a painted Renaissance ceiling, and covetable pieces of furniture hidden under piles of junk.

I like best the cheapest room (350f, twin beds, feminine rose-spattered chintz, bath) and the most expensive (500f, sunshine yellow-draped four-poster, elaborately pleated and swagged, French Revolution-design curtains, which C-H admits are highly inappropriate in this aristocrat's residence, antique bath, shower and loo), but all the rooms are spacious and have their own bathrooms.

The dinner, eaten by the extravagant light of thirty candles, is expertly cooked by the ubiquitous Charles-Henry and served by loyal local wenches, who are only too willing to contribute to the renaissance of the château which was always the heart and raison d'être of the village that St. Paterne used to be. There are four courses, always with fresh vegetables from the kitchen garden; with apéritif, wine and coffee, they cost 220f; there is no obligation to eat in, but you'll be missing a treat if you don't.

No doubt about the arrow here.

Map 5E **ST. PIERRE-SUR-DIVES** 14170 Calvados. 26 km SE of Caen

Ⓜ *Mon. a.m.*

A disappointing little town, in my view, apart from the covered market halls, rebuilt in 1944 after a fire destroyed the original 11C building. The reincarnation is certainly a triumph, with not a single nail or screw used in the construction, but 300,000 chestnut pegs, faithful to its model. It sits in a vast market square, which solves the parking problem.

The old abbey church, dating back to the 12th century, with a fine lantern tower, contains 'The Meridian', a copper strip running from the south aisle to the organ, but in fact the true meridian is slightly to the east. Don't bother with the cheese museum – a very disappointing visit except perhaps for the professionals.

In fact, the whole day looked as if it would turn into a disaster. A glorious April morning had seduced me into planning a picnic. The drive through the leafy valleys of the Auge, dotted with bluebells, cowslips and wild garlic, threaded with streams, had whetted the appetite for a super lunch sur l'herbe. But, at 1 o'clock precisely, the storm clouds gathered and the first of the April showers spattered down. I found the centre of the town a hole in the ground, with bulldozers abandoned like childrens' toys, for the sacred lunch break. It rained harder than ever, and even the abbey was closed. I began to think more in terms of shelter than a gastronomic thrill. A good rule in France, when in doubt, is to make for the station or the market place. In the latter I came across:

Restaurant du Marché
R(S)

A drink or perhaps just a crêpe was all I had hoped for, but one look at the hors d'oeuvres convinced me that at last my luck had changed. Indeed its thirty odd ingredients included those I had chosen earlier for my picnic, at a price in the charcuterie well in excess of the 40f asked for a three-course meal, of which these were but an appetiser. And none of your tinned beans and sweetcorn here. The rillettes, pâtés, stuffed tomatoes, céleri remoulade, mayonnaise, were all home-made and of highest quality.

Course two could have been escalope de veau or chicken cooked in cider, but by now the rain had settled down in earnest and so had I, determined to get best value, with a petit salé, a substantial peasant dish of boiled ham and sauerkraut. Followed by cheese or dessert – baked apple, apple tart, apple clafoutis.

I reckon this the best example I found anywhere in Normandy of a breed fast disappearing – a simple café with fuss-free, cheap, freshly cooked food. How confidence-restoring. Arrowed.

Map 6B   **ST. QUENTIN-SUR-LE-HOMME** 50220 Ducey, Manche. 5 km SE of Avranches

---

 Thurs.

A charming oddly-named village on the D 78.

Le Gué du Holme
(R)M   *33.60.63.76   Cl. Sun. p.m.; Mon.; 30/6–15/7; 22/1–10/2*

A solid bourgeois house near the church has been converted into a comfortable and elegant restaurant, decorated in contemporary style. It has become the gastronomic refuge of the businessmen from

Avranches – always a good sign – and looks like becoming one of the Manche's premier restaurants.

The food based on local produce and specialising in fish, is sophisticated without being chi-chi – a ragoût of lotte cooked in Gamay wine, a gratin of apples cooked in cider – and the 80f weekday menu is a bargain.

In summer this is a particularly pleasant treat – to sit outside in the garden and be spoiled by the attentive patron, M. Leroux and his staff. More reports please for this potential arrow.

Map 4E   **ST. SAMSON** 14670 Troarn, Calvados. 15 km E of Caen

---

A turning marked off the N 175.

Auberge du Domaine de la Brousse
(R)M   *31.23.31.49*

Recommended by a local gourmet for unusually interesting cooking. The Domaine is unusually interesting too. It's a rambling Norman manor-house of uncertain date, part black and white, part turreted and gabled.

Unusually too, it offers the afternoon tea in addition to the more Gallic preoccupation with lunch and dinner; it is a very pleasant diversion from the autoroute to sit and sip in the courtyard, surrounded by nothing more stressful than cows and birds in fields and trees.

The food, on menus from 85f, calls itself nouvelle cuisine, which is enough to put anyone off these days, but dishes like trout with basil, rillettes of hare or casserole of fruits de mer are all well presented and offer quantity as well as quality.

Map 6B   **ST. SENIER-SOUS-AVRANCHES** 50300 Avranches, Manche. 5 km E of Avranches

---

A village in rolling countryside. Two km south of the village is:

Le Château du Champ du Genêt
(C)M   *Route de Mortain   33.60.52.67*

A small but imposing 18C château, complete with turrets and towers. The four guest rooms all have private bathrooms and are good value for 195f a double. Mme Annette Jouvin will produce an evening meal upon request, but there are several restaurant alternatives within easy reach. Breakfast can be taken round a massive oak table in the imposing dining-room furnished with antiques, or on the terrace outside if the sun smiles.

Map 5E   **ST. SYLVAIN** 14190 Grainville Langannerie, Calvados. 18 km S of Caen

Turn E off the N 158 onto the D 132. The auberge is in the centre of the village.

Auberge de la Cremaillère
(R)M   *31.78.11.18   Cl. Tues. p.m.; Wed.   AE, DC*

Very much the centre of the village and usually full of locals (book ahead), who realise how lucky they are to have a 'relais gastronomique' on their doorstep.

It's run by nice Mme Potignon, who welcomes – and I mean welcomes – and husband, Philippe, who cooks, divinely. Between them they contrive a warm and old-fashioned atmosphere – lace cloths, raised fire, fresh flowers – with warm old-fashioned food, on affordable menus,80 and 140f. The cooking is classic without being dull – oyster soup, salad with three terrines, duck in red wine with onion feuillété. Just the kind of set-up that we go to France for.

More reports please, so that I can award an arrow.

Map 2B   **ST. VAAST-LA-HOUGUE** 50550 Manche. 30 km E of Cherbourg

(T) *Quai Vauban*   (M) *Sat.*

A real fishing village on the eastern coast of the Cotentin peninsula, where the far-receding tide leaves vast stretches of muddy sand and rock. At low water you can walk out to the little island of Tatihou; another splendid walk is past the bijou Mariners' Chapel along the sea wall to the fort, via the isthmus that links the former island of La Hougue to St. Vaast. In every direction there are little sandy beaches and that romantic horizon of rocks and islands, with the great bay curving south past the landing beaches to Grandcamp-Maisy, clearly visible most days, as are the islands of St. Marcouf.

The new marina, highly popular with British yachties, has brought renewed life and vigour to the town, and more fresh paint and new bars than I ever remember. Much has remained unchanged, however, including the faces of the fisherfolk here, uniquely ruddy and full of character, begging to be painted.

The Saturday morning market, which takes over the whole of the rue du Port, hasn't changed either, and is still one of the best outings in the peninsula. I defy you to walk down the street and not buy something from one of the colourful stalls.

Another great attraction is M. Josselin's shop, advertised throughout the town by his handsome, brilliantly painted vintage van. Here is a mini-Fortnum's, stocking everything you did not find in the market, and of very high quality. His wine cellar is especially remarkable.

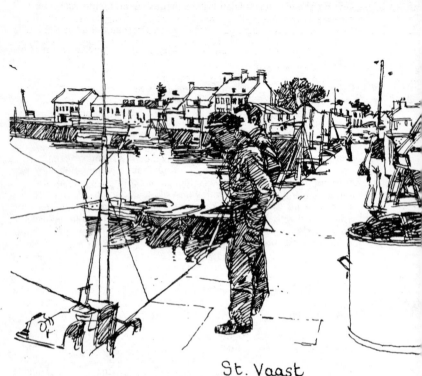

St. Vaast

➤ Hotel France et Fuchsias
(HR)M   *18 r. du Mal. Foch   33.54.42.26   Cl. 9/1–25/2; Mon.   CB, AE, DC*

I would have doubted that the F. et F. could improve. For so many years it has been a favourite with French and English alike, best-loved and most recommended by word of mouth of all F.E.3's Manche entries. Secure in its reputation, in its favoured situation, an easy drive from the ferry port, in one of the most attractive areas of the peninsula, with the recent bonus of the marina bringing yet more British customers straight from heaving and tossing to the delights of its shore-bound comfort and cuisine, the odds were heavily, if cynically, loaded in favour of the management resting on its fuchsias and cashing in.

What a great pleasure then to report that I found the place better than ever. The only disappointment in fact is that the famous fuchsias that used to rampage up its walls so dramatically have been cut back by a severe frost. The good news is that their lusty replacements are making a bid to catch up.

The fuchsia theme has been delightfully exploited, featured on the curtains and china now used in the nice old beamed dining-room, echoing the pink of walls and table linen. Very pretty indeed. Their blossoms continue to drip from the walls of the conservatory dining-room too. It's the colour of their leaves that recurs in the table linen. In short, someone (young Mme Isabelle Brix in fact) has taken a lot of time and trouble over the details that make the whole so attractive.

The bedrooms in the new annexe are a delight, approached by a long and leafy garden curving unexpectedly behind the restaurant and linking the original building with one two streets away. Mine had fresh sharp green chintz curtains and bedspread, and a smart bathroom. At 350f it was a bargain, overlooking the terrace dotted with white tables and chairs for drinks, coffee, gossip, or in my case writing up my notes.

A popular innovation has been the 'manifestations musicales' – concerts in the garden during the last fortnight of August, free to clients of the hotel, which have been such a success that Isabelle Brix intends to develop and extend their range.

The food has kept pace with the general uplift. Superb value and superb quality. I like the way they manage to walk the tightrope between the avant-garde and the boring. The ingredients are local – many of them from the Brix farm – but prepared in the modern way, with lovely light, well-reduced sauces, fish and meat cooked à point and not a minute more.

On the Menu de la Marée (others appealing at 70f and 100f), I ate a mousse of smoked salmon served with a hot blini, then a substantial feuilleté of monkfish, sole and salmon, in a beurre blanc flecked with chervil. Then a choice from a good cheeseboard and rather over-decorated desserts (too many glacé cherries!). All excellent value at 150f.

The only criticisms of the hotel in a very hefty file have been of the smaller cheaper rooms in the main building – 'we were forced to live out of suitcases because the first-floor twin-bedded room was so badly equipped' – and of the clientele 'mostly Brits'. I can only say that the kind of Brits who are discriminating enough to patronise a hotel like the Fuchsias must be worth meeting; as for the rooms, I'm afraid it's a matter of booking early and bagging the new ones. Rooms from 125–345f. Demi-pension obligatory in high season at 180–290f per person.

No doubt in my mind about this arrow, for charm, cooking, value.

L'Escale
(R)M

One of several – I think the best – of the fish restaurants overlooking the harbour. Very pleasant to sit outside, making the most of the prospect of fishing boats and yachts going about their business, and then to eat the freshest of the local catch.

A bonus for the customers at l'Escale is the exceptionally pleasant patronne. St. Vaast's new prosperity has not had an adverse effect here. When she discovered it was my companion's birthday, out came a bottle of champagne on the house, even though we had only ordered a modest fruits de mer between the two of us. (We were glad we had been so parsimonious as two portions would certainly have defeated us.) Menus from 65f.

La Granitière
(HR)M *33.54.58.99   64 bis r. Maréchal Foch*

A relatively new addition to the St. Vaast hotel scene, and particularly useful when, as so often happens, the Fuchsias is full. As its name implies, the Granitière is a granite house, substantial, immaculate, on the approach road to the town. The interior has been luxuriously furnished with repro. antiques. The nine rooms are spacious and very well equipped; seven of them have private bathrooms, of the dark blue or maroon persuasion, from 350f. Owners M. and Mme Boullin-Delabrière are anxious to make a success of their new venture and take every care of their guests' needs. When I visited there were plans to get the restaurant going, with the appointment of a new chef. More reports welcome.

Map 1F **ST. VALÉRY EN CAUX** 76460 Seine-Mar. 32 km W of Dieppe; 32 km E of Fécamp

---

(T) *pl. Hotel de Ville (May–Sept.)* (M) *June–September Fri. a.m.*

Considering that its centre was razed in June 1940, the little fishing town retains a good deal of character. Several of the old buildings survived across the drawbridge, but the market place and its surroundings are uniformly post-war. A forest of masts rises from the yachts tied up in the mouth of the river and fish is sold straight from the fishing boats along the quays. The beach is stony and seems forever windswept, but St. Valéry has a loyal following of holidaymakers, both French and British.

Les Terrasses
(HR)M *35.97.11.22   Cl. Jan.   CB, DE, EC*

Readers have been quick to come to the defence of Les Terrasses, which I described as austere. Its façade may be just that, but several of the rooms have been brightened up, and are now well-equipped and comfortable. Try and get one facing out to sea, of course. They cost 210–310f. Menus from 85f.

'The room was adequate, but the dining was something else. A lovely room, attractive furniture and drapery. The food matched it. Marvellous fish, wonderful cheeseboard, and an apple tart to remember. Charming service.' – Jem Miller.

Les Bains
(HR)S *pl. Marché   35.97.04.32   Hotel cl. 15/12–15/2; rest. cl. Mon. and 1/12–15/2   EC, V*

Very simple, very central, very cheap. Reader-approved. Rooms are 90–190f and menus from 65f.

Pigeon Blanc
(R)M   *near the old church   35.97.03.55   Cl. Thurs. p.m.; Fri.; 15/12–15/1*

A little chalet restaurant in a nice garden just outside the town. Bargain meals from 65f.

Map 3G   **ST. WANDRILLE-RANÇON** 76490 Caudebec-en-Caux, Seine-Mar. 4 km E of Caudebec

---

The hamlet of St. Wandrille is famous for its Benedictine Abbey, where mass with the Gregorian chant can be heard in an old 15C tithe barn at 9.25 a.m. on weekdays, 10 a.m. on Sundays. It is possible for men to stay in the Abbey and live with the monks.

Stroll around the ruins of the 14C nave and take an agreeable walk to the Saturnin chapel.

Auberge Deux Coronnes
(R)M   *35.96.11.44   Cl. Sun. p.m.; Mon.; 24/1–10/2; 5/9–22/10   EC, V*

A charming old Norman building in the village street, opposite the Abbey – quite small, full of flowers, colourful table linen and oak beams of course. Menus from 100f; carafe wine.

Map 3E   **STE. ADRESSE** 76310 Seine-Mar. 2 km NW of Le Havre

Ⓜ *Tues. and Fri. a.m.*

Those in the know turn left from the ferry disembarkation queue and avoid the lack-lustre hotels of Le Havre altogether by making for the leafy residential suburb of Ste. Adresse. It's a pleasantish beach resort, lined with wooden huts on the cobbles and rising sharply up the hill to gain a good view back over the windsurfers, the marina and the commercial port.

Les Phares
(H)S   *29 r. Gén. de Gaulle   35.46.31.86*

A tall narrow white-shuttered, gravel-fronted, iron-gated house, quintessentially French, that has been one of French Entrée's most successful discoveries. This has been not entirely due to its position in a quiet leafy road, nor to the cheapness of its bedrooms (150–190f), but in great measure to the personality of its previous owner M. Morgand, for whom nothing was too much trouble if it affected the well-being of his guests. Many of them became personal friends and considered a trip to France hardly worth while if it did not start and end at Les Phares.

Michel Beaumont who also owns the Hotel Atlantic in Le Havre, has taken over and is gradually improving the bedrooms, while retaining their character. He mercifully retains too the tradition of always being open, year round. His rooms cost 210f to 308f and he now serves meals – lunch and dinner for 62 or 80f.

Reports eagerly awaited. Meanwhile the old-established arrow has to go.

A consoling end to a good holiday can be an evening spent at Ste. Adresse before catching the night ferry. It is very agreeable to sit on the seafront, high above the beach, and watch all the marine activity. An equally good view can be had from any of the four restaurants on the front, and we often use the Beau Séjour on a Sunday, when most Havre restaurants shutter themselves up.

Beau Séjour
(R)M   *3 pl. Clemenceau   35.46.19.69   Open every day   AE, DC, EC, V*

One reader wrote that he used the Beau Séjour as a refuge when the weather was wet and Le Havre proved inhospitable. I know exactly what he means. It is comfortable, warm, friendly, with a wonderful view over the water and open when you need it most. I personally don't think the food is marvellous, but it's not bad if you play safe – with straightforward fish perhaps. Expect to pay at least 120f and to meet several fellow-refugees.

Yves Page
(R)M   *7 pl. Clemenceau   35.46.06.09   Cl. Sun. p.m.; Mon.; 10/2–26/2; 15/8–6/9   AE, EC, V*

You pays your money and you takes your choice between the Beau Séjour's easy options, user-friendly opening hours and British clientele, and Yves Page's infinitely better food, French clientele, and opening hours geared to locals not ferry-catchers. They both have the splendid outlook in common, but at Yves Page you don't get the same quick turn-round and you have to be quick off the mark to book a window table.

Yves Page is a serious cook, in the traditional vein. His fish is of unsurpassed freshness, as indeed are all his ingredients. He has trained his young brigade well and the service is professional and smiling. Menus from 148f.

Map 2F   **SASSETÔT-LE-MAUCONDUIT** 76540 Valmont, Seine-Mar. 15 km NE of Fécamp

---

The coast road north from Fécamp, the D 79, is altogether more attractive, with its valleys and wooded hills, than the rather dull countryside that lies only a few km inland. Well worth a drive to the hamlet, centred round its imposing château, of Sassetôt.

Au Relais des Dalles
(R)M   *35.27.41.83   Cl. Mon. p.m. and Tues.*

Attractively low-beamed little restaurant with a particularly pleasant garden, making an excursion even more worthwhile, even for a cuppa. It is a well-known Sunday jaunt, so be sure to book then. The food is predictable but reliable, with the price of the midweek menu (65f) indicating where most of the trade comes from (weekend menus from 107f).

Domaine du Château
(HR)M-L   *35.28.00.11   Open every day*

An exciting new development in an area sadly lacking in accommodation. The rooms in this lovely 18C château, well restored, are spacious and furnished with stylish antiques. Floor-length windows make the most of the view over the large park and venerable trees. Good value at 335f (go soon), and breakfast is well above average. There is a restaurant but so far the food is not up to the high standard of the rooms, service and welcome. More reports please for this potential arrow.

Map 7E   **SÉES** 61500 Orne. 23 km SE of Argentan; 22 km N of Alençon

---

Ⓣ *pl. Gén.-de-Gaulle (April–Sept.)   33.28.74.79* Ⓜ *Sat.*

Not everyone has agreed with my liking for Sées; several readers have found the little town dull and nondescript. Perhaps it was the cathedral and the surrounding square, lined with other ancient buildings, that blinded me to other shortcomings. Its character comes, in my view, from the former seminaries, Bishop's Palace and convents, their functions changed perhaps, the town demoted from its bustling Gallo-Roman provincial importance to a drowsy backwater. But surely that cathedral makes up for a lot. I have never managed to catch the Son-et-Lumière which floodlights the building and the whole town on summer evenings, but it must be an uplifting vision, inspired by the 14C pilgrims who used to spend the night of the summer solstice in the cathedral, a contemporary version of the 'alchimie des couleurs, magie des lumières', which then derived from the natural light which always seems to flood the interior. Michelin enthuses 'one of the finest examples of 13th and 14th century Norman Gothic' and, apart from the buttresses that had to be added to prop up the subsiding porch, I would agree that it is an absolute gem. However, I can see that, having done the culture bit, Sées' other resources are a bit limited. Of night life there is none; not even a decent café.

Le Cheval Blanc
(HR)S   *1 pl. St. Pierre   33.27.80.48   Cl. Thurs. p.m.; Fri. p.m. and Sat. o.o.s.   EC, V*

Another dichotomy here. I found the Cheval Blanc all that one could

Sées.

wish for in a really simple country hotel. Black and white timbering, windows opening onto a vista of trees, flowery bedrooms, helpful proprietors, pleasant dining-room, all for 175–235f; menus from 60f. Readers were divided, however, and it is obvious that the unhappy ones had all been allotted rooms at the back, which were gloomy and had only skylights. The lucky ones were as pleased as I was:-

'The hotel is charming. We had the best room, looking out over the trees to the cathedral. It was very cheap and included an excellent shower and washroom cubicle, very good bed – spotless. Food is first-class. We had the second menu (at 65f) and this included the most delicious seafood pancakes as a starter (we had them three days in a row, they were so good); ris de veau à la Normande also excellent. Only worth staying there for one night to visit Chateau d'O – a gem, as the town is so dull.' – Susan Leyden.

There has been one warning note, however, in a 1990 report, which could mean the end of a beautiful friendship with the Cheval Blanc:

'Things are not the same. The twin bedroom is now 230f, with the only window at ceiling level. When we arrived three menus were displayed outside at varying prices. When we returned after a stroll we found they had been changed to a buffet meal at 78f, incl house wine, served in a gloomy room behind the reception area. Two teenagers, dressed ready for the local disco, served the clients.'

This confounds two theories – that the patrons aim to please their customers and that Sées and discos are unthinkable. More reports would help to decide these puzzling discrepancies.

Le Dauphin
(HR)S   *pl. des Halles*   33.27.80.07   *Cl. Mon. o.o.s; Feb.*   CB, V, AE, DC

The rival Logis de France. Not so obviously attractive as the Cheval Blanc, but trying hard to please: rooms are 80–120f. Menus from 85f.

'Food is a treat in more ways than one. All sorts of extras, such as an extra starter, sorbet and home-made petits fours with dessert. Breakfast was 25f but worth every centime – apple, fruit juice, boiled egg and croissants.' – Margaret Ostle.

Another reader has discovered a new addition to the Sées scene, so far unvisited by me:-

Hotel du Normandy
(H)M   *12 r. des Ardrillers*   33.27.98.27   EC, V

'Excellent spacious room with bathroom en suite. Under new management, with new decoration in progress throughout. Friendly welcome. Husband Australian, French wife speak English. Dearest room 150f for two people.' – Mrs. J. Stevenson.

To the south-west of Sées runs the Forest of Écouves, well-manicured, neat piles of logs, shade, quiet, good for shady picnics on benches provided, or for long walks down the avenues. Boar, roe and red deer are among its population. The road through the forest west of Sées, the D 908, is very beautiful; it leads to the rather boring little town of **Carrouges**, but, unusually sited in a dip below the town, lies the enormous 16C castle, moated, chequered bricks, visitable for 8f from April to October from 9–12 and 2–6 except Tues. (See also Château d'Ô, Médavy, and Haras du Pin.)

Map 3F   **TANCARVILLE** 76430 St. Romain de Colbosc, Seine-Mar. 29 km E of Le Havre

---

Right under the bridge, with a fascinating view of all the river activity.

La Marine
(HR)M   *35.39.77.15   Cl. Sun. p.m.; Mon.; School hols.; 15/7–10/8   CB*

I cannot understand why there has never been any feedback on the Marine. It is so strategically sited for first and last meals and overnight stops, and yet it appears that no F.E. readers cast a second glance. I must confess that I have not eaten there myself since the glory-days when it had a Michelin star, and perhaps it is the lack of welcome that I have encountered on recent recces that has deterred others. I include it because of its convenience, not because of the ambience, but that view does make up for a lot.

The 14 bedrooms are very comfortable and overlook the river and the gardens. They are good value at 170–250f. The sophisticated food in the restaurant, with panoramic-view windows, cooked by Jean-Pierre Sedon, is also good value, particularly on the 130f menu, which includes wine, and the next one up, at 170f.

Give it a try someone.

Map 7C   **LE TEILLEUL** 50630 Manche. 19 km SW of Domfront

 Thurs.

On the N 176 between Domfront and St. Hilaire. 1 km E of Le Teilleul.

Clé des Champs
(HR)S-M   *33.59.42.27   Cl. Sun. p.m. o.o.s.; Feb.*

A modern chalet-type building set well back from the road, which has been most popular with F.E. readers for an overnight stop. Most rooms are double-bedded but a few of the more expensive ones (235f) have twins and bathroom. The cheapest are 110f. Menus from 65f.

'A first-class stop at a most reasonable price. We had a clean comfortable room with bath at the back overlooking an étang. Fresh pretty flowered wallpaper, comfy bed. Reception and breakfast room a bit clinical, but the dining-room offering menus from 62–140f was excellent. Chef patron cooks. We had terrine trois poissons, carbonade

of beef, île flottante. Breakfast wasn't bad either – a bit ordinary, but coffee o.k.' – Eileen Broadbent.

Map 5C　　**TESSY-SUR-VIRE** 50420 Manche. 18 km S of St. Lo

 Wed.

In the heart of some very pretty green unspoiled hilly countryside.

Hotel de France
(HR)S　　*33.56.30.01　Cl. 1/2–15/2　CB, V, EC*

A little Logis de France recommended by local residents as the best value for miles around. Rooms cost 88–220f; menus start at 46f. M. and Mme Amiot are the hosts; there is a garage and a little garden.
　　'Ambiance great – sweet people – warm welcome – delicious dinner for 48f. Room with two double beds, loo and shower for 155f. We invited friends to dinner and chose the 54f menu, which was excellent – terrine of lotte, médaillon of veal, vallée d'Auge, cheese and crème caramel. Highly recommended.' – Judy Wright.

Map 2B　　**TEURTHEVILLE-BOCAGE** 50630 Quettehou, Manche. 5 km W of Quettehou

---

The best advice I can give you to find this flowery hamlet is to get lost. Make for the quadrangle formed by the D roads 901, 26, 902 and 24, and with any luck and a lot of pleasure you will stumble across Teurtheville-Bocage. Make for the church to find:-

Le Moulin à Poivre
(R)S　　*33.54.11.97*

I wrote about this tiny rustic restaurant in F.E.1, then heard it had changed hands and had to drop it from F.E.3 for lack of information. Now I have confirmation that it is just as good as when I first loved it.
　　'The food is outstanding. I've been eating there for four years and never had a bad course.' – M. Saxton.
　　It has changed its formula since I was there, but is still good value. Allow around 60f and you will feed well and copiously on simple fresh country food.
　　'For 36.80 we got four courses – salade niçoise, steak fried in Normandy butter brought to table in beautiful copper frying-pan, cheese and succulent white-fleshed peaches.'

Map 4F   **THIBERVILLE** 27230 Eure. 17 km E of Lisieux

Ⓜ *Mon.*

> An uninteresting village, useful perhaps for a victualling stop, now by-passed by the N 13.

Hotel de la Levrette
(R)S   *32.46.80.22   Cl. Sun. p.m.; Tues.*

> You know that sinking feeling, when you've postponed a lunch-time stop until it's nearly too late, and in desperation (and usually with some marital aggro) you say you'll take the next one, however awful it is? That's how it was with us one wet autumn day, en route for somewhere much more interesting. The Levrette did not lend encouragement – it's one of those old-fashioned, rather grim-faced, grey buildings that exist in most French provincial towns. Only the cars in the car park gave us a clue that all was not lost. Far from lost – we had a splendid 65f inclusive lunch in the steamily full dining-room, and were only sorry that it had to be a quick one. A very useful, *very* simple pub.
>
> There are seven rooms, but I did not have time to check.

Map 5D   **THURY-HARCOURT** 14220 Calvados. 26 km S of Caen

Ⓣ *pl. St. Sauveur (in season)   31.79.70.45*

> I can hardly blame Thury-Harcourt for being destroyed in the war, but it is sad to see the disappointing reincarnation. Its situation, however, in the heart of the enchanting Suisse Normande, makes it a popular base, and it is well served with accommodation and restaurants.

Relais de la Poste
(HR)M   *r. de Caen   31.79.72.12   Cl. 15/11–1/2   CB, AE, DC, EC*

> The big hotel of the town, which has had its ups and downs. Currently I hear that it's more down than up, but still offers a good value menu at 120f. The rooms are very comfortable, especially those on the first floor, which cost 365f. I cannot approve of demi-pension being obligatory in the summer.

Le Val d'Orne
(HR)S   *31.79.70.81*

> A nice old-fashioned hotel, down by the bridge over the river, which has proved popular with readers. Both meals and rooms are simple honest good value. A double will cost around 140f and menus start at 45f. A good cheap base from which to explore the rewarding valley of the Orne.
>
> 'Pleasantly surprised by the food, which was not as basic as you led

us to believe. We had the second-price menu, which was excellent and quite up-market. Local cuisine, apart from the chips.' – Helen Davis.

Suisse Normande
(R)S   *Cl. Wed.*

Very popular with the locals. In high season you should certainly book to get a place in the pretty Norman-style restaurant. Excellent regional cooking on menus from 60f.

'The end of our holiday and the cheapest menu had to suffice, as we were low on francs and credit cards didn't appear to be accepted. However, we had fish soup, ratatouille and sausages, and pineapple and ice cream with Martini. Excellent house wine at 30f.' – Helen Davis.

'For 45f we had a tureen of fish soup, croutons, plus the rarely-encountered rouille, lovely braised ham in Madeira sauce and pruneaux au vin rouge. Beautifully cooked, remarkable value. A family enterprise, with a charming wife and a must on the way back to the ferry. Surely it deserves an arrow?' – Geoff Woollen.

It does, Mr. Woollen, and here it is.

Map 6C   **TINCHEBRAY** 61800 Orne. 16 km SE of Vire

(M) *Mon.*

Not an especially interesting village but a useful stop on the route from Cherbourg southwards.

Le Relais
(R)S   *pl. Général Leclerc   33.66.60.54   Cl. Sat.*

I stopped to telephone and chanced upon this pleasant little Relais Routier, with spotless bar. Further investigation revealed a four course menu for 45f and items like steaks and pork chops for a mere 40f. My omelette and frites with salad cost an unbelievable 20f. Pleasant owner, Michel Coupry, cooks special 'repas gastronomiques' on Sundays, which could be very good news indeed.

Map 5C   **TORIGNI-SUR-VIRE** 50160 Manche. 13 km SE of St. Lo

(M) *Mon.*

A useful stop on the N 174, a good fast road south. The nice little town is dominated and given character by the restored château, on whose terraces the market is held. Very pleasant wandering round here peering into the baskets of hens, speckled guineafowl and doves and feeling sorry for the rabbits stunned in the cramped runs. The surrounding park and lakes are pleasant places to stroll and the river Vire splashes agreeably through the town.

A most spectacular beauty spot is only 6 km away – the Roches de Ham. Park in a flat meadow and walk to the edge prepared to have your breath taken away. With no warning, the land comes to an end and hundreds of feet below, at the bottom of an escarpment of white cliffs, runs the river, through a panorama of Normandy. You can walk down a pleasant winding lane to the river and puff back up again to take tea and crêpes in the garden of the café by the car.

Hotel de la Gare
(HR)S

No more information, but easy enough to find – in the station yard. Driven by franc-shortage and a gaggle of hungry youth to feed, we investigated here some years ago and it was tentatively included in F.E.3, with many cautions as to its simplicity and basic character. Since then many readers have agreed that our experience of excellent value for money and good home cooking was not an isolated one. It is a Relais Routier, and relais routiers don't tolerate small helpings, so it's still the best choice for miles around to fill up for a small bill.

'Obviously this is not everyone's idea of elegance, but the bedroom was clean, the place was quiet, the helpings large. If we had stayed there for some time we could have put on a lot of weight. We would gladly visit again.' – Alwyn L. Harland.

Rooms 75f; menu 55f.

And a new idea:

'Finally could I recommend L'Auberge Fleurie, 20 rue Danican. A chance stop on a Sunday evening (not the easiest). Pleasant service, a wonderful coq-au-vin and an excellent house wine.' – Rowan J. Cherrington.

Map 3E   **TOUQUES** 14800 Deauville, Calvados. 3 km SE of Deauville by the N 834

Only three kilometres inland from Deauville, on the river from which it takes its name, lies the charming little medieval town of Touques. No longer an important port, as it was in the 11th century when some of its old houses along the river and the church of St. Pierre were built, it attracts few tourists now. That is a pity, since its mature charms contrast well with those of its more popular parvenu neighbour and its brassy *port de plaisance* .

Thomas à Becket built a church here and gave it his name and the Dukes of Normandy were regular visitors. A few small ruins of William the Conqueror's castle at Bourneville-sur-Touques are reminders of the town's early eminence.

Aux Landiers
(R)N   *90 r. Louvel-et-Briers   31.88.00.39   Cl. Tues. p.m., Wed.   CB, AE, DC, EC*

A pleasant little Norman-style restaurant, offering excellent value for those suffering cheque-book embarrassment from Deauville. The nice patron, M. Girard, cooks straightforward dishes like grilled salmon on menus from 58f. More reports please.

Map 7F   **TOUROUVRE** 61190 Orne. 10 km NE of Mortagne on the D 32 off the N 12

 Fri.

An unspectacular village on the edge of the Perche forest.

Hotel de France
(HR)S   *19 r. du 13 Août 1944   33.25.73.55   Cl. Sun. p.m.; Mon.   20/12–10/1*

No beauty spot from the outside, but an example of a little French country hotel where the family interest more than makes up for lack of glamour. Rooms are 95–360f and menus now start at 60f.
  'The welcome was the warmest we have met for years. The dining-room was impeccably turned out. Whilst we were waiting for our 56f menu we were given, for nothing, not just the usual plate of feuilletés but a large jar of rillettes to help ourselves from. The menu itself was excellent and there were a number of French guests of all types partaking with obvious relish. The bedrooms which we looked at seemed to be everything you could wish for. An absolutely charming couple, M. et Mme Feugueur, run it.' – R. F. Ash.

Map 5B   **TRELLY** 50660 Quettreville sur Sienne, Manche. 12 km S of Coutances

 Sat.

Trelly lies between the D 971 and D 7 south of Coutances, but whenever I pass a sign towards it on these two fast roads it always takes me by surprise that anything so intrinsically rural should be even within striking distance of 'civilisation'. The lanes round the Verte Campagne, in the hamlet of Le Chevalier, are the heart of Normandy; best of all in the spring, when starred with primroses and the cowslips that are sadly so rare in England nowadays, and when the lambs look up in astonishment as the car edges its way between the high hedges, but green all year round, if not with bud then with mistletoe. Aptly named therefore is:

La Verte Campagne
(HR)M   *Hameau Chevallier   33.47.65.33   Cl. Sun. p.m.; M. and Mon o.o.s.; 15/2–1/3; 15/11–5/12   CB, AE*

Well known, well beloved to generations of Brits, who took to their heart Madame Meredith, the widow of an English naval officer, who still runs this modest 18C farmhouse, with grey stone, white paint and climbing roses. Inside are flagged floors, beams, flowers, chintzes, log fires in winter.

Reports on welcome, food and accommodation have varied widely, from horror – 'No more returning until she has handed over the reins' – to affectionate enthusiasm – 'We found Mme Meredith in her usual good form.'

At best, you will enjoy the atmosphere of staying in a private home, with tea by the fire, drinks in the garden, a personal service hard to find in these plastic days. Be prepared by chat to your fellow guests.

The eight rooms vary considerably, though all are very pretty. The best cost 310f and are definitely worth the money; the smallest are 160f. There is not a lot of choice on the menus but the food is good and imaginative on menus from 105f.

'There have been more changes recently. No evidence of the Desnos half of the parternship. Maybe M. Desnos – if he was the rather gorgeous Maître d' in evidence during our last visit – did not match up to Madame's standards which, I can assure you, have not slipped. The salon, with its gallery, has become the dining-room, and vice versa, crowded with oversize comfortable seats, so one cannot help but be friendly. But the atmosphere and rooms have not changed. The food was excellent – not too nouvelle cuisine, and good use of vegetables. There are two set menus, both consisting of a starter, two choices of main course, cheese and choice of sweet. Excellent value, beautifully cooked and presented. The problem is that if you stay more than one night your choice of dinner becomes very limited.' – A. J. Wilson.

Map 4E   **TROARN** 14670 Calvados. 13 km E of Caen on the N 175

 Sat. a.m.

Clos Normand
(HR)S   *10 r. Pasteur M. Malhaire   31.23.31.28 Cl. Sun. p.m. o.o.s.; 27/8–10/9; 24/1–7/1*

A substantial Logis de France in the corner of the market square, with simple comfortable rooms at 120–145f and menus from 60f. Nothing special gastronomically, unless you happen to be a wine buff:-

'The food was reasonable but nothing more. Certainly not expensive. The wine list contained some amazing bargains, of which we sampled two – a 1983 Gewurtztraminer at 103f and a 86 Moulin à Vent at 96f.

Amazing bargains truly. Perhaps you can keep this a secret!' – R. Furber.
I never was any good at keeping secrets.

Map 3E   **TROUVILLE** 14360 Calvados. 74 km W of Le Havre; 2 km E of Deauville

---

(T) *32 bvd. F-Moureaux   31.88.36.19* (M) *Wed.; daily a.m. 1 July–31 August*

Deauville's lively, blowsy sister, no distance across the bridge in miles but a world apart in character. Where Deauville dies o.o.s., deprived of its chic clientele, Trouville gets on with its busy life as a fishing port. Deauville is for the jeunesse dorée (and sometimes for the not-so-jeune); Trouville more for Mum, Dad and the kids, with a splendid beach for the latter, and a Casino to keep Dad amused. The fish market is the hub of the town, with enviable mounds of patently fresh specimens providing the interest for passers-by and shoppers.

The town starts seedily near the bridge and gets progressively smarter towards the Casino end, where quiet streets, lined with stylish old houses, refer back to the town's Edwardian roots. Here there are one or two nice little hotels and my favourite restaurant:-

La Petite Auberge
(R)M   *7 r. Carnot 31.88.11.07   Cl. Tues. p.m. o.o.s. and Wed. except Aug.; Jan   EC, V*

Small, rustic, unpretentious, serving excellent fresh fish, on menus from 95f. Very popular, so do book.

Les Vapeurs
(R)M   *160 bvd. F. Moureau   31.88.15.24   Cl. Tues.; Wed.*

Along the quay are numerous restaurants and bars, of which the most famous is Les Vapeurs. A narrow bustling brasserie, Parisian-style in more ways than one – the service is brusque. In order to enjoy Les Vapeurs (which I do very much), you must accept that you will probably have to wait for a table, even if you have booked, and that you will be treated with that special brand of condescension and impatience that only Parisian waiters perfect. Resign yourself to that, and to the fact that the food is far from cheap because the place is so popular, and give them the credit for providing a seat at a floor show in the hub of the town, in a quintessentially French atmosphere. In summer you play a kind of musical chairs to grab a table on the pavement (the waiter will shrug his shoulders if you appeal to him for fair play); in winter you sit inside, by the zinc bar, reflected in the many mirrors, and will probably receive slightly better treatment from the waiters and waitresses in their black and white gear.

The menus are limited, and it is probably better to go for one piece of superb fish, perfectly cooked. Even so, with wine and coffee, the bill will probably touch 150f.

For those rejected from Les Vapeurs, consolation is at hand:
   'Much to my wife's sorrow, Les Vapeurs closes some lunch-times (market days out of season). However, we went next door to Le Central, bigger and just as busy. Food just as good. In fact it could be a clone of Les Vapeurs.' – Keith R. Whettam.

Hotel Carmen
(HR)M   *24 r. Carnot   31.88.35.43   Cl. Jan.; 17/4–24/4; 16/10–23/10 Rest. cl. Mon. p.m. and Mon. o.o.s.*

Just 300 yards from the beach, a little hotel with fifteen rooms that has pleased readers by its welcome from Madame Bude and by its simple, clean rooms at 140–275f. A bonus for some too to be able to eat in the hotel. Menus from 75f.
   'Wednesday and La Petite Auberge closed, so we tried the Carmen and were not disappointed, even after a wait of an hour for a second sitting. Very busy Logis, local clientele mostly. Very happy staff.' – R. B. Hood.

Les Sablettes
(H)M   *15 r. P.-Besson   31.88.10.66   Cl. 1/12–31/1   EC, V*

Well kept, central but quiet. 155–240f.

Map 2F   **TROUVILLE-ALLIQUERVILLE** 76210 Bolbec, Seine-Mar. 13 km W of Yvetot

---

Le Moulin à Grains
(R)M   *35.38.04.46   Cl. Sun. p.m.; Mon.   CB, AE*

Particularly useful because of its position, apparently in the heart of nowhere and a gastronomic desert, but in fact just a minute off the main N 15. What is more, it is open in winter, when what little other opportunity for good eating there is in this area shuts down; in summer you can eat in the garden.
   It's a picturesquely timbered old Norman mill, specialising in huge grills and with a good comprehensive 110f menu which includes wine.

Map 2B   **VALOGNES** 50700 Manche. 20 km SE of Cherbourg

(T) *pl. Château 33.40.11.55* (M) *Tues., Fri.*

For those who remember the pre-1944 Valognes, the present concrete town must be a sad sight. It clings still to its old title the Normandy Versailles, but like an old man dreaming of past glories. There is little now to be proud about, except perhaps one or two 18C houses, like the Hôtel de Beaumont, or the Hôtel de Granvol-Caligny, both open to the public in July, August and September. There is a regional cider museum located in the 15C Logis du Grand Quartier.

However, it is still an important market town for the surrounding agricultural area, with a huge market filling the square on Fridays.

Because of its position, it is also a useful halt to and from the ferry for easy stocking up, and you will hear plenty of English spoken in the bars and cafés. La Galetière, an excellent crêperie, is a favourite refreshment stop.

Hotel de l'Agriculture

(HR)S 16. r. Léopold-Delisle 33.95.02.02 Rest. cl. Sun. p.m. o.o.s.; Mon. CB, V, EC

A Valognes institution, as French as they come. Creeper-clad, ancient, in a quiet back street, it is popular with locals, who know value for money when they see it, travellers who relish this distinctive first taste of France (at prices they are regrettably unlikely to encounter in other smarter destinations) and habitués who like to make this a cheap weekend base.

There is a huge dining-room, often completely full, where the cheapest menu – expect at least four courses – has now risen to 56f; rooms from 86–196f, the higher price for a family room with bathroom in the annexe a few doors down the road.

Mme Boucher-Botton somehow continues to struggle on under her enormous workload, and manages to make her guests feel wanted.

Le Louvre

(HR)S 28 r. Religeuses 33.40.30.40 Sat. EC, V

Good value again. Straightforward cooking from patronne Mme Mesnil on menus from 50f, with carafe wine. Rooms vary in style, comfort and appeal, as you might expect from the price range – 80–190f.

One reader has solved the mystery as to what happened to the once-recommended Le Doyen in Cherbourg, now sadly characterless. The owner, Gerard Bellet, fell ill and had to retire. He has now opened up not far from Valognes, at Brix, 8 km NW, in a simple bar-restaurant called Chez Gée.

'If you are calling, take a taxi, his hospitality can be overwhelming.' – Peter Wagstaff.

I look forward to reactions to this one.

Hotel Saint-Mâlo

(HR)S 7 r. St. Mâlo 33.40.03.27

A young couple are working hard to up-date and improve this simple hotel. Reports about their enthusiasm and welcome have been encouraging. Rooms from 85f.

Map 1G   **VARENGEVILLE-SUR-MER** 76119 Seine-Mar. 8 km NW of Dieppe

A popular excursion from Dieppe, 12 km away to the east. Turn off the D 75 on to the V 13 for an area of unspoiled Norman countryside. Down the country lane stands the ancient church, buffeted by the sea gales, its graveyard running down to the very edge of the high cliffs. Braque is buried there and inside the church his Tree of Jesse, burning blue, brings a steady stream of tourists. Nearby is the Parc des Moutiers, an 'English' garden, surrounding a Lutyens house. The French are mad about it, but it's comforting for a *chauviniste* to discover that it's not really a patch on any self-respecting English equivalent.

I didn't think much of the well-publicised 15f-worth offered by the Manoir d'Ango either. This fascinating 1530-ish manor was built by Jéhan Ango, a complete Renaissance man, developer of the ports of Rouen, Honfleur, Le Havre, a great shipowner, Governor of Dieppe, banker, explorer. Here he entertained François I and Diane de Poitiers; from a high window in the manor he showed the King a fleet of fifteen galleons riding at sea – a gift to support the King's projected attempt to seize Calais back from the English.

All fascinating stuff and the Italian Renaissance-style architecture is rare in France, but with a quick peep inside the courtyard to see the distinctively patterned dovecot, you can take it all in from the outside for free, even being cheeky enough to picnic in the shade of the avenue leading to the gatehouse.

La Terrasse
(HR)S   *2 km NW at Vasterival, by the D 75*   35.85.12.54   Cl. 1/10–15/3   CB, EC

Readers have been well pleased with a relaxing stay here, taking the obligatory demi-p. in their stride. It's a large, old, very French house, paint peeling from the balconies, set peacefully in the pine trees above the sea. There are good walks in the neighbourhood and an interesting little beach. Could be a wise choice in this area, short of accommodation, for a weekend, or longer. 170–210f per person demi-p.

'*All was clean and comfortable, although it must be said that some of the decorations were a little faded. We found the food very good with a choice of four or five items on each course and an emphasis on seafood. The dining room was very pleasant, with views out to sea, the service friendly and helpful and the whole atmosphere one of people enjoying themselves. The hotel was full, mainly with French people. We would be very happy to stay there again.*' – O. J. Cheeseman.

Map 5E   **VENDEUVRE** 14170 St. Pierre-sur-Dives, Calvados. 30 km SE of Caen

Le Château de Vendeuvre
and **le Musée International du Mobilier Miniature.**
31.40.93.83   Open from Easter to All Saints Day. From Easter–1/6 and from 15/9–All Saints Day, Sats., Suns. and fêtes from 2 p.m.–7 p.m.; from 1/6–15/9 every day, same hours. 27f for both château and museum. Guided tours every half hour.

One of the most interesting diversions in Normandy but strangly little-known and under-appreciated. The 18C château stands on the banks of the river Dives, which defines the area of the Auge from that of Falaise.

Guy de Vendeuvre, his wife and children, spend a good deal of time here and are frequently accessible to talk to their visitors and point out details of special interest in their lovely home. The château is packed with so many treasures that it would justify a whole guidebook to describe them all. Look at the damask cloth on the elegantly-laid table, with 36 covers of crystal, silver and porcelain, and spot the facade of the château woven in the cloth. The furniture everywhere is stunning – exquisite marquetry, tapestries, panelling, carpets, a fumoir with smoking accessories from the 17C when gentlemen liked to retire to indulge in the practice, glorious paintings in oils and pastels, four-poster beds, and a newly restored kitchen, gleaming with copper, brass and polished wood. In fact the whole place gleams – it must be the *cleanest* stately home I've ever seen. Just two dedicated ladies from the village scrub, dust and polish every inch.

This alone would be good reason to visit Vendeuvre, but another unique experience awaits in the lovely vaulted orangery. There Mme de Vendeuvre has arranged, in well-researched settings, her exceptional collection of miniature furniture, assembled from all over the world. If you have in mind doll's house furniture, think again. These are miniatures made by master craftsmen in the same wood and with the same care as the full-size articles, as a proof of their skill. The fine details and intricate workmanship are truly a wonder to behold. There are dozens of little 'rooms', each depicting a different period, with contemporary accessories, like a micro-cupboard containing a carpenter's tools, or a gaming table with pieces, or canopied beds; alabaster, mahogany, ivory, gold, porcelain, embroidery, all contribute to this miniature world. Don't miss it.

Map 6G   **VERNEUIL-SUR-AVRE** 27130 Eure. 50 km S of Rouen

Ⓣ *129 pl. de la Madeleine*   Ⓜ *Sat.*

On Normandy's border, defined by the river Avre, and therefore fortified in the 11th century to hold the frontier against France. Lots of splendid old houses in the area between the Tour Grise, the 1120 drum tower, and the 15C church of La Madeleine, three storeys high,

} Le SAUMON - Verneuil.

crowned with a double diadem of lantern and Flamboyant tower. Notre Dame is another interesting church to visit in this fascinating little town, with wide market square full of colour on Saturdays, ramparts to explore and the river Avre nearby. An excellent choice for a weekend, particularly with the bonus of:

➤ **Le Saumon**
(HR)M   *89 pl. de la Madeleine   32.32.02.36   Cl. 24/12–31/12*

The youthful M. and Mme Simon have taken over from M. Poisson, now retired, and redecorated the dining-room of this old coaching inn in the market place in refreshingly light and airy colours, with green and yellow trellised paper in the dining-room and blue and white iris pattern in the DIY breakfast rooms.

They are gradually doing up the bedrooms too. Those in the rear annexe (quieter but somewhat characterless) have already been repainted and those in the older part overlooking the square are taking their turn. These are particularly attractive, also in fresh pastels, and are more spacious than the newer ones, but there is the chance of traffic noise during the day. Verneuil goes to bed early (on Mondays all day) and so there shouldn't be too much of a problem. 250f with bath is excellent value.

M.Simon is now in charge of the cooking and his 65f menu is very good news. The 140f menu gastronomique likewise, with five courses on offer and the hotel's namesake featuring in many guises.

The Saumon is a well-run and inexpensive little French hotel, with good food, in an attractive town in a lovely part of Normandy. Arrowed on all these counts.

'A sure thumbs-up, double arrow, and we feel a contender for Normandy's Hotel of the Year. Our stay there will be remembered for a long time. Very friendly welcome, super room – No. 19 featured on back of their promotional leaflet and the most stupendous meal in the evening. I did opt for the 120f menu, but it was well worth it. Five courses of smoked fish platter, monkfish in curry sauce, pork fillet in mustard sauce, cheese, blackcurrent mousse. The sauces were superb, decliate and subtle flavours, while the meal must have been cooked by an expert, probably M. Simon. My companion's 68f menu was excellently prepared – salade Normande, chicken Normande and bilberry tart. Carafe house wine is 38f.'

Another view: 'All you say. Wonderful value dinner. We had a room in the new wing, functional indeed but with everything you might need and some you did not. I would much prefer a real bar where you could happily spend an hour go by than the expensive 'convenience' of a bedroom mini-bar.' – Diana Holmes.

▶ **Le Clos**
(HR)L   *98 r. Ferte-Vidame   32.32.21.81   Cl. Mon.; 1/2–26/11   AE, DE, EC, V*

An eccentric-looking, turreted brick-patterned Belle-Époque manor-house, member of the Relais et Châteaux chain, has proved very popular with readers prepared to spend a little more for a lot more pampering. Madame Simon welcomes with dignity and efficiency; husband Patrick cooks superbly. Fish is his speciality, particularly the more luxurious ones, like lobster, cooked in a kind of mille-feuille, and crawfish in an imaginative salad, so the bill is not going to be modest. There is an excellent 230f menu, midweek, which includes wine, but otherwise it's 160f, 280f, or around 400f if you tackle the carte.

The atmosphere is luxurious too, with top-quality china and silver and napery, elegant furniture. There is a delightful terrace for summer sipping and the ensemble will undoubtedly provide a lovely peaceful spoiled weekend break – longer if you can afford it.

The bedroom prices have shot up since F.E.3, but with justification since the rooms have all been improved. There are three apartments, with their own terrace, at 800–1100f, and 8 rooms for 480–700f. Demi-pension at 580–800f per person is obligatory in high season. Arrowed for comfort and elegance in a charming setting.

'We agree entirely with your assessment. The Hotel is 'L' and you pay accordingly. We had a very nice twin room with bath, and I was particularly impressed by the quality of the bed linen and of the taste displayed in the furnishings (although I did think some of the cider press conversions a bit heavy.) The brickwork is marvellous in its variety and despite the hotel being very close to the N 12 Verneuil by-pass, it was pleasantly quiet. Altogether we thought Le Clos scored on the little elegances.' – Jill and Alastair Wilson.

Map 5H **VERNON** 27200 Eure. 63 km SE of Rouen

(T) *36 r. Carnot 35.51.39.60* (M) *Sun., Tues., Wed., Sat.*

An appealing small town on the Seine; some attractive old houses still stand in tree-lined avenues near the 12C Notre Dame and there is an extensive and bustling Saturday market. The liveliness unusually extends into Sunday, when many of the shops stay open, making it a good base for a weekend.

There is plenty to see and do in the neighbourhood, following the convolutions of the Seine or exploring the banks of the two other local rivers, the Eure and the Epte. On the latter, **Fourges** is a pleasant destination for an excursion. You can picnic there, where a massive old waterwheel revolves hypnotically against the background of a picturesque old inn (the Moulin de Fourges, regrettably looking a bit too seedy to recommend further).

The dignified 18C **Chateau of Bizy** (closed Fri.) is another popular excursion and a drive in that direction, taking the D 52 through the forest, is particularly worthwhile in the autumn, when the beech and chestnut leaves are at their most colourful.

But the best reason for making Vernon a base is its most famous known tourist attraction, the house and gardens of Claude Monet at nearby *Giverny*. With the nearby autoroute making Paris very accessible, and the lure of Giverny, the area is studded with restaurants, many of them expensive, but Vernon itself seems badly served both for food and beds. The best on offer are:-

Hotel Evreux
(HR)M *11 pl. Evreux 32.21.16.12 Open every day CB, AE, DC, EC*

Rooms have been completely renovated in this old hotel in the centre of town. It does have a garden and a restaurant, but lacks smiles and welcome. Rooms cost 160–320f. Menus from 70f.

Strasbourg
(HR)M *6 pl. Evreux 32.51.23.12 Rest. cl. Sun. p.m.; Mon.; 24/12–10/1 EC, V*

Old-fashioned, just opposite the Evreux: *'perfectly respectable overnight stop'* – Janet Lockett – just about sums it up. Rooms cost 130–280f.

➤ Restaurant de la Poste
(R)S *26 av. Gambetta 32.51.10.63 Cl. Wed*

A happy discovery that has been approved of by many readers. Particularly popular with the stallholders and shoppers after the market days. Lots of variety on the 70f five-course menu, with duck and Dover sole particularly commendable. I think an arrow is indicated for reliable good value, at low prices, in a gastronomic desert.

'179f for two, including aperitifs and cider and coffee, charmingly served and presented and with the guest French onion soup ever tasted.' M. H. and D. C. Rogers.

LES VERTUS 76550 Offranville, Seine-Mar. 7 km S of Dieppe on N 27

Auberge de la Bûcherie

(H)M *35.84.83.10 Cl. Sun. p.m.; Mon.; 5/1–13/1 CB*

The most luxurious (and pricey) of Dieppe's affiliated restaurants. Glossy, always gleaming with fresh paint, thick carpets, flowers, shining cutlery and glasses, cocktail bar. Chef-patron Delauney is ambitious, dedicated, and determined to use only the best produce, regardless of cost. Its position on the nationale, near the airport, is somewhat unfortunate and makes the pleasant-surrounding garden hard to enjoy. Increasing costs lose the arrow, but the standard is impeccably high, and readers have been pleased. Menus start at 160f.

'It was worth buying your book just to know of this place. I had to book early for the Bank Holiday weekend – they had been fully reserved for weeks. We were the only Brits there. Everything about the place was perfect, including the sumptuous loos. The 5-course cheapest menu was excellent value, with each course gorgeously presented, and the wine prices were reasonable. My three companions were impressed by my choice of a 'climax to our eating and drinking week.' – Ken Bell.

VEULES-LES-ROSES 76980 Seine-Mar. 24 km W of Dieppe

(T) *r. Dr. Girard (July–August) 35.97.63.05* (M) *Wed.*

The village's name is apt indeed. The Veule 'le plus petit fleuve de France' trickles down through the main street to the sea, and the cottages along its way are indeed miles covered in roses. The days when Veules was a fashionable resort with the Parisian bohemians are 150 years past. Nowadays it is a sleepy little seaside resort, whose pebble beach (pebbles-galets) gives the name to a much-esteemed restaurant:-

Les Galets

(R)L *3 r. V. Hugo 35.97.61.33 Cl. Sun. p.m. o.o.s.; Tues. p.m.; Wed.; Jan.; last week Nov. CB, AE, DC*

Delightful of an evening, when the candlelight is reflected in the polished silver, or on a hot summer's day, when the terrace is the most favoured place to eat, but at any time my first choice for a memorable meal for many miles around.

For over twenty years Gilbert Plaisance has been cooking inspired food at Veules (why no second Michelin star?). Here is one Norman chef who is not content to rely solely on the reputation of the prime local produce from sea and field, but is always ready to experiment, taste, improvise, improve, combining the best of traditional and the new concept of cooking, instigated by nouvelle cuisine. Trust him and go for his menus. 170f for lunch, or an unbeatable 220f, which will bot offer a well-balanced indication of what he can do. Scallops with chicory, a sauté of sole and lobster in a delicate cream sauce and wonderful desserts are what I remember most fondly, but you can't really go wrong. All the extras are special too – a galette of potatoes, the appetisers and the petits fours are alone worth the visit.

A confident arrow.

'We've followed your recommendation of Les Galets and were delighted in every way. It was quite charming, the staff were thoroughly professional and the food was superb. As you warned, it wasn't cheap. With aperitifs, and good wine our lunch came to 800f, but I don't begrudge a single centime.'

Map 1F   **VEULETTES-SUR-MER** 76450 Cany-Barville, Seine-Mar. 26 km NE of Fécamp

---

Ignore, if you can, the nuclear power station to the north and turn to this little family resort in the wide green valley of the Durdent. It hasincongruous casino and disco, but ignore these too and make for the 11–13C church with fine lantern tower half-way up the hill overlooking the bay.

Frégates
(HR)M   *35.97.51.22   Cl. Sun. p.m.; Mon.; lunch o.o.s. 20/12–10/1   AE, DC, EC, V*

A little Logis de France in prime position overlooking the sea. The rooms are modest but comfortable and well maintained. They cost 175–195f; menus (this is really a restaurant with rooms, so the food has to be good enough to attract non-residents) start at 85f with good carafe wine.

Map 6B   **VILLEDIEU-LES-POËLES** 50800 Manche. 34 km S of St. Lo

Ⓣ *pl. Gostils (June–Sept.)   33.61.05.69; Mairie (o.o.s.)   33.61.00.16* Ⓜ *Tues.*

'God's Town of the Frying Pans', where the streets are lined with shop selling the locally-made copper ware, is one of the most popular *French Entrée* destinations. It's a pleasant little town, particularly busy on Tuesdays, when its wide market square gets taken over from an early hour with colourful market stalls.

Le Fruitier
(HR)S   *r. Gén. de Gaulle   33.51.14.24   Cl. 15/2–28/2   EC, V*

A popular little hotel, particularly so because of the friendliness and efficiency of patronne Mme Lebargy. 16 rooms cost from 139–200f, and menus are from 58f–125f.

'Mme Lebargy welcoming, friendly, and her young staff also very capable. Hotel charming, comfortable and clean. Our room, on the minor road, was reasonably quiet. We stuck to the second menu, which was good value and my husband happily swallowed 8 oysters as his regular starter. The more expensive menus read well.'

'Excellent value for money, plus a lock-up garage.' – C. James Jones.

Hotel St. Pierre et St. Michel
(HR)S   pl. République   33.61.00.1   Cl. Fri. o.o.s.; 23/12–28/2   EC, V

This used to be everyone's favourite – mine too. It's in a commanding position in the High Street, and looks very much the part of a typical French coaching inn. The food is still good enough to earn a Michelin red R on menus from 79f, and I would still choose it en passant, but there have been criticisms of the welcome and service. Rooms at the front suffer from lorry noise, especially on market days. Rooms are from 120–210f.

Map 3F   **VILLEQUIER** 76490 Caudebec en Caux, Seine-Mar. 45 km E of Le Havre

---

From Caudebec take the D 81, following the Seine, and 3 km towards the Tancarville Bridge is the village whose doubtful claim to fame is that Victor Hugo's daughter drowned there. Turn left off the busy main road to find:

Hotel de France
(HR)S   quai Victor Hugo   35.56.78.70   Cl. Sun. p.m.; Mon.

I am delighted that the France continues to please F.E. readers, in spite of its lack of first-impression appeal from the roadside and in spite of lack of second-impression appeal from the bedrooms. I cannot stress strongly enough that when I say simple here I mean basic. The rooms have good views, a shower and loo, and that's it. Decoration and electric light are minimal. What else do you expect for a fiver a head?

No, you go here for excellent cooking in a very pretty dining-room, overlooking the river (or courtyard in summer), and a warm welcome by M. and Mme Loisel. Shy M. Loisel cooks with obvious respect for his ingredients. All his menus are good value, from the basic 60f up to the one that includes half a lobster. Mme Loisel does front-of-house with smiling efficiency.

'Basic menu was excellent value – some of the best cooking we met. Service was quiet and friendly. M. et Mme Loisel were kindness itself.' – Susan Leyden.

'Room very basic, as we expected (no door on loo/shower room). Excellent meal. I thoroughly approve of this friendly young couple

concentrating on cuisine and wines rather than plush accommodation,
5 courses on cheapest menu including jambon de Bayonne, assiette d
jardin, sorbet au Calvados, truite au beurre, côte de porc Normand,
excellent cheese, and tarte Normande. Long may they flourish.'

Grand Sapin
(HR)S   *35.56.78.73   Cl. Tues. p.m. and Wed. o.o.s.; 15/11–1/12–10/2*

The more obvious choice in Villequier, in a prime position, with lovely
terrace overlooking the Seine. The food is not as good as at the France
but it is a much larger operation and worth considering if the France is
full or closed. No information recently about the bedrooms, which
used to be lovely, old-fashioned and spacious. Menus start at 55f.

Map 5D   **VILLERS-BOCAGE** 14310 Calvados. 26 km S of Caen

(T) *pl. Petit Marché (June–Sept.)   31.77.16.14*   (M) *Wed.*

Les Trois Rois
(HR)M   *Rte de Vire   31.77.00.32   Cl. Sun. p.m.; Mon.; Feb.; 26/6–2/7   CB, AE, DC*
EC

On the main road, the N 175 between Caen and Vire, and therefore
highly useful for an overnight stop. The proprietors, Henry and Aline
Martinotti, do not cash in on their tourist potential, however, and
continue to make their guests most welcome and pampered.

Perhaps the large dining-room does lack character, but M.
Martinotti's cooking makes up for a lot. His specialities are very
sophisticated, and he has won numerous prizes in gastronomic
competitions. Michelin give him a red R for his 115f menu, which is
well deserved.

The bedrooms are designed for over-nighters – small but
comfortable, with good bathrooms and sound-proofing – 185–300f.
Lock-up garage makes this a sensible transit stop with the benefit of an
excellent dinner.

'Very clean, excellent service. Clearly M. Martinotti is going for a
Michelin star. Perfect tripes à la mode de Caen, imaginative salads,
stunningly good cheeses on the cheapest menu. For our second dinner
we lashed out on the 100f menu, which I cannot praise too highly.

May I also recommend the Vrai Normande next door. Unpretentious
but really excellent value.' – Jem Miller.

Map 5E   **VIMOUTIERS** 61120 Orne. 27 km S of Lisieux

(T) *10 av. Gén.-de-Gaulle   33.39.30.29*   (M) *Mon. p.m.*

The centre of the dairy produce area. A statue to Marie Harel, who get
the credit for having 'invented' Camembert, stands at the entrance to
the little post-war town.

The hamlet of Camembert lies 3 km to the south-west, with another memorial to the farmer's wife who is said to have neglected her cheesemaking one day and found it strangely and deliciously transformed the next. The farms along the *Route des Fromages* display signs offering their version of the local speciality.

Don't be afraid to ask to taste, either here or at the **Camembert museum**, *10 av. Gén. de Gaulle (open daily, except Mon. a.m. 1/4–31/10. Not Sat. a.m., Sun., Mon. a.m. in winter)*. Vimoutiers is altogether a fine place for freebies. You can see Calvados being distilled and taste the result at Anée, 27 r. du Pierre, Mon.–Fri., and there are as many apples as you can eat at the Apple Fair in mid-Oct.

Escale de Vitou

HR(S)   *Centre de Loisirs, rte Argentan   33.39.12.04   Rest. cl. Sun. p.m.; Mon.   EC, V*

A few km out of the town on the D 916 lies this complex of sports facilities – vast open-air swimming-pool, grass skiing, stables, tennis courts, fishing, pedalos on the lake, with artificial beach and well-equipped playground. A fine place for a children's holiday you might say, but fat chance of finding a good eatery here. Wrong. Le Vitou is an above-average restaurant, and open in winter; on our last visit, it lit a log fire specially for us and dished up some comforting fare on a dark and dirty night when we were the only customers. Good menus from 65f.

The accommodation is in 17 little Norman-style gîtes, varying in size and price, but all bright and well-equipped. It is best to write for details, since prices depend on length of stay and date, but I assure you it is all a very good deal.

Map 6C   **VIRE** 14500 Calvados. 39 km SE of St. Lo

ⓣ *pl. Résistance (cl. Mon. o.o.s.)   31.68.00.05*   Ⓜ *Fri.*

High above the rolling Norman countryside, the site is attractive enough, but the town was annihilated during the war, and I can't say I find its reincarnation is one of my favourites. Its specialities are sausages – boudins and andouilles. Not everyone's taste, but this is the place to try them at least once.

Vire does make a useful stopping place on the route south from Cherbourg, and it is useful to have some suggestions for the vicinity.

Hotel de France

(HR)M   *4 r. d'Aignaux   31.68.00.35   Cl. 18/12–10/1   CB*

On a central crossroads, but the rooms are quiet, and not expensive at 140–250f. Not exciting, just practical, with all mod. cons., including air conditioning.

Hotel des Voyageurs
(HR)S   *av. Gare   31.68.01.16   EC, V*

No beauty, but beloved by F.E. readers for the welcome from the patron-chef Patrick Denian, and for his cooking. Good value all round, with rooms at 100–180f and menus from 45f, with reliable house wine.

Le Relais Normand
(HR)S   *Martilly   31.68.08.67   Cl. Sat. o.o.s.*

'The service was friendly and good and the food, which included local specialities, was the best home cooking of all my meals. Wines were good quality and value.' –G. Jeffs.

This is the consensus of opinion on this simple hostelry on the Villedieu road. Mme Goure speaks good English; her husband is chef and cooks local specialities like rabbit in cider, veal vallée d'Auge and of course andouille de Vire. Still excellent value with rooms from 75f and menus starting at 50f.

Le St. Clair
(R)S   *2. r. de Rennes   31.68.12.56*

Recommended by a local resident as the best value in town. Run by a Parisian/Anglophile. Grills particularly good. Menus from 60f.

Manoir de la Pommeraie
(R)M   *31.68.07.71   2 km SE on Rte de Paris   Cl. Sun. p.m.; Mon.; Feb. school hols.   CB, AE, DC*

For more up-market dining, M. Lesage's attractive old manor-house, converted into a light and airy restaurant, cannot be bettered. His weekday menus are especially good value, at 102f or 210f including good wine. Otherwise it's 153f upwards for fish specialities and clever desserts.

Map 2G   **YVETOT** 76190 Seine-Mar. 51 km E of Le Havre; 53 km SW of Dieppe

Ⓣ *pl. V. Hugo April–Sept.*   Ⓜ *Wed. a.m.*

A fair-sized market town centre, rebuilt, whose ferro-concrete St. Pierre church has a hard-to-miss free-standing belfry/scaffolding encasing Max Ingrand stained glass; I'm told it's glowingly impressive from inside. Not a lot of interest otherwise nowadays, and hard to believe that from the 14th century to the Revolution the town was an independent territory with its own King. Lying at the hub of several routes nationales, it might, however, prove a useful overnight stop.

Hotel Du Havre
(HR)M *pl. Belges   35.95.16.77   Cl. Fri. p.m.; Mon.; 24/10–4/11   EC, V*

> A typical French provincial hotel, old-fashioned in concept, busy, commercial, in the centre of the town.
>
> *'We have just spent five days here, using it as a base to tour Normandy and have found it very pleasant in every way. It is clean and comfortable and good value for money.'* – Mrs. J. A. Ellaway.
>
> Rooms, recently renovated (not altogether successfully), some in a garden annexe, are 256–325f. Menus from 90f with good carafe wine.

Auberge du Val au Cesne
(HR)M *le Val au Cesne   35.56.63.06   Open every day   CB, AE*

> A few km SE of Yvetot, the D 5 follows the valley of the little river Cesne in deep green countryside. A lovely place to stay for those looking for absolute quiet, and an oasis in generally rather dull countryside. The Auberge is an old Norman house, timbered, with just five pretty rooms opening directly into a flowery garden. They cost 290f. I have no details of the restaurant yet and I look forward to more reports on this potential treasure.

Map 2B   **YVETOT-BOCAGE** 50700 Valognes, Manche. 2 km W of Valognes

---

> A hamlet on the Bricquebec road.

Le Moulin de la Haulle
(R)S *33.40.21.37   Open weekends only from Easter–15/6 and from 15/9–15/10; from 15/6–15/9 every day except Tues.*

> A picturesque old stone converted windmill at the side of the road, with trout fishery appended, recommended for excellent crêpes and light meals in most agreeable surroundings.

Wines and spirits by John Doxat

AN INTRODUCTION TO FRENCH WINES

Bonne cuisine et bons vins, c'est le paradis sur terre. (Good cooking and good wines, that is earthly paradise.)

King Henri IV

French food positively invites accompaniment by wine, albeit only a couple of glasses because one is driving on after lunch. At dinner one can usually be self-indulgent. Then wine becomes more than a sensory pleasure: with some rich regional meals it is almost imperative digestively. Civilised drinking of wine inhibits the speedy eating that is the cause of much Anglo-Saxon dyspepsia.

The most basic French wine generically is *vin ordinaire*, and very ordinary indeed it can be. The term is seldom used nowadays: *vin de table* is a fancier description – simple blended wine of no particular provenance. *Vins de table* often come under brand-names, such as those of the of the ubiquitous Nicolas stores (Vieux Ceps, etc.) – and highly reliable they are. Only personal experience can lead you to your preference: in a take-away situation I would never buy the absolute cheapest just to save a franc or so.

Nearly every restaurant has its house wines. Many an owner, even of a chain of establishments, takes pride in those he has chosen to signify as *vins de la maison, vin du patron* or similar listing. In a wine-rich area, house wines (in carafe or bottle) are likely to be *vins de pays*, one step up from *vins de table*, since this label indicates that they come from a distinct certificated area and only that area, though they may be a blend (thus sometimes an improvement) of several wines.

Ever since they invented the useful, if frequently confusing, *Appellation d'Origine Contrôlée* (AC) the French have created qualitative sub-divisions. An AC wine, whose label will give you a good deal of information, will usually be costlier – but not necessarily better – than one that is a VDQS. To avoid excessive use of French, I translate that as 'designated (regional) wine of superior quality'. A newer, marginally lesser category is VQPRD: 'quality wine from a specified district'.

Hundreds of wines bear AC descriptions: you require knowledge and/or a wine guide to find your way around. The intention of the AC laws was to protect consumers and ensure wine was not falsely labelled – and also to prevent over-production, without noticeable reduction of the 'EEC wine lake'. Only wines of reasonable standards should achieve AC status: new ones are being regularly admitted to the list, and the hand of politics as much as the expertise of the taster can be suspected in some instances. Thus AC covers some unimportant wines as well as the rarest, vastly expensive vintages.

Advice? In wine regions, drink local wines. Do not hesitate to ask the opinion of patron or wine-waiter: they are not all venal, and most folk are flattered by being consulted. By all means refer to a vintage chart, when considering top class wines, but it cannot be an infallible guide: it has no bearing on blended wines.

OUTLINE OF FRENCH WINE REGIONS

Bordeaux

Divided into a score of districts, and sub-divided into very many *communes* (parishes). The big district names are Médoc, St Emilion, Pomerol, Graves and Sauternes. Prices for the great reds (châteaux Pétrus, Mouton-Rothschild, etc.) or the finest sweet whites (especially the miraculous Yquem) have become stratospheric. Yet château in itself means little and the classification of various rankings of châteaux is not easily understood. Some tiny vineyards are entitled to be called château, which has led to disputes about what have been dubbed 'phantom châteaux'. Visitors are advised, unless wine-wise, to stick to the simpler designations.

Bourgogne (Burgundy)

Topographically a large region, stretching from Chablis (on the east end of the Loire), noted for its steely dry whites, to Lyons. It is particularly associated with fairly powerful red wines and very dry whites, which tend to acidity except for the costlier styles. Almost to Bordeaux excesses, the prices for really top Burgundies have gone through the roof. For value, stick to simpler local wines.

Technically Burgundies, but often separately listed, are the Beaujolais wines. The young red Beaujolais (not necessarily the over-publicised *nouveau*) are delicious, mildly chilled. There are several rather neglected Beaujolais wines (Moulin-à-Vent, Morgon, St Amour, for instance) that improve for several years: they represent good value as a rule. The Mâconnais and Chalonnais also produce sound Burgundies (red and white) that are usually priced within reason.

Rhône

Continuation south of Burgundy. The Rhône is particularly associated with very robust reds, notably Châteauneuf-du-Pape; also Tavel, to my mind the finest of all still *rosé* wines. Lirac *rosé* is nearly as good. Hermitage and Gigondas are names to respect for reds, whites and *rosés*. Rhône has well earned its modern reputation – no longer Burgundy's poore[r] brother. From the extreme south comes the newly 'smart' dessert *vin doux naturel*, ultra-sweet Muscat des Beaumes-de-Venise, once despised by British wine-drinkers. There are fashions in wine just like anything else.

Alsace

Producer of attractive, light white wines, mostly medium-dr[y] widely used as carafe wines in middle-range French restaurants. Alsace wines are not greatly appreciated overseas and thus remain comparatively inexpensive for their quality; they are well placed to compete with popular German varieties. Alsace wines are designated by grape – principally Sylvaner for lightest styles, the widespread and reliable Riesling for a large part of the total, and Gerwürztztraminer for slightly fruitier wines.

Loire

Prolific producer of very reliable, if rarely great, white wines, notably Muscadet, Sancerre, Anjou (its *rosé* is famous), Vouvray (sparkling and semi-sparkling), and Saumur (particularly its 'champagne styles'). Touraine makes excellent whites and also reds of some distinction – Bourgueil and Chinon. It used to be widely believed – a rumour put out by rivals? – that Loire wines 'did not travel': nonsense. They are a successful export.

Champagne

So important is Champagne that, alone of French wines, it carries no AC: its name is sufficient guarantee. (It shares this distinction with the brandies Cognac and Armagnac.) Vintag[e] Champagnes from the *grandes marques* – a limited number of 'great brands' – tend to be as expensive in France as in Britain. You can find unknown brands of high quality (often off-shoots of *grandes marques*) at attractive prices, especial[ly] in the Champagne country itself. However, you need information to discover these, and there are true Champagnes for the home market that are *doux* (sweet) or *demi-sec* (medium sweet) that are pleasing to few non-French tastes. Champagne is very closely controlled as to region, quantities, grape types, and is made only by secondary fermentation in the bottle. From 1993, it is prohibited (under EEC law) to state that other wines are made by the 'champagne method' – even if they are.

Minor regions, very briefly

Jura – Virtually unknown outside France. Try local speciality wines such as *vin jaune* if in the region.

Jurançon – Remote area; sound, unimportant white wines, sweet styles being the better.

Cahors – Noted for its powerful *vin de pays* 'black wine', darkest red made.

Gaillac – Little known; once celebrated for dessert wines.

Savoy – Good enough table wines for local consumption. Best product of the region is delicious Chambéry vermouth: as an aperitif, do try the well distributed Chambéryzette, a unique vermouth with a hint of wild strawberries.

Bergerac – Attractive basic reds; also sweet Monbazillac, relished in France but not easily obtained outside: aged examples can be superb.

Provence – Large wine region of immense antiquity. Many and varied *vins de pays* of little distinction, usually on the sweet side, inexpensive and totally drinkable.

Midi – Stretches from Marseilles to the Spanish border. Outstandingly prolific contributor to the 'EEC wine lake' and producer of some 80 per cent of French *vins de table*, white and red. Sweet whites dominate, and there is major production of *vins doux naturels* (fortified sugary wines).

Corsica – Roughish wines of more antiquity than breeding, but by all means drink local reds – and try the wine-based aperitif Cap Corse – if visiting this remarkable island.

Paris – Yes, there is a vineyard – in Montmartre! Don't ask for a bottle: the tiny production is sold by auction, for charity, to rich collectors of curiosities.

HINTS ON SPIRITS

The great French spirit is brandy. Cognac, commercially the leader, must come from the closely controlled region of that name. Of various quality designations, the commonest is VSOP (very special old pale): it will be a cognac worth drinking neat. Remember, *champagne* in a cognac connotation has absolutely no connection with the wine. It is a topographical term, *grande champagne* being the most prestigious cognac area: *fine champagne* is a blend of brandy from the two top cognac sub-divisions.

Armagnac has become better known lately outside France, and rightly so. As a brandy it has a much longer history than cognac: some connoisseurs rate old armagnac (the quality designations are roughly similar) above cognac.

Be cautious of French brandy without a cognac or armagnac title, regardless of how many meaningless 'stars' the label carries or even the magic word 'Napoléon' (which has no legal significance).

Little appreciated in Britain is the splendid 'apple brandy', Calvados, mainly associated with Normandy but also made in Brittany and the Marne. The best is *Calvados du Pays d'Auge*. Do taste well-aged Calvados, but avoid any suspiciously cheap.

Contrary to popular belief, true Calvados is not distilled from cider – but an inferior imitation is: French cider *(cidre)* is excellent.

Though most French proprietary aperitifs, like Dubonnet, are fairly low in alcohol, the extremely popular Pernod/Ricard *pastis*-style brands are highly spirituous. *Eau-de-vie* is the generic term for all spirits, but colloquially tends to refer to local, often rough, distillates. Exceptions are the better *alcools blancs* (white spirits), which are not inexpensive, made from fresh fruits and not sweetened as *crèmes* are.

Liqueurs
Numerous travellers deem it worth allocating their allowance to bring back some of the famous French liqueurs (Bénédictine, Chartreuse, Cointreau, and so on) which are so costly in Britain. Compare 'duty free' prices with those in stores, which can vary markedly. There is a plethora of regional liqueurs, and numerous sickly *crèmes*, interesting to taste locally. The only *crème* generally meriting serious consideration as a liqueur is *crème de menthe* (preferably Cusenier), though the newish *crème de Grand Marnier* has been successful. *Crème de cassis* has a special function: see *Kir* in alphabetical list.

Condensed glossary
of French wine and ancillary terminology

Abricotine – Generic apricot liqueur. Look for known brand-names.

Alcool blanc – Spirit distilled from fruit (not wine); not to be confused with fruit-flavoured cordials.

Aligoté – Burgundy wine (from grape of same name); light and dry.

Anis – Aniseed; much used in aperitifs of Pernod type.

Aperitif – Any drink taken as an appetiser (literally 'opener'). France has a huge range of proprietary aperitifs.

Appellation (d'Origine) Contrôlée – AC; see An Introduction to French Wines.

Armagnac – Superb brandy of the Gascon country, now achieving something of a rediscovery. See Hints on Spirits.

Barsac – Sweet Bordeaux wine (officially part of Sauternes); wide range from excellent to sickly boring.

Basserau – Sparkling red Burgundy; unusual if nothing else.

Beaune – Prestigious Burgundy name (red), the best very costly.

Blanc de Blancs – White wine from white grapes only. White wine is often made from black grapes, skins being removed before fermentation – as this is.

Blanc de Noirs – See immediately above: these are essentially type descriptions; some prestige accrues to *Blanc de Blancs*.

Bordeaux – See An Introduction to French Wines.

Bourgogne – Burgundy; see An Introduction to French Wines.

Brut – Very dry; particularly with good Champagne.

Cabernet – Noble grape, especially Cabernet-Sauvignon. Just its name on a label denotes a sound red wine.

Cacao – Cocoa; usually as *crème de cacao.*

Calvados – Apple brandy; see Hints on Spirits.

Cassis – Blackcurrant; *crème de cassis* widely favoured, notably in Kir (q.v.).

Cave – Cellar.

Cépage – Indication of grape variety; e.g. *cépage Sauvignon.*

Chai – Ground-level wine store, exclusively used in Cognac, frequently also in Bordeaux.

Champagne – See An Introduction to French Wines.

Clairet – Unimportant little-known Bordeaux wine, but probably origin of English word Claret (red Bordeaux).

Clos – Principally Burgundian word for vineyard enclosed, or formerly protected, by a wall.

Cognac – see Hints on Spirits.

Côte – Vineyard on a slope; no particular quality significance

Coteau(x) – Hillside(s); much the same as *côte*.

Crème – Sweet, mildly alcoholic cordials of many flavours. Not rated as true liqueurs, but one exception is *crème de menthe* (mint). See also *cassis*.

Crémant – Sparkling wine, without lasting champagne-style effervescence.

Cru – Literally 'growth'. Somewhat complicated term. *Grand cru* only meaningful if allied to good name. *Grand cru classé* (officially classified great wine) covers greatest wines, but not all *cru classé* is *grand*.

Cuve close – Sealed vat; describes production of sparkling wine by bulk secondary fermentation as opposed to bottle fermentation of 'champagne method'.

Cuvée – Wine from one vat, unblended. Another confusing word; *cuvée spéciale* can have more than its literal meaning.

Demi-sec – Translates as 'medium dry'; in practice means sweet.

Domaine – Mainly Burgundian word; broadly equivalent to château.

Doux – Very sweet.

Eau-de-vie – Generic term for all distilled spirits.

Frappé – Drink served on finely crushed ice.

Glacé – Iced by immersion of bottle, or other refrigeration.

Goût – Taste. In some regions also describes rough local spirit.

Haut – 'High'; denotes upper part of wine district. Not necessarily a mark of quality, though Haut-Medoc produces notably better wines than its lower areas.

Izarra – Ancient, Armagnac-based Basque liqueur.

Kir – Excellent, now very popular aperitif: very dry chilled white wine (properly *Bourgogne Aligoté*) with a teaspoon of *crème de cassis* (q.v.) added, Kir Royale employs champagne.

Liqueur – originally *liqueur de dessert*, denoting post-prandial digestive use. Always sweet, so to speak of a 'liqueur Cognac' is absurd.

Litre – 1.7 pints; 5 litres equals 1.1 gallons.

Méthode Champenoise – Wine made by the champagne method.

Marc – Usually roughish brandy distilled from wine residue, though a few *Marcs* (pronounced 'mar') – notably *Marc de Bourgogne* – have some status.

Marque – Brand or company name.

Mise – As in *mise en bouteilles au château* (bottled at the château) or . . . *dans nos caves* (in our own cellars), etc.

Moelleux – On the sweet side.

Mousseux – Semi-technical term for sparkling; applies to the greatest champagne and to artificially carbonated rubbish.

Nouveau – New wine, particularly Beaujolais; made for drinking within a few months of harvest.

Pastis – General description, once more specific, for strong anis/liquorice-flavoured aperitifs originating in Marseilles; Ricard is a prime example.

Pétillant – Gently effervescent; sometimes translated as 'prickly' or 'crackling'.

Pineau – Unfermented grape juice fortified with grape spirit. Made in many regions: *Pineau des Charantes* (Cognac area) is best known. Well chilled, an attractive aperitif.

Porto – Portwine. The French are very big consumers, often using it (chilled) as an aperitif.

Primeur – Basically the same as *nouveau*. However, much fine Bordeaux and Burgundy is sold '*en primeur*' for long maturing by buyer.

Rosé – 'Pink wine'. Made by leaving skins of black grapes briefly in contact with juice; also by addition of red wine to white.

Sauvignon – Splendid white grape.

Sec – 'Dry', but wines thus marked will be sweetish. *Extra sec* may actually mean what it says.

Sirop – Syrup; akin to non-alcoholic *crème*.

Vermout – Vermouth.

Vin de Xérès – 'Vin de 'ereth'; sherry.

Glossary of cooking terms and dishes

(It would take another book to list comprehensively French cooking terms and dishes, but here are the ones most likely to be encountered.)

Aigre-doux	bittersweet
Aiguillette	thin slice (*aiguille* – needle)
Aile	wing
Aiolli	garlic mayonnaise
Allemande (à l')	German style, i.e.: with sausages and sauerkraut
Amuse-gueules	appetisers
Anglaise (à l')	plain boiled. *Crème Anglaise* – egg and cream sauce
Andouille	large uncooked sausage, served cold after boiling
Andouillettes	ditto but made from smaller intestines, usually served hot after grilling
Anis	aniseed
Argenteuil	with asparagus
Assiette Anglaise	plate of cold meats
Baba au rhum	yeast-based sponge macerated in rum
Baguette	long, thin loaf
Ballotine	boned, stuffed and rolled meat or poultry, usually cold
Béarnaise	sauce made from egg yolks, butter, tarragon, wine, shallots
Beurre blanc	sauce from Nantes, with butter, reduction of shallot-flavoured vinegar or wine
Béchamel	white sauce flavoured with infusion of herbs
Beignets	fritters
Bercy	sauce with white wine and shallots
Beurre noir	browned butter
Bigarade	with oranges
Billy By	mussel soup
Bisque	creamy shellfish soup
Blanquette	stew with thick, white creamy sauce, usually veal
Boeuf à la mode	braised beef
Bombe	ice-cream mould
Bonne femme	with root vegetables
Bordelais	Bordeaux-style, with red or white wine, marrowbone fat
Bouchée	mouthful, e.g. *vol-au-vent*
Boudin	sausage, white or black
Bourride	thick fish-soup
Braisé	braised

Brandade (de morue)	dried salt-cod pounded into mousse
Broche	spit
Brochette	skewer
Brouillade	stew, using oil
Brouillé	scrambled
Brûlé	burnt, e.g. *crème brûlée*
Campagne	country style
Cannelle	cinnamon
Carbonnade	braised in beer
Cardinal	red-coloured sauce, e.g. with lobster, or in *pâtisserie* with redcurrant
Cassolette or cassoulette	small pan
Cassoulet	rich stew with goose, pork and haricot beans
Cervelas	pork garlic sausage
Cervelles	brains
Chantilly	whipped sweetened cream
Charcuterie	cold pork-butcher's meats
Charlotte	mould, as dessert lined with sponge-fingers, as savoury lined with vegetable
Chasseur	with mushrooms, shallots, wine
Chausson	pastry turnover
Chemise	covering, i.e. pastry
Chiffonade	thinly-cut, e.g. lettuce
Choron	tomato Béarnaise
Choucroute	Alsatian stew with sauerkraut and sausages
Civet	stew
Clafoutis	batter dessert, usually with cherries
Clamart	with peas
Cocotte	covered casserole
Cocque (à la)	e.g. *oeufs* – boiled eggs
Compôte	cooked fruit
Concassé	e.g. *tomates concassées* – skinned, chopped, juice extracted
Confit	preserved
Confiture	jam
Consommé	clear soup
Cou	neck
Coulis	juice, purée (of vegetables or fruit)

Court-bouillon	aromatic liquor for cooking meat, fish, vegetables	Galette	Breton pancake, flat cake
Couscous	N. African dish with millet, chicken, vegetable variations	Garbure	thick country soup
		Garni	garnished, usually with vegetables
Crapaudine	involving fowl, particularly pigeon, trussed	Gaufre	waffle
		Gelée	aspic
Crécy	with carrots	Gésier	gizzard
Crème pâtissière	thick custard filling	Gibier	game
		Gigot	leg
Crêpe	pancake	Glacé	iced
Crépinette	little flat sausage, encased in caul	Gougère	choux pastry, large base
		Goujons	fried strips, usually of fish
Croque-Monsieur	toasted cheese-and-ham sandwich	Graine	seed
		Gratin	baked dish of vegetables cooked in cream and eggs
Croustade	pastry or baked bread shell		
Croûte	pastry crust	Gratinée	browned under grill
Croûton	cube of fried or toasted bread	Grecque (à la)	cold vegetables served in oil
Cru	raw	Grenadin	nugget of meat, usually of veal
Crudités	raw vegetables	Grenouilles	frogs; cuisses de grenouille – frogs' legs
Demi-glâce	basic brown sauce	Grillé	grilled
Doria	with cucumber	Gros sel	coarse salt
Émincé	thinly sliced	Hachis	minced or chopped
Étuvé	stewed, e.g. vegetables in butter	Haricot	slow cooked stew
		Hochepot	hotpot
Entremets	sweets	Hollandaise	sauce with egg, butter, lemon
		Hongroise	Hungarian, i.e. spiced with paprika
Farci	stuffed		
Fines herbes	parsley, thyme, bayleaf	Hors-d'oeuvre	assorted starters
Feuilleté	leaves of flaky pastry	Huile	oil
Flamande	Flemish style, with beer		
Flambé	flamed in spirit	Île flottante	floating island – soft meringue on egg-custard sauce
Flamiche	flan		
Florentine	with spinach	Indienne	Indian, i.e. with hot spices
Flûte	thinnest bread loaf		
Foie gras	goose liver	Jambon	ham
Fondu	melted	Jardinière	from the garden, i.e. with vegetables
Fond (d'artichaut)	heart (of artichoke)		
		Jarret	shin, e.g. jarret de veau
Forestière	with mushrooms, bacon and potatoes	Julienne	matchstick vegetables
		Jus	natural juice
Four (au)	baked in the oven		
Fourré	stuffed, usually sweets	Lait	milk
Fricandeau	veal, usually topside	Langue	tongue
Frais, fraîche	fresh and cool	Lard	bacon
Frangipane	almond-cream pâtisserie	Longe	loin
Fricadelle	Swedish meat ball		
Fricassé	(usually of veal) in creamy sauce	Macédoine	diced fruits or vegetables
		Madeleine	small sponge cake
Frit	fried	Magret	breast (of duck)
Frites	chips	Maïs	sweetcorn
Friture	assorted small fish, fried in batter	Maître d'hôtel	sauce with butter, lemon, parsley
Froid	cold	Marchand de vin	sauce with red wine, shallots
Fumé	smoked		
		Marengo	sauce with tomatoes, olive oil, white wine
Galantine	loaf-shaped chopped meat, fish or vegetable, set in natural jelly		

Marinière	seamens' style e.g. *moules marinière* (mussels in white wine)
Marmite	deep casserole
Matelote	fish stew, e.g. of eel
Médaillon	round slice
Mélange	mixture
Meunière	sauce with butter, lemon
Miel	honey
Mille-feuille	flaky pastry, lit. 1,000 leaves
Mirepoix	cubed carrot, onion etc. used for sauces
Moëlle	beef marrow
Mornay	cheese sauce
Mouclade	mussel stew
Mousseline	Hollandaise sauce, lightened with egg whites
Moutarde	mustard
Nage (à la)	poached in flavoured liquor (fish)
Nature	plain
Navarin (d'agneau)	stew of lamb with spring vegetables
Noisette	nut-brown, burned butter
Noix de veau	nut (leg) of veal
Normande	Normandy style, i.e. with cream, apple, cider, Calvados
Nouilles	noodles
Onglet	beef cut from flank
Os	bone
Paillettes	straws (of pastry)
Panaché	mixed
Panade	flour crust
Papillote (en)	cooked in paper case
Parmentier	with potatoes
Pâté	paste, of meat or fish
Pâte	pastry
Pâte brisée	rich short-crust pastry
Pâtisserie	pastries
Paupiettes	paper-thin slice
Pavé	thick slice
Paysan	country style
Périgueux	with truffles
Persillade	chopped parsley and garlic topping
Petits fours	tiny cakes, sweetmeats
Petit pain	bread roll
Piperade	peppers, onions, tomatoes in scrambled egg
Poché	poached
Poêlé	fried
Poitrine	breast
Poivre	pepper
Pommade	paste
Potage	thick soup

Pot-au-four	broth with meat and vegetables
Potée	country soup with cabbage
Pralines	caramelised almonds
Primeurs	young veg
Printanier (printanière)	garnished with early vegetables
Profiteroles	choux pastry balls
Provençale	with garlic, tomatoes, olive, peppers
Purée	mashed and sieved
Quenelle	pounded fish or meat boun with egg, poached
Queue	tail
Quiche	pastry flan, e.g. *quiche Lorraine* – egg, bacon, crea
Râble	saddle, e.g. *râble de lièvre*
Ragoût	stew
Ramequin	little pot
Râpé	grated
Ratatouille	Provençale stew of onions, garlic, peppers, tomatoes
Ravigote	highly seasoned white sau
Rémoulade	mayonnaise with gherkins, capers, herbs and shallots
Rillettes	potted shredded meat, usu fat pork or goose
Riz	rice
Robert	sauce with mustard, vinega onion
Roquefort	ewe's milk blue cheese
Rossini	garnished with *foie gras* an truffle
Rôti	roast
Rouelle	nugget
Rouille	hot garlicky sauce for *soup poisson*
Roulade	roll
Roux	sauce base – flour and butt
Sabayon	sweet fluffy sauce, with eg and wine
Safran	saffron
Sagou	sago
St-Germain	with peas
Salade niçoise	with tunny, anchovies, tomatoes, beans, black oliv
Salé	salted
Salmis	dish of game or fowl, with r wine
Sang	blood
Santé	lit, healthy, i.e. with spinacl and potato
Salpicon	meat, fowl, vegetables, chopped fine, bound with sauce and used as fillings

Saucisse	fresh sausage	Thé	tea
Saucisson	dried sausage	Tiède	luke warm
Sauté	cooked in fat in open pan	Timbale	steamed mould
Sauvage	wild	Tisane	infusion
Savarin	ring of yeast-sponge, soaked in syrup and liquor	Tourte	pie
		Tranche	thick slice
Sel	salt	Truffes	truffles
Selle	saddle	Tuile	tile, i.e. thin biscuit
Selon	according to, e.g. selon grosseur (according to size)		
		Vacherin	meringue confection
Smitane	with sour cream, white wine, onion	Vallée d'Auge	with cream, apple, Calvados
		Vapeur (au)	steamed
Soissons	with dried white beans	Velouté	white sauce, bouillon-flavoured
Sorbet	water ice		
Soubise	with creamed onions	Véronique	with grapes
Soufflé	puffed, i.e. mixed with egg white and baked	Vert(e)	green, e.g. sauce verte, with herbs
Sucre	sugar (sucré – sugared)	Vessie	pig's bladder
Suprême	fillet of poultry breast or fish	Vichysoisse	chilled creamy leek and potato soup
Tartare	raw minced beef, flavoured with onions etc. and bound with raw egg	Vierge	prime olive oil
		Vinaigre	vinegar (lit. bitter wine)
		Vinaigrette	wine vinegar and oil dressing
Tartare (sauce)	mayonnaise with capers, herbs, onions	Volaille	poultry
		Vol-au-vent	puff-pastry case
Tarte Tatin	upside down apple pie		
Terrine	pottery dish/baked minced, chopped meat, veg., chicken, fish or fruit	Xérès	sherry
		Yaourt	yoghurt

FISH – Les Poissons, SHELLFISH – Les Coquillages

Alose	shad	Daurade	sea bream
Anchois	anchovy	Écrevisse	crayfish
Anguille	eel	Éperlan	smelt
Araignée de mer	spider crab	Espadon	swordfish
		Étrille	baby crab
Bar	sea bass	Favouille	spider crab
Barbue	brill	Flétan	halibut
Baudroie	monkfish, anglerfish	Fruits de mer	seafood
Belon	oyster – flat shelled	Grondin	red gurnet
Bigorneau	winkle	Hareng	herring
Blanchaille	whitebait	Homard	lobster
Brochet	pike	Huître	oyster
Cabillaud	cod	Julienne	ling
Calamar	squid	Laitance	soft herring-roe
Carpe	carp	Lamproie	lamprey
Carrelet	plaice	Langouste	spring lobster, or crawfish
Chapon de mer	scorpion fish	Langoustine	Dublin Bay prawn
Claire	oyster	Lieu	ling
Coquille St-Jacques	scallop	Limand	lemon sole
		Lotte de mer	monkfish
Crabe	crab	Loup de mer	sea bass
Crevette grise	shrimp	Maquereau	mackerel
Crevette rose	prawn	Merlan	whiting

Morue	salt cod	*St-Pierre*	John Dory
Moule	mussel	*Sandre*	zander
Mulet	grey mullet	*Saumon*	salmon
Ombre	grayling	*Saumonette*	rock salmon
Oursin	sea urchin	*Seiche*	squid
Palourde	clam	*Sole*	sole
Pétoncle	small scallop	*Soupion*	inkfish
Plie	plaice	*Thon*	tunny
Portugaise	oyster	*Tortue*	turtle
Poulpe	octopus	*Torteau*	large crab
Praire	oyster	*Truite*	trout
Raie	skate	*Turbot*	turbot
Rascasse	scorpion-fish	*Turbotin*	chicken turbot
Rouget	red mullet		

FRUITS – Les Fruits, VEGETABLES – Les Légumes, NUTS – Les Noix

HERBS – Les Herbes, SPICES – Les Épices

Ail	garlic	*Cornichon*	gherkin
Algue	seaweed	*Courge*	pumpkin
Amande	almond	*Courgette*	courgette
Ananas	pineapple	*Cresson*	watercress
Aneth	dill	*Échalote*	shallot
Abricot	apricot	*Endive*	chicory
Arachide	peanut	*Épinard*	spinach
Artichaut	globe artichoke	*Escarole*	salad leaves
Asperge	asparagus	*Estragon*	tarragon
Avocat	avocado	*Fenouil*	fennel
Banane	banana	*Fève*	broad bean
Basilic	basil	*Flageolet*	dried bean
Betterave	beetroot	*Fraise*	strawberry
Blette	Swiss chard	*Framboise*	raspberry
Brugnon	nectarine	*Genièvre*	juniper
Cassis	blackcurrant	*Gingembre*	ginger
Céléri	celery	*Girofle*	clove
Céléri-rave	celeriac	*Girolle*	edible fungus
Cêpe	edible fungus	*Grenade*	pomegranate
Cerfeuil	chervil	*Griotte*	bitter red cherry
Cerise	cherry	*Groseille*	gooseberry
Champignon	mushroom	*Groseille noire*	blackcurrant
Chanterelle	edible fungus	*Groseille rouge*	redcurrant
Châtaigne	chestnut	*Haricot*	dried white bean
Chicorée	endive	*Haricot vert*	French bean
Chou	cabbage	*Laitue*	lettuce
Chou-fleur	cauliflower	*Mandarine*	tangerine, mandarin
Choux de Bruxelles	Brussels sprouts	*Mangetout*	sugar pea
Ciboulette	chive	*Marron*	chestnut
Citron	lemon	*Menthe*	mint
Citron vert	lime	*Mirabelle*	tiny gold plum
Coing	quince	*Morille*	dark brown crinkly edible fungus
Concombre	cucumber	*Mûre*	blackberry
Coriandre	coriander	*Muscade*	nutmeg
		Myrtille	bilberry, blueberry
		Navet	turnip
		Noisette	hazelnut

Oignon	onion	*Pomme*	apple
Oseille	sorrel	*Pomme de terre*	potato
Palmier	palm	*Prune*	plum
Pamplemousse	grapefruit	*Pruneau*	prune
Panais	parsnip	*Quetsch*	small dark plum
Passe-Pierre	seaweed	*Radis*	radish
Pastèque	water melon	*Raifort*	horseradish
Peche	peach	*Raisin*	grape
Persil	parsley	*Reine Claude*	greengage
Petit pois	pea	*Romarin*	rosemary
Piment doux	sweet pepper	*Safran*	saffron
Pissenlit	dandelion	*Salsifis*	salsify
Pistache	pistachio	*Thym*	thyme
Pleurote	edible fungi	*Tilleul*	lime blossom
Poire	pear	*Tomate*	tomato
Poireau	leek	*Topinambour*	Jerusalem artichoke
Poivre	pepper	*Truffe*	truffle
Poivron	green, red and yellow peppers		

MEAT - Les Viandes

Le Boeuf	Beef	*Le Porc*	Pork
Charolais	is the best	*Jambon*	ham
Chateaubriand	double fillet steak	*Jambon cru*	raw smoked ham
Contrefilet	sirloin	*Porcelet*	suckling pig
Entrecôte	rib steak		
Faux Filet	sirloin steak	*Le Veau*	Veal
Filet	fillet	*Escalope*	thin slice cut from fillet
L'Agneau	Lamb	*Les Abats*	Offal
Pré-Salé	is the best	*Foie*	liver
Carré	neck cutlets	*Foie gras*	goose liver
Côte	chump chop	*Cervelles*	brains
Épaule	shoulder	*Langue*	tongue
Gigot	leg	*Ris*	sweetbreads
		Rognons	kidneys
		Tripes	tripe

POULTRY – Volaille, GAME – Gibier

Abatis	giblets	*Lièvre*	hare
Bécasse	woodcock	*Oie*	goose
Bécassine	snipe	*Perdreau*	partridge
Caille	quail	*Pigeon*	pigeon
Canard	duck	*Pintade*	guineafowl
Caneton	duckling	*Pluvier*	plover
Chapon	capon	*Poularde*	chicken (boiling)
Chevreuil	roe deer	*Poulet*	chicken (roasting)
Dinde	young hen turkey	*Poussin*	spring chicken
Dindon	turkey	*Sanglier*	wild boar
Dindonneau	young turkey	*Sarcelle*	teal
Faisan	pheasant	*Venaison*	venison
Grive	thrush		

Notes

Other French Entrée Guides

French Entrée 5	Brittany	£4.95
French Entrée 6	Coast to Capital – Boulogne, Pays d'Opal, Picardy	£4.95
French Entrée 7	Calais, Champagne, the Ardennes and Bruges	£5.95
French Entrée 8	The Loire	£4.95

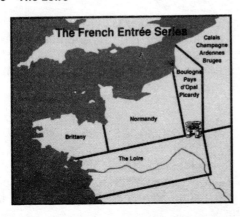

"She doesn't care what she says". *Observer*

"Well worth looking through for anyone wondering where to spend the first (or last) night of a holiday in France". *Country Life*

"Makes you want to drive down to Dover and onto a cross-Channel ferry right away". *Sunday Telegraph*

"An excellent, evocative but crisp little guide to the neglected North of France". *Good Book Guide*

"... a very objective and highly readable book for visitors to the three ports of Calais, Le Havre, Cherbourg and their environs". *Autosport*

"Can there be an auberge or dockside café that Ms Fenn has failed to report on?" *Books and Bookmen*

"Patricia Fenn's immensely reliable guides to the places to eat and sleep need no recommendation to anyone who has used them". *Evening Standard*

"Time and again she has got to good places and chefs before the news reached Michelin or Gault-et-Millau". *Guardian*

"Lively, humorous and above all immensely readable". *Country Life*

"Makes you want to dash across on the ferry immediately". *Good Housekeeping*

In preparation:
FRENCH ENTRÉE 10 The South of France
FRENCH ENTRÉE 11 Paris   and many others.

Also published by Quiller Press
— two companions to French Entrée to help you enjoy your holiday more.

LEGAL BEAGLE GOES TO FRANCE
Bill Thomas   £3.95
All you need to deal with problems involving the law in France – accidents, houses, travel – even births and deaths. Includes: legal and customs formalities; daily life in France; eating, sleeping and drinking; en route; getting around without a car; renting a gîte and buying a house.

CONTINENTAL MOTORING GUIDE 1991
Paul Youden   £3.95
A concise and highly illustrated full-colour guide for motorists. Gives essential facts on continental road signs and regulations, as well as tips to make your drive more enjoyable right from the time you leave the ferry.

Please order from your bookshop or, in case of difficulty, write with payment to:
Quiller Press, 46 Lillie Road, London SW6 1TN.